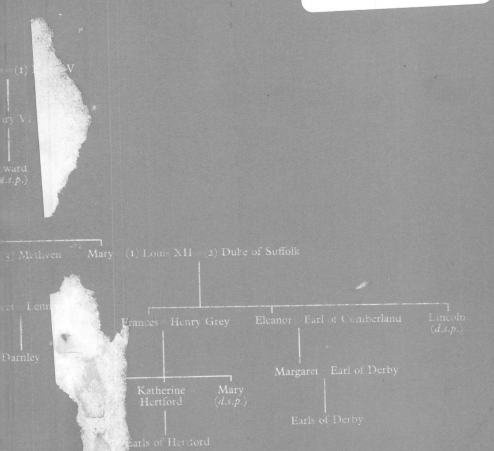

(1) ... V

... ry V.

... ward
(d.s.p.)

(3) Methven — Mary = (1) Louis XII = (2) Duke of Suffolk

... Lenn...

... Darnley

Frances = Henry Grey     Eleanor — Earl of Cumberland     Lincoln
                                                            (d.s.p.)

                                                Margaret — Earl of Derby

Katherine =     Mary
Hertford     (d.s.p.)

                                                Earls of Derby

Earls of Hertford

# THE SISTERS OF
# HENRY VIII

GORONW- AND MYFANWY-AP-TUDOR FYCHAN
*(from the church of St Gredifael, Pynmynydd, Anglesey)*

# THE SISTERS OF HENRY VIII

*Margaret Tudor, Queen of Scotland*
(November 1489 – October 1541)

*Mary Tudor, Queen of France
and Duchess of Suffolk*
(March 1496 – June 1533)

BY HESTER W. CHAPMAN

JONATHAN CAPE
THIRTY BEDFORD SQUARE LONDON

FIRST PUBLISHED 1969
© 1969 BY HESTER CHAPMAN

JONATHAN CAPE LTD
30 BEDFORD SQUARE, LONDON, WCI

SBN 224 61743 5

TO ANNE CUBITT

PRINTED IN GREAT BRITAIN
BY EBENEZER BAYLIS AND SON LTD
THE TRINITY PRESS, WORCESTER, AND LONDON
ON PAPER MADE BY JOHN DICKINSON AND CO. LTD
BOUND BY A. W. BAIN AND CO. LTD, LONDON

# Contents

## MARGARET TUDOR

## MARY TUDOR

# CONTENTS

# List of Illustrations

# *Acknowledgments*

THE portrait of Queen Margaret of Scotland in Holyroodhouse is re-produced by gracious permission of Her Majesty Queen Elizabeth II. Grateful thanks are due to the Master and Fellows of St John's College, Cambridge, for leave to present that of Lady Margaret Beaufort; to the Provost of Eton for that of Henry VII; to the Marquess of Bute for that of Queen Margaret and the Earl of Angus; to Lt.-Col. W. J. Stirling for that of James IV; to the Scottish National Portrait Gallery for that of James V; to the English National Portrait Gallery for those of Henry VIII and Elizabeth of York; and to the Earl of Yarborough for that of the Duke and Duchess of Suffolk.

The author has very great pleasure in thanking Mr William Evans of Llangefni for the print—taken under extremely difficult conditions—of the monument of Goronw- and Myfanwy-ap-Tudor in the Church of St Gredifael, Penmynydd. The print of Louis XII is reproduced from an engraving by A. Berthold. Finally, grateful acknowledgments are offered to Miss Rosamond Lehmann and Mr George Rylands for their acute and sensitive criticisms in matters of treatment and style.

# *Foreword*

THE process known as getting one's own way may be partially effected by the consciousness of being in the right, and sometimes, in the case of those subscribing to an orthodox faith, maintained through direct contact with and orders from the Almighty. Thus, instructions from above are generally carried out regardless of consequences and in the face of apparently insurmountable difficulties.

The outstanding characteristic of the Tudor family was an inspired, yet persistent and methodical pursuit of aims they saw as altruistic, beneficial and above criticism. The acknowledgment of 'private' sins, weakness or — the terms were synonymous — failure to achieve these aims was their only concession to the current belief in repentance as being the surest means of access to paradise. The Tudors knew that they could never have acted wrongly — although they might have faltered in their efforts — because God had guided them. In their minds, ambition, self-aggrandisement and the fulfilment of desire had no connection with successes brought about by obedience to the only Being higher than themselves.

In varying degrees, this attitude was evolved and then sustained by the founders of the dynasty, reaching its apotheosis in the triumphs of its last and greatest member. Queen Elizabeth's grandfather, Henry VII, acquired the crown to which he had a faint — in fact, an almost non-existent — claim, through a combination of patience, forethought and resolve. Yet after the battle of Bosworth Field he announced that he had been commanded by the Deity to rescue England from the tyranny of Richard III, having no other motive for his skilfully planned invasion.

The ruthless and subtle manoeuvres of his magnificent successor precipitated the long-overdue Reformation in an atmosphere of hostility, but with a national support on which few dictators would have dared to count. Henry VIII's only surviving son and elder daughter, equally dedicated to the cause of religion, enhanced the Tudor legend: Edward VI by his attempted enforcement of an exaggerated Protestantism, which Mary I determined to eradicate. The supreme

9

genius of Elizabeth I guided her away from doctrinal controversy;
she chose to perfect the union — she saw it as her marriage — of the
monarchy with the realm, in order to strengthen their joint power
and security.

So the Tudors established an ineffaceable and intensely personal
pattern on our history. That pattern was reproduced in the actions
of Henry VIII's sisters, Margaret and Mary. Both became queens:
the first of Scotland, the second of France; both revolutionized the
careers marked out for them by their father.

There the resemblance ends. Margaret was plain, clever, capricious
and self-willed. She became highly unpopular, lived too long and
died unlamented. Mary was beautiful, naive, passionate and charm-
ing; her death was mourned by all but one: the man on whom she
had lavished an unfailing and romantic devotion.

These two princesses obtained, against seemingly impossible odds,
their hearts' desire; Margaret impermanently and Mary with reservations. The story of their lives, dramatically contrasting, and over-
shadowed by the fame of Henry VII and Henry VIII, is now almost
forgotten. So perhaps the time has come for the recapitulation of
their adventures.

# MARGARET TUDOR

'Thou shalt no more be called, The lady of kingdoms ...
Therefore, hear now this, thou that art given to
pleasures, that dwellest carelessly, that sayest in thine
heart ... I shall not sit as a widow, neither shall I know
the loss of children ... But these two things shall come
upon thee in a moment ... the loss of children and
widowhood ... for the multitude of thy sorceries, and
for the great abundance of thine enchantments.'

*Isaiah, 48, 47*

# I

## *The Founders of the Dynasty*

ON THE south-east side of the Isle of Anglesey, some ten miles from the Menai Straits, lies the hamlet of Penmynydd. Its setting is treeless, rocky and rather austere than picturesque. A group of whitewashed, fifteenth-century cottages surrounds the church of Saint Gredifael.

The interior of this small, solid building is unremarkable but for the alabaster monument of a medieval knight and his lady in the chancel. This commemorates Goronw-ap-Tudor Fychan and his wife Myfanwy, whose coffins were placed in a recess behind their effigies after their removal from a neighbouring monastery destroyed under Henry VIII.

They lie side by side, their hands clasped in prayer, a middle-aged, respectable couple. His features appear rather homely than distinguished; his thin, drooping moustachios fall neatly over the chainmail of his hauberk, in the fashion set by his friend and patron, the Black Prince. The plain folds of her gown are relieved by a necklace and brooches. She looks plump-faced and determined. Her feet rest on a pair of lap-dogs, his on a lion. Angels support their headrests. Although conventionally designed, the memorial gives the impression of a likeness, in both cases.

Goronw-ap-Tudor, a cousin of Owen Glendower, was Forester of Snowdon and Lord High Constable of Beaumaris. Returning from the French wars in 1382, he was drowned, and his descendants built the church of Saint Gredifael to his memory, providing other amenities still to be seen—some brightly coloured windows, an octagonal font, and a pair of tongs for removing dogs' messes, or, if necessary, the dogs themselves.[1]

After Henry IV defeated Owen Glendower, Goronw-ap-Tudor's son Meredith became steward to the Bishop of Bangor. He then killed a man, and escaped into England, where he remained till his death. His son, Owen Tudor, entered the service of Henry V, fought at Agincourt and was made esquire of the body to his master. In 1420

13

Henry married Katherine de Valois, youngest daughter of the insane Charles VI and Isabeau of Bavaria. They had one child, Henry VI, who succeeded his father as King of France and England in 1421, at the age of nine months.

Owen Tudor remained with the Queen-Dowager as Clerk of the Wardrobe. He was tall and fair: a handsome athlete. Katherine, a lonely widow of twenty-five, first became aware of him at a dance. As she watched him pass, he tripped, stumbled forward, and fell into her lap.[2]

Such accidents are seldom fortuitous: and this one, whether planned or not, changed the course of English history. Katherine fell in love with her Welsh gentleman—and married him. 'This woman', says a contemporary chronicler, 'being young and lusty ... following more her own appetite than her open honour, took to husband, privily, a goodly gentleman and a beautiful person, garnished with many gifts, both of nature and of grace.'[3]

Between 1425 and 1430 Katherine and Owen Tudor had four children—Edmund, Jasper, another Owen and a girl who died in infancy. Their union was indictable on two counts: marriage with a Welshman was forbidden by statute, and the Queen-Dowager should not have taken a second husband without the permission of the Regent-Protector—her brother-in-law, John Duke of Bedford—and the Privy Council.

The young couple managed to keep their marriage, and the existence of their children, secret; but Katherine seems to have had some qualms about having made a mésalliance, which Owen disposed of by claiming descent (he may even have been able to prove it) from the royal house of Caedwallader. He introduced several of his relatives into her household in Bermondsey; but as they spoke only Welsh, Katherine dismissed them, so the story goes, with, 'They are the goodliest dumb creatures that ever I saw.'[4]

Shortly after Katherine's death in 1437 (in her will she made no mention of Owen or of their family) their marriage was discovered, with the result that the children were placed in the care of the Abbess of Barking, and Owen, who had left London, was summoned before the Privy Council.

He refused to appear without a safe conduct. Summoned again, he returned and took sanctuary in Westminster Abbey, where he remained for several days. Here he was visited by a number of old comrades who urged him to accompany them to the taverns, and when he demurred, taunted him with cowardice. Characteristically, he at once emerged and faced the Council. His having taken out papers of nationalization five years earlier availed him nothing, and he was committed, with his priest and a body-servant, to Newgate. With their help, he escaped — in the ensuing struggle he wounded a gaoler — but was recaptured. He then escaped again, this time successfully, and took refuge in Wales, where he remained until his stepson, Henry VI, reached his majority.[5]

In the years preceding the Wars of the Roses the King restored the fortunes of the Tudor family. Owen was given a pension and several appointments; in 1453 Edmund received the earldom of Richmond, and Jasper that of Pembroke. (The younger Owen had become a monk, and remained in obscurity until he died in 1502.)[6] When the Yorkists, headed by Edward IV, as he later became, and the Earl of Warwick, rose against Henry VI and the Lancastrians, the Tudors fought for Henry with stubborn gallantry and intermittent success.

Meanwhile, Edmund had done even better than Jasper. In 1454 he married Margaret Beaufort, only child of the Duke of Somerset and great-granddaughter of John of Gaunt, youngest son of Edward III. In 1456 Edmund died, and two months after that, Margaret, who was not quite fourteen, gave birth to a son, Henry. Twenty-nine years later, he became Henry VII — the first Tudor king.

Margaret Beaufort's attitude towards her marriage had shown the forethought and caution for which her only son was to become famous. In 1444, when she was two, her father died, and she became the ward of the Duke of Suffolk. Seven years later, he was hesitating as to whether she should be married to his son, John de la Pole, or to Edmund Tudor; eventually, he contracted her to John. Naturally, there was then no question of any young girl, of whatever standing, being consulted as to her choice of a husband; but Suffolk was suspected — and Margaret must have heard these rumours — of intriguing with the King of France about a plan to invade England. The nine-year-old heiress therefore called upon Saint Nicholas to advise her. His status enhanced by episcopal robes, the saint appeared to her in a dream, and said that she should marry Edmund Tudor.[7] Shortly afterwards, the Suffolk plot was discovered, the Duke attainted, Margaret's contract to his son annulled, and she was betrothed to Edmund.* She remained under her mother's care until her marriage.

* There was no connection between the de la Pole Suffolks and the Duke who married Mary Tudor.

She and Edmund then occupied Pembroke Castle, where Henry was born.

From the moment of his birth Henry of Richmond's life was one of danger and uncertainty. In the first place, the legitimacy of his mother's Plantagenet descent was doubtful, for John of Gaunt's children had not been legitimized until after his marriage to his former mistress, Katherine Swynford. (In 1407 Henry IV disqualified them and their descendants from inheriting the throne by Act of Parliament, although he confirmed their legitimacy.) The Lady Margaret's dynastic situation was therefore anomalous; but her determination and intelligence were such as to overcome this and many other disadvantages. Her grandchildren — Henry VIII, Margaret and Mary Tudor — were not only influenced by her, rather than by their parents: they inherited her gift for dominating their circumstances, however unpromising.

Henry was not quite three years old when the struggle between his York and Lancaster relatives began. In 1459 his mother married her second husband, Lord Henry Stafford, youngest son of the Duke of Buckingham. Henry Tudor's Uncle Jasper became his guardian; but in that same year Jasper had to leave Pembroke to fight the Yorkists. Henry's stepfather was politically negligible, and could do nothing for him.

In February 1461 Jasper and Owen Tudor were defeated at Mortimer's Cross. Jasper escaped, to find himself attainted; his title and estates — with the care of his nephew — were given to Lord William Herbert. For the next few years Henry, although officially a prisoner, was fortunate. He became one of the Herbert family, and his education continued on the lines laid down by his mother.[8]

Owen Tudor, now in his sixties, was captured and sentenced to death at Hereford. Counting on a reprieve, he refused to kneel, until the headsman tore away the collar of his red velvet jerkin. 'That head which was wont to lie on Queen Katherine's lap', he is reported to have said, 'shall lie on the stock —' and so perished. His head was then placed on the highest step of the market cross. An old woman washed away the blood, combed out the hair and surrounded it with candles. Presently head and body were shovelled into a coffin and buried in the nearest monastery.[9]

A month later Edward IV was crowned and Henry VI imprisoned in the Tower. Still the fighting continued. In 1468 the Lancastrians triumphed, and Edward had to take refuge in Holland. Henry VI,

LADY MARGARET BEAUFORT *(artist unknown)*

who had been insane for some years, was freed, and, temporarily
restored to power, regained some measure of mental stability. Jasper
then returned to Pembroke, to find his nephew had been left in the
charge of a Welsh servant. Lord William Herbert had been killed, his
widow and children had fled, and Margaret and Stafford were with
the Court at Westminster. Jasper took his ward up to London, where
he was kindly received by Henry VI, who placed him at Eton. A few
months later, Edward IV reappeared, and Jasper sent his nephew
back to Pembroke. In May 1471 Edward finally defeated the Lancastrians at Tewkesbury, and Henry VI was murdered in the Tower.

For some time, Jasper had managed to organize rebellions in Scotland, Ireland and Wales; now he accepted defeat, and, with Henry
Tudor, who was in his sixteenth year, escaped to Brittany, where
Duke Francis II placed them both in honourable confinement. There
Henry remained for fourteen years, in constant danger of being
handed over, first to Edward IV and then to Richard III, both of
whom continued, unsuccessfully, to bribe Francis to release him.
Henry himself gave up all hope of return, and decided to become a
priest.[10]

In 1482 Stafford died, and Margaret of Richmond (all her life she
retained her first husband's title) married Lord Thomas Stanley,
brother of William, Earl of Derby. Then, with the death of Edward IV
and the coup d'état of Richard III, the dynastic situation was revolutionized, and with it the fortunes of Henry of Richmond.

Paradoxically, Richard's seizure of the crown from the twelve-
year-old Edward V strengthened Henry's position. With the imprisonment and 'disappearance' of the two Yorkist Princes, and the death
of Richard's only son, his claim to the throne through his mother
appeared in a much more favourable light; in fact, it became paramount, or nearly so. She therefore renounced her rights in his favour,
and began to discuss with the Queen-Dowager his marrying Elizabeth
of York, Edward IV's eldest daughter.

Agreement was reached; and after a false start in 1484 Henry
escaped shipwreck and capture in the English Channel and made his
way to Paris, where he raised an army of exiled Lancastrians and
French mercenaries partially financed by Charles VIII and commanded by himself and Jasper. In August 1485 he landed at Milford
Haven, where he consulted David Lloyd, the local seer, about his
chances. The prophet would not commit himself, and Henry went
gloomily to bed. That night, Mrs Lloyd told her husband to assure

their guest of success — she herself was certain of it — and he did so.[11]

The last-minute desertion of the Stanleys from Richard's army ensured Henry's success at Bosworth Field and he entered London in triumph. A year after his coronation he and Elizabeth of York were married, and eight months later she gave birth to a boy, Arthur. In October 1489 she again 'took her chamber', according to the elaborate ordinances laid down by her mother-in-law. On November 30th a daughter, Margaret, was born at the Palace of Westminster.

---

## NOTES

1 *Inventory of Ancient Monuments* (Anglesey), pp. 129–31; *Archaeologia Cambrensis*, p. 147.
2 H. Evans, *Wales and the Wars of the Roses*, pp. 22, 67, 72.
3 E. Hall, *Chronicle*, p. 175.
4 Evans, ibid.
5 Ibid.
6 A. L. Rowse, *Bosworth Field*, p. 225.

7 M. Domvile, *The King's Mother*, p. 8. C. Cooper, *The Lady Margaret*, p. 72.
8 Commines, *Mémoires*, vol. II, p. 66.
9 Calendar of Patent Rolls; Rowse, p. 145.
10 Hall, p. 395.
11 *Archaeologia Cambrensis*, p. 49.

## II

## *Background and Education*

THE first fourteen years of Margaret Tudor's life had a medieval
setting. Until she left England — as she thought, for ever — in 1503,
her surroundings were Gothic. The palaces and castles which formed
her background, the London in which she spent most of her childhood, and the country beyond them had changed very little since the
days of the Angevin kings.

The kingdom her father ruled with an ingenuity and care amount-
ing to genius had greatly diminished in extent, as in power. Only a
few coastal towns remained of the continental territory — some two-
thirds of modern France — acquired by his forbears. And thirty years
of civil war, while not seriously impoverishing the population, had
depleted the Treasury, affected the hierarchy and modified the class
system.

Yet visiting foreigners, however critical and disapproving of
English customs, were unwillingly impressed by what an anonymous
Venetian describes as a triangular island inhabited by an unreliable,
arrogant, but surprisingly prosperous race. One could not believe a
word these people said; they were boastful, violent and unscrupulous,
extravagantly dressed and recklessly quarrelsome; but their scorn of
convention and their exuberant hospitality had a certain charm. And
when it came to display — they were superb.[1]

Indeed, the splendour of Henry VII's Court was staggering; he
and his family seem to have moved in a series of gorgeous processions,
in which Margaret Tudor took part as soon as she could walk.
Accomplishments, gracefully formal manners and an undeviating
stateliness of bearing were taught her from infancy. The ritual preceding her birth was a foretaste of her daily routine.

On this occasion, Queen Elizabeth, led by the Earls of Oxford and
Derby, and preceded by a number of officials, heard Mass before
entering the state bedchamber, where spiced wine and cakes were
served. Her Chamberlain then desired the company to pray for 'a

good hour' for her labour, after which the men departed, and
Elizabeth, with some twenty ladies and their attendants, entered the
inner chamber. This was 'hanged ... with rich cloth of blue arras
with fleurs de lys of gold', and contained a bed canopied in gold and
embroidered with red roses.[2]

The Princess was born at nine o'clock in the evening, and
christened in the chapel of Westminster two days later. A torch-lit
procession escorted the Lady Governess carrying the child; she was
accompanied by a concourse of courtiers, Plantagenet relatives and
clergy. Margaret of Richmond, the Duchess of Norfolk, the Earl of
Shrewsbury and Lady Berkeley were godparents. The baby was undressed and dipped in the font by the Archbishop of Canterbury. A
taper having been placed in her hand — and presumably bound to it —
she was carried up to the high altar, where the service concluded.
Refreshments followed, and the presents — jewelled vessels of gold —
were laid before the Princess. 'And thus in order, to the sound of
trumpets', she was taken back to her room, where four nurses, with
their attendants, and six rockers, with theirs, awaited her. She was
then placed in an oaken cradle lined with ermine and draped in cloth
of gold.[3]

Thereafter, Margaret and the four-year-old Prince Arthur were
daily presented to, and blessed by, their parents. Family gatherings
were infrequent. The children had their own households, at Eltham,
Windsor and Westminster. As they grew old enough to share in
Court ceremonies — all Henry's children appeared in public before
they were five — the formalities were implacably sustained; yet there
was no lack of affection.

Margaret loved her father, and became dependent on his approval.
Her grandmother supervised her education. Her mother, a gentle,
delicate creature, too often ailing to count for much in her life, took
third place. The Queen's motto, 'Humble and reverent', typified her
attitude towards her family.

Because Elizabeth of York was subordinated to her formidable
mother-in-law, some of Henry VII's biographers have assumed that
he was an unkind husband, and a stern father. This last supposition
may have sprung from the view, circulated by a number of foreign
residents, that all English children hated their parents, who treated
them with cold brutality.[4]

This was not true of Henry VII. Danger, misfortune and suspense
had outwardly hardened him; his self-control was phenomenal; his

reserve gave those who did not know him well (and few did) an impression of coldness, and even of potential cruelty.

In fact, he was neither cold nor cruel. He had great dignity, a dry sense of humour and a passion for hard work. He generally appeared unresponsive and withdrawn, and so did not become a popular public figure; he could never have been described as Bluff, Bold, or Good. He was a brilliantly clever man, highly educated (he spoke and wrote four languages, and was well read in all of them), many of whose ideas were far in advance of his time; he became an enthusiastic economist, a shrewd bargainer, a generous and discriminating patron of the arts, a subtle politician, a strangely merciful ruler—and an indulgent father. It was to him that Margaret wrote of her unhappiness as a homesick exile; and his mother's letters, beginning, 'My own sweet and most dear King', and answered in the same terms, are proof of the devotion he could inspire.[5]

Henry's marriage—he had promised to become Elizabeth's husband several years before they met—was entirely successful. He remained faithful, considerate, and as dependent on his wife's love and obedience as on his mother's companionship and advice. So his children, Arthur, Margaret, Henry and Mary—five others died in infancy—fitted into a pattern, rare in any age, of serene and dutiful family life.

That Margaret of Richmond should dominate that life was inevitable, for the King was over-worked and the Queen often absent through illness. She was a very remarkable woman, and her influence on her grandchildren became paramount—although not so much, perhaps, in the case of her namesake. She failed to interest Margaret Tudor in the intellectual projects for which she herself became celebrated. Margaret of Richmond is an early example of Renaissance scholarship. She was the first person to translate *The Imitation of Christ* into English; she founded the Colleges of Christ's and St John's at Cambridge; she was the friend and patroness of More, Fisher, Caxton, and many other such persons. In her own day, her *Ordinances* for Court etiquette became the text-book of that circle.[6] Although she liked to retire to her estate of Collyweston in Nottinghamshire, she spent the greater part of her time at Court, often taking her daughter-in-law's place. She never interfered in politics; and there is no record of her sharing her son's private hobbies.

These show Henry VII as a domesticated, cheerful character, as easily approached by his children as by those of his subjects who provided him with informal entertainments—when he had time for them. Before, and long after, Margaret's birth, Henry had many problems. In the first year of his reign, plague swept the country; then came the rebellions of Lambert Simnel and Perkin Warbeck, then war with France. Yet the King often enjoyed, as his children did, the distractions provided by a number of humble persons, all of whom he rewarded, noting down the sums paid them in his own hand.[7]

His favourite pursuits, shared by Margaret, were music and hunting. She learnt to play the lute and the clavichord at an early age, and seems to have been a fair shot with the bow. Both she and her father had their own consort of minstrels. Such items as 2s. 6d. 'to a woman that singeth with the fiddle', £1 'to him that playeth on the bagpipe' and 3s. 4d. 'to the children for singing in the garden' illustrate relaxations which included watching May-games, morris-dancers, acrobats and freaks.[8] Henry's payments to those making cages for his parrots and monkeys, or for the fruit, vegetables and flowers offered during his country progresses may have contributed towards Margaret's habit of buying whatever she fancied, and thus becoming a reckless spendthrift as she reached maturity.

Her background had many bewildering contradictions. England was half ruined by past and present civil wars; yet the magnificence of her surroundings seem to have given this princess the impression that her father would deny her nothing, in dress, at least; and high fashion then, as now, entailed vast expenditure.

In the last decade of the fifteenth century jewelled cauls and high-waisted gowns were not being worn by the upper classes. Head-dresses were broader and larger, and ladies no longer stood or walked as if pregnant. Brocade, velvet and cloth-of-gold dresses with fur trimmings swept the ground in immense folds, contrasting exotically with bare bosoms. Hair was strained back and shaved in front; the resultant exaggerated oval of the face was further emphasized by plucked eyebrows and a uniform pallor.

The men's hair was grown into a long, sometimes a frizzed bob, surmounted by a flat cap. Their straight gowns reached the ankle, opening at the neck to reveal frilled shirts. Both men and women wore a mass of jewellery. The general effect was one of perverse elaboration, as if showing off persons too richly clothed to do more than parade themselves.

In fact, both sexes hunted the whole day, shot at the butts or in the forests for many hours, and frequently danced half the night. Walking, confined to galleries and terraces, was a means of display. Meals, generally eaten in silence to a musical accompaniment, took a long time; at the tables of the great, forty dishes to a course were customary. Breakfast was at seven, dinner at ten and supper at four o'clock. The last two repasts were often preceded or followed by spiced wine and little cakes, served from trays, taken standing and described as voiders.[9]

Hygiene was non-existent. The great cities were stinking, filthy — and exquisitely beautiful. (Dunbar's famous tribute to London was not mere flattery.) Indoors, during cold weather, heat from blazing fires contended with icy draughts and general dampness. In summer, scented rushes were beginning to give way to carpets from the East; and here and there medieval tapestries alternated with portraits or sacred pictures. Furniture was massive, sombre and so carved as to give the feeling of stealthy animation. Most rooms, whether large or small, were dark, fusty and oppressively bare.

Religion was the mainspring of all activity. No one embarked on any pursuit, either of pleasure or business, without first hearing Mass. In Henry's Council lawyers' authority was shared, as in previous reigns, with cardinals and bishops.

All these advisers were good linguists; but neither this section of the community nor those below it were well read in English literature. Caxton's popularization of the Arthurian Saga (his edition of Malory's *Morte d'Arthur* appeared in 1485) then appealed to a small public only, of which the King was one; for his solitary youth had been spent in a country where that pervasive and extraordinary legend was regarded as factual and he himself, though far from credulous, may have liked, sometimes, to believe in the deeds and the semi-divinity of its hero, whose name he had given to his elder son. This imaginative gesture (which was also politic, for Wales must be won over) would not have been made by Margaret. Her vigorous intellect turned her towards the practical aspect of her own career.

That career had been planned and was being carried out before she reached her sixth year. Her marriage was under discussion soon after the birth, in 1491, of the future Henry VIII; by the time her sister Mary was born, five years later, negotiations had begun for her betrothal to the King of Scotland.

This arrangement was the result of the Perkin Warbeck rebellion, which lasted intermittently from 1491 till 1499. During those eight years Henry VII had only one ally, Spain, against the countries supporting Warbeck, who was not even English, but a native of Picardy. As Ferdinand and Isabella had agreed to the marriage of their daughter Katherine of Aragon with Prince Arthur, they wished to ensure peace in England before the Princess arrived. Without their intervention, the war between Henry's forces and the Scottish, Irish and French mercenaries of the young man calling himself Richard of York might have continued indefinitely. A truce with Scotland was made in 1493, on the understanding that permanent peace would follow with an Anglo-Scots alliance.

At about this time the four-year-old Prince Henry had been proclaimed Duke of York and ridden through the city in state. He and Margaret were much alike, remaining a little apart from the Prince of Wales. Arthur was a thoughtful, quiet boy of intellectual tastes, and very like his father in looks and temperament. Margaret and Henry resembled their maternal grandfather, Edward IV: bursting with energy and high spirits, they excelled in dancing, hunting and all outdoor games. Henry was more accomplished than Margaret, and could have competed in scholarship with his brother, had he cared to do so; but from an early age he preferred sports to indoor amusements. All three children had been trained to appear as triumphant public figures, and were thus acclaimed by the people.

Margaret's fifth birthday and her younger brother's dukedom were celebrated by a tournament at Westminster in November 1494. Her head nurses, Alice Bywimble and Alice Davy, had been pensioned off; she was therefore dressed by her ladies in a gown for which eleven yards of buckram and velvet trimmed with gold lace had been ordered, and fitted with one of the white, winged caps now generally associated with Dutch and Flemish costume.[10]

Such attire could hardly have suited this dumpy, round-faced child: but Margaret's fair hair and fresh complexion were well set off, and her behaviour during the course of the three-day tournament was faultless. Attended by her ladies, who wore white damask gowns with crimson velvet sleeves, gold chains and circlets, 'the right high and excellent Princess, the Lady Margaret' was announced by the herald, and took her place beside her grandmother and her parents. When the tourney ended, she thanked the jousters and presented the prizes — rings set with rubies. She was not allowed to stay up for the banquet which followed, and a few days later returned, with her brothers, to the newly built Palace of Shene, later known as that of Richmond.[11]

Meanwhile, the Warbeck rebels had reached Scotland, where they were welcomed and reinforced by James IV, who allowed his cousin, the Lady Katherine Gordon, to marry their leader. In the following August Henry offered Margaret's hand to James, who replied by an attempted invasion in September 1496. A year later, Warbeck was captured, brought to London and given honourable confinement at Westminster, while Henry continued his discussions with Ferdinand and Isabella about their daughter's settlements. At last, just after Margaret's ninth birthday (February 1498) agreement was reached, and the proxy marriage of Katherine and Arthur was celebrated at Westminster.

By this time, the betrothal of Margaret and James IV had been set in hand, and Henry placed the terms before the Privy Council. Some members, perhaps recalling the Prince of Wales's delicacy, objected. As the King's eldest daughter, the Princess might inherit the crown; then, her marriage having been consummated, England would become the 'appanage' of Scotland. 'Supposing, which God forbid,' Henry replied, 'that all my male progeny should become extinct, and the kingdom devolve by law to Margaret's heirs, will England be damaged thereby? For since it ever happens that the less becomes subservient to the greater, the accession will be that of Scotland to England, just as formerly happened to Normandy, which devolved on our ancestors in the same manner, and was happily added to our kingdom by hereditary right — as a rivulet to a fountain.'[12]

After some discussion, the comparison was accepted, and arrangements for the betrothal continued. Neither Henry nor his advisers thought it a disadvantage that James IV was more than twice the age of the Princess. This discrepancy was to have serious consequences.

---

### NOTES

1 C. A. Sneyd (ed.), *Relazione d'Inghilterra*, pp. 8–54.
2 J. Leland, *Collectanea*, vol. IV, p. 249.
3 Op. cit., p. 253.
4 Sneyd, ibid.
5 Domvile, p. 159.
6 Ibid.
7 *Excerpta Historica*, pp. 85–133.
8 Ibid.
9 Sneyd, ibid.
10 *L. & P. Henry VII*, vol. I, p. 395.
11 Ibid.
12 Bishop Lesley, *History of Scotland*, p. 208.

# III

## *Proxy Marriage*

MARGARET TUDOR was more carefully educated than most princesses of her day. She grew up in a court where learning and the arts were highly valued. One of her brothers' tutors was Skelton, who received a degree in rhetoric; the post of what came to be known as Historiographer-Royal fell to a Frenchman, Bernard André; and his compatriot, Giles d'Ewes, was Margaret's writing-master. A group of distinguished visitors headed by Sir Thomas More included Erasmus, who spent several years in England during Margaret's childhood; an Italian expatriate historian, Polydore Vergil, was permanently established in this country. Torrigiano, the architect of Richmond Palace and the decorator of Henry VII's Chapel of Westminster was in frequent consultation with her father. Finally, both his and the young Princes' interest in music, poetry and painting combined with her grandmother's patronage of scholars to make her background one of variegated culture. Her amusements covered an equally wide range: archery, cards, dancing and practice of the lute and the regals alternated with sport and appearances at banquets, tourneys and receptions.

Yet all the time, from her earliest years, she was aware that this existence must come to an end, and that one day she would leave her home and family for a strange country, on the understanding that she might never see them again. All she knew of her future husband was that he had been her father's enemy, and had now become, through her, his ally. (She may have seen his portrait: there is no record of its presentation.) She could have had no notion of what her new life would be like. Admired, busy and indulged, she lived without any responsibility but that of conforming to the customs and manners of those who served or directed her.

Such an upbringing may produce a certain rigidity of outlook, and an inclination to self-will. This was Margaret's case. Her temperament was robust but unyielding; she assumed, as her subsequent

history shows, that she would always get her own way. Meanwhile,
she neither rebelled against nor failed in her share of the pageantry
organized by her father and grandmother. This seems to have become
more elaborate with the peace which followed Perkin Warbeck's
escape and recapture, and his execution in 1499.

In the following year Sir Thomas More brought Erasmus to the
Palace of Eltham, where Margaret, Prince Henry and the four-year-
old Princess Mary received them. 'When we arrived in the hall,' says
Erasmus, 'the attendants were all assembled. In the midst stood
Prince Henry, now nine years old, and having already something of
royalty in his demeanour ... On his right was Margaret.' Sir Thomas
More then presented Henry with a Latin poem. Erasmus, who had
nothing to offer, apologized, and after some talk he and More with-
drew and went in to dinner. During the meal a little note from the
Prince was given to Erasmus, 'to challenge something from my pen.
I was angry with More', he adds, 'for not having warned me. I went
home and, in the Muses' spite, finished the poem within three days.'
With this tribute, he sent Henry a letter, congratulating him on his
care for learning.[1] This young Prince was not only noted for his
insistence on correct behaviour, but for his concern over precedence.
When he realized that Margaret would shortly be known as Queen of
Scots, and thus announced before him at all public ceremonies, he
flew into a rage; he seems to have accepted the situation as soon as the
festivities for her proxy wedding began.[2]

These were preceded by the arrival of the fifteen-year-old Katherine
of Aragon, and her marriage to Prince Arthur in the autumn of 1501.
For the feast in Westminster Hall Margaret wore a gown of crimson
velvet edged with fur. Two wooden stools covered with scarlet cloth
and ornamented with gilt nails had been ordered for her and Prince
Henry, who sat on either side of their parents. The wedding ceremony, and the jousts and banquets preceding it, had tired Prince
Arthur, who danced only once. Henry and Margaret performed
together; she correctly, he with abandon. The courtiers were delighted when he threw aside his gown of state, and continued the
volta in his jacket, 'in so goodly and pleasant a manner that it was to
the King and Queen a great and singular pleasure'[3] — as also to the
Scots ambassadors, who had been asked to the wedding in order to
inspect their future Queen, and formally commissioned by James IV
to betroth the Princess on his behalf, 'or to marry her at once, as
might be most convenient and advisable'.[4]

The leaders of the embassy were Blacader Bishop of Glasgow, Patrick Earl Bothwell and the Bishop of Moray. The preliminaries had been gone through some time before they arrived; these included a correspondence between the twelve-year-old Princess and the Borgia Pope, Alexander VI, on the subject of consanguinity, for James IV's great-grandmother, Joan Beaufort, was one of her Gaunt ancestresses. Her request for a dispensation to marry 'our dearest son in Christ' was granted, 'as a gift of special favour', by His Holiness, with his assurance of the legitimacy of their children. It was then agreed that 'the singular desire, frequent entreaties and continual solicitations' of King James for Margaret's hand should be rewarded by a proxy marriage in January 1502, but that she should remain in England for another year. By that time she would have reached the age of puberty, and so be ready for child-bearing.[5]

There followed a final wrangle over her dower lands. James agreed to be responsible for 'the apparatus of her body, the ornamenting of her residences, her vehicles, stud, furniture, dress, private and domestic affairs, and all other things whatsoever necessary and becoming the honour, state and dignity of the said Lady Margaret', including the salaries of her English attendants. Her marriage portion was 30,000 gold nobles, to be paid into the Scots exchequer over a period of three years. The first instalment arrived when King James's capital had sunk to £100, exclusive of plate and jewels.[6]

Shortly after the Prince and Princess of Wales left for Ludlow as Viceroy and Vicereine of that kingdom, this highly profitable bargain was celebrated at Richmond Palace. Prince Henry and Princess Mary attended their sister, her proxy bridegroom Earl Bothwell, and their parents, at High Mass.

The whole assembly, including the continental ambassadors and their suites, then proceeded to Queen Elizabeth's presence-chamber. The peace treaty was signed, the Lord High Treasurer announced the purpose of the meeting, and the bill of dispensation was read out. The Archbishop of Glasgow turned to King Henry, and said, 'Doth Your Grace know of any impediment other than there is dispensed withal? Doth the Queen likewise? Or the Princess?' All three replied, 'There is none,' and the King asked the Archbishop, 'Is it the very will and mind of the King of Scotland that the said Earl Bothwell should in his name assure the said Princess?' Assurance given, the Archbishop turned to Margaret. 'Are you content without compulsion, and of your own free will?' She replied, 'If it please my lord and father the King, and my lady mother the Queen.' 'It is my will and pleasure,' said Henry, and she knelt for her parents' blessing.

Bothwell, taking her hand, repeated the marriage promises on his master's behalf. Now everyone was looking at the short, solid figure of the bride. In a clear and penetrating treble she announced, 'I, Margaret, the first begotten daughter of the right excellent, right high and mighty prince and princess, Henry by the Grace of God King of England, and Elizabeth Queen of the same, wittingly and of deliberate mind, having twelve years complete in age in the month of November last past, contract matrimony with the right excellent, right high and mighty prince, James King of Scotland, and the person of whom, Patrick Earl of Bothwell, procurator of the said prince, represents, and take the said James King of Scotland into and for my husband and spouse, and all other for him forsake, during his and mine lives natural, and thereto I plight and give to him, in your person as procurator aforesaid, my faith and troth.' 'That done,' says the herald reporter, 'the trumpets ... blew up, and the loud noise of minstrels played in the best and most joyful manner.'[7]

The women then separated from the men. Henry escorted the Scots to dinner in his presence-chamber; the Queen took her daughter's hand and led her up to the dais, where they sat as equals. For the next three days tournaments and shows alternated with banquets—in Westminster Hall, morris-dancers and 'goodly disguisings' of masked ladies and gentlemen appeared from behind screens painted to resemble windows—and after an exchange of presents the Scots embassy departed. In the streets, bonfires blazed; the people danced round them, and drank from the twelve hogsheads of wine provided by the King. Quantities of bad verse were produced; services of thanksgiving were held throughout the country. Meanwhile, Margaret, Prince Henry and their parents sat for their portraits. These were sent to King James, who had to pay for them.[8]

Then tragedy came to the Tudors and their people. The Prince and Princess of Wales fell ill. She recovered; he died within two days.

When the news reached the Privy Council they desired the King's confessor, a friar Observant, to break it to him. Having asked for a private audience, he bowed and began, '*Si bona de manu Dei suscipimus, mala autem quare non sustineamus?*' The King did not answer, and he continued bluntly, 'Your dearest son hath departed to God.' Henry seemed dazed; some time passed before he took in what had happened: then he sent for his wife.

His grief was so painful, so alarming, that she mastered her own, and begged him not to sink into despair, 'for the comfort of your realm, and of me. God by His Grace hath ever preserved you and brought you where you are,' she went on. 'Over that, God hath left you yet a fair Prince and two fair Princesses.' With unconscious pathos, she added, 'God is where He was — and we are both young enough.'

He managed an assent, and she left him. In her own apartments she gave way. Her sobs were so violent that her frightened ladies sent for King Henry, and once more they wept together. A few weeks later she became pregnant again; her health did not improve, and she sank into permanent invalidism.[9]

After Arthur's burial in Worcester Cathedral, Katherine began her journey south. She remained a widow — and the pensioner of her father-in-law — for the next eight years. By the time she married Henry VIII a few weeks after his accession, she must have long ceased to mourn her first husband. She was young, handsome, and more than half in love with the seventeen-year-old King. She knew, and declared, that she was still a virgin; and all Europe believed her.

Arthur's death seems not to have deeply affected Margaret. Henry was her favourite brother; and she was preparing herself for greater triumphs. What she saw as the first step in her professional career had brought her pride of place, and thus increased her innate self-confidence. She was Queen of Scots; and she occupied the position as if she had been born in it.

This attitude was facilitated by her being given establishments of her own at Windsor and Westminster, where she was served on the knee from plate especially made for her and inscribed with the Scottish arms. Meanwhile, the preparations for her journey began with orders for a litter lined with blue velvet and cloth of gold. The litter-bearers had suits of green and black, the footmen white and green liveries. Margaret's gilded state chariot was lined with bearskin; the horses' trappings were of black-and-crimson velvet; her saddle was embroidered with red roses. A bed of green velvet with curtains to match, and altar-cloths with needlework decorations (some showing coats-of-arms, others pictures of Our Lady) were put in hand.[10]

Then came the orders for her trousseau; her entire wardrobe, down to laces, pins and ribands, was renewed. Her state gowns were of cloth of gold, and purple-and-crimson velvet; the sleeves were detachable, some of lynx, some of orange-and-white satin; her velvet head-dresses were set with semi-precious stones. Her consort of musicians had new liveries of Tudor white and green; at the last moment two sackbut players, five trumpeters, a pursuivant-at-arms and a herald were added to her suite.[11]

For the next eighteen months Margaret's life was uneventful. As the Queen's health deteriorated and Margaret of Richmond came less to court, the King made fewer public appearances. He would look in at a banquet and then return to his own rooms, where he wrote his diary and dealt with his personal accounts. This insistence on privacy irritated his courtiers, and they were rather pleased when his pet monkey tore the diary to pieces.[12]

Henry was chiefly occupied with negotiations for keeping Katherine of Aragon in England until the dispensation for her marriage to his younger son had been obtained; for it was essential that her dowry should remain in his hands. The year's mourning observed for Prince Arthur cut down the celebrations for Margaret's birthday, and her daily routine was less crowded. Lessons gave way to accomplishments; she practised assiduously, acquired a new lute, and spent more time with her father than with her mother.[13]

In the first week of February 1503 Queen Elizabeth retired to the Tower for her ninth confinement. There, having given birth to a daughter who survived only a few weeks, she died, in her thirty-eighth year. The King left for one of his country estates to mourn in private. Thenceforward, he lived only for his work, and acquired the cold manner, stingy habits and grasping policy which made him unpopular and unapproachable. So Margaret's last months at home must have been melancholy, and slow in passing. Far from dreading separation from her family, she seems to have looked forward to it; that at least is the impression given by the accounts of her farewells and of her journey north.[14]

Margaret left Richmond Palace on July 2nd, 1503, and reached that of Dalkeith on September 3rd. Every daylight hour of those eight weeks was spent in public receptions, church-going and formal converse with local potentates. Henry VII and his advisers had planned her progress so as to display the wealth and glory of his dynasty, and also to emphasize its origin. The vast concourse centring on the fourteen-year-old bride, the crowds flocking to greet her were surrounded by Tudor emblems — white-and-green uniforms, and banners embroidered with red dragons, a dun cow on a yellow field, a portcullis, and the hawthorn bush bearing the crown abandoned at

Bosworth. Henry and his courtiers accompanied her as far as Colly-weston, where they were received by his mother. Then came the ceremony of farewell.

At this point, the principal herald, John Young, joined Margaret's train. Every night he sat down to record the events of the day. His account is of considerable length, and abounds in repetitive detail and gloating admiration. He took it for granted that the little Queen of Scots would never, at any moment, make a single mistake, or even falter throughout the series of public appearances, its concomitant changes of clothing (more than once these had to be made by the roadside) and appropriate speeches to civic authorities, great nobles and clerical grandees. If the procedure had been confused or halted, he would certainly have noted it, as his accounts of other ceremonies show. It never was; nor did that determined, pink-and-white central figure complain or hesitate. Her farewells to her father and grand-mother were made with the same self-assurance that informed her receptions of abbots, mayors, land-owners and bishops.

Outside the manor-house of Collyweston she knelt to receive King Henry's blessing; he then gave her a short, private admonition about her future duties. They embraced, and she took her place in an ordered concourse of some four hundred persons. So she progressed into Lincolnshire, and thence, ever more slowly and magnificently, through Yorkshire, Durham, Northumberland, Berwick and East Lothian, making her penultimate halt some miles outside Edinburgh.[15]

In each county, lay and clerical representatives emerged from castles, abbeys and town halls to welcome her, themselves accom-panied by some hundreds of attendants. And all the way along, whether in cities, villages or the countryside, the common people lined the route, cheering, throwing flowers, crowding round her to present fruit, nosegays or farm produce. Gorgeous in velvet and cloth of gold, glittering with jewels, and sometimes wearing a train so heavy that four pages were required to carry it, Margaret descended from her litter, mounted her palfrey, stood to receive addresses, kissed holy relics, heard Mass, feasted, danced and conversed, with changeless aplomb and unbroken serenity. Since infancy she had absorbed the rules of precedence. The Earl and Countess of Northum-berland, the Earl of Derby, the Archbishop of York, the Scots dignitaries who crossed the Border to welcome her — sheriffs, priors, burgesses and knights — all were received according to etiquette. Some ladies were kissed, the salutations of others greeted with a bend

HENRY VII *(artist unknown)*

ELIZABETH OF YORK
*(artist unknown)*

of the head; smiling courtesy and pretty speeches of thanks were vouchsafed to every host and hostess.[16]

Her stay in York was the longest of the journey. Some miles from that city, the Earl of Northumberland, 'upon a fair courser, with a footcloth to the ground of crimson velvet ... his arms very rich ... himself arrayed of the said crimson ... and black velvet boots', came to meet her with his train. To the music of the town band, he conducted her to the Minster, where she was received by the Archbishop, the Bishop of Durham and the Lord Abbot of St Mary's. She then heard Mass and was lodged in the episcopal palace, 'to refresh', while the bells rang out over the city.[17]

Next day, surrounded by nobles and 'richly arrayed', she heard Mass again, received the Countess of Northumberland and her ladies, and dined in public to the sound of 'trumpets and other instruments, rung to the ancient manner and lasting the said dinner'.[18]

The Northumberlands, with some four hundred followers, then escorted her across the Border. Here the quantity of Scots personages outnumbered that of the English, and Margaret's new subjects thronged about her. She was now so loaded with jewels that her golden dress was barely visible; its train spread out behind her for some twelve yards. Whether on foot or on horseback, she supported the weight of these splendours without difficulty or, it would seem, the faintest concern. Success, down to the minutest detail, was assured. Her triumph must be as flawless as her mastery of its elaborations. And so it was. Nothing went wrong, from first to last.

At Berwick, Northumberland took his leave, sprang on his 'gambading' steed without touching the stirrup and rode away. With the Earl and Countess of Surrey (afterwards Duke and Duchess of Norfolk) who were to attend her temporarily, Margaret proceeded through Haddington to Dalkeith, the last of the twenty-two places in which she stayed. She was now within a short ride of Edinburgh, and her first sight of her husband.

At the gates of the palace she was received by the Countess of Morton, who, curtsying low, greeted her as lady and mistress. A number of presents from James IV, including a crown of rubies, diamonds and emeralds, awaited her. Their public meeting was to take place next day, at the Canongate. Then, suddenly, a change of schedule, a breaking away from formality was announced.

In fact, this so-called surprise was one of the chivalric customs of the day. Margaret was informed, as most royal brides then were, that her gallant husband could not endure further waiting. Nor would he suffer the appraisal of the crowds; he longed to welcome and embrace her, privately and at once.

She was at cards with the Surreys when the news — not wholly unexpected — of James's departure from Holyrood Palace thrilled through courtyards, galleries and ante-chambers. 'The King! The King of Scots is on his way!'[19]

---

## NOTES

1 J. Nichols, *Epistles of Erasmus*, vol. I, p. 201.
2 A. Strickland, *Queens of Scotland*, vol. I, p. 9.
3 Leland, vol. V, p. 362.
4 Ibid.
5 Ibid.
6 M. A. Everett Green, *Princesses of England*, vol. IV, p. 63.
7 Leland, vol. IV, p. 262.
8 Ibid.
9 Ibid.
10 Leland, op. cit., pp. 265–82. Green, op. cit., pp. 71–82.
11 Ibid.
12 F. Bacon, *Life of Henry VII*, p. 243.
13 Green, ibid.
14 Ibid.
15 Ibid.
16 Ibid.
17 Ibid.
18 Ibid.
19 Ibid.

# IV

## *Queen of Scots*

JAMES IV was in his sixteenth year when a group of lords led by the Humes and the Hepburns made him the figurehead of a revolt against his father, James III. In the summer of 1488 the struggle reached its climax at the battle of Sauchieburn.

After the death of his wife, Margaret of Denmark, in 1486, the King had become something of a recluse. A brilliant, self-willed Renaissance prince, he avoided the company of his brutal and illiterate nobles, preferring to spend his leisure hours with persons of culture, many of whom were artists or craftsmen. This infuriated the heads of the clans, who identified aesthetic taste with effeminacy, and the King's disregard of their complaints was a further cause of enmity. He then enraged them to the point of open rebellion by uniting the Priory of Coldingham, for several centuries the unofficial property of the Humes, to the Chapel Royal. Both the Vatican and Parliament agreed to this annexation, which became law in 1487.

During the next six months the Humes collected an army, persuaded the young Prince to join them and tried to force his father to abdicate. The King rallied his followers, buckled on the sword worn by Robert the Bruce and marched to Sauchieburn. There he saw his son, in the vanguard of the rebel troops. He halted, uncertain whether to charge or not. His enemies seized the advantage, and descended on his front line, which began to give way after some hours' fighting.

Urged to fly, the King galloped from the field. He was thrown from his horse outside a mill, whose owners carried him into the barn and asked him who he was. 'I was your King this day morn,' he said, and begged them to fetch a priest. The miller's wife ran out into the street, crying, 'A priest—a priest for the King!' and was answered by a stranger with, 'Here am I, a priest—where is the King?' She led him inside and he knelt down by James, who gasped out, 'Shrive me.' 'That will I do hastily,' his pursuer replied, and stabbed him through the heart.

Having been long estranged from his father, James IV was eager to succeed, but he did not foresee exactly how he would do so, for he had chosen to believe the rebels' assurance that they would spare the King's life. Now, realizing once and for all what such a promise — in fact, what any Scottish promise — was worth, he set himself to rule more ruthlessly than his predecessor, while suffering from a sense of guilt which nothing could efface. High-spirited, handsome, of protean talent, and successful in much that he did, he yet felt himself stricken and haunted. That he had been to some extent forced into treachery and patricide was little consolation. His crown was stained with his father's blood; thenceforward, all his enterprises were shadowed by the memory of his share in the crime.

Piety was then the concomitant of kingship; in this respect James went to extremes. He wore an iron chain about his waist, made constant pilgrimages to the shrine of St Ninian, his patron, and at intervals retired to a monastery to pray and fast. As these practices did not remove the whole burden of remorse, he distracted himself with a series of mistresses — his establishment contained five bastards — while a frenzied restlessness drove him from one part of his kingdom to another, hunting, playing football and golf, studying and even practising surgery, dentistry and medicine. He was an accomplished musician and an ingenious diplomat; he became an expert ruler in circumstances which would have defeated most monarchs and had helped to destroy his father.

For although Scotland was entering upon a period of comparative prosperity, and had begun to show signs of civilized living — even of concern for learning and the arts — it remained, as ever, impoverished, commercially backward and in that state of internal chaos which was part of the national way of life. The clans were not subdued, much less intimidated, by James's authority, because his government was not, and never became, centralized.

Indeed, it could not be otherwise. The monarchy was as short of bullion as of land; so if the nobles chose to combine against the government and civil war ensued, the regal power was further weakened, and the laws were defied with impunity. Parliament, the civic authorities and the wealthy burgesses were helpless in the face of the nobles' and their followers' bestial savagery, and the support of the English kings, who paid them to betray their country. This they did as it suited them: sometimes they accepted bribes and did nothing; sometimes they preferred to fight one another. And in many cases their privileges had a legal basis. If one of their tenants was summoned before the King's justiciar, he could demand trial by his landlord's court, and so might escape punishment. This ensured his loyalty to his chief in the event of a revolt against the crown.

This primitive and tottering feudalism was further confused by divisions of language and territory, which separated the Western Isles and the Highlands from the rest of the kingdom. The Macdonalds ruled the Hebrides, which had been taken from Norway in 1266. At intervals they, or the 'wild Scots' of the Highlands, or both together, made war against the monarchy; these expeditions were encouraged and sometimes financed by the English. When repulsed, the Hebrideans would retire to their sea-bound fortresses to make ready for the the next raid, in which the Highlanders might join.

In the fifteen years between his accession and his marriage James IV mastered many of his problems. His greatest mistake was his backing of Perkin Warbeck; this was eradicated by the Anglo-Scots peace of 1497 and his alliance with France. Having failed to achieve marriage with a princess of Spain, he seems to have considered a love-match with the Lady Margaret Drummond, whom he installed in his Palace of Linlithgow. Then, aware of the dangers of marrying a subject, he began negotiations for the hand of Margaret Tudor, while continuing his relationship with the beautiful Mistress Drummond. She and their daughter were still established at Linlithgow when the younger Margaret's proxy marriage was celebrated at Richmond.[1]

James's ministers, who feared that this long-planned alliance might even now fall through—there were rumours that he had secretly married Margaret Drummond—were much relieved when she and both her sisters suddenly died, presumably of poison, in the spring of 1502.

The King's grief was deep and lasting; although he took another mistress, Janet Kennedy, almost at once, he never got over Margaret Drummond's death. Her loss intensified the underlying melancholy of his address, outwardly that of a gracious and popular ruler, whose care for his subjects was unremitting and whose vitality seemed inexhaustible. The best of his portraits shows something of this dichotomy; a strange unease, a lurking morbidity can be discerned beneath that gallant self-assurance.

James now made it his business, as much for his people's sake as for his own, to receive Margaret as became his Queen, and the representative of a richer and more powerful country. Scottish pride required an immense outlay on splendours which must equal if not surpass those borne by a Tudor heiress. Also, it was to be made clear, especially to Surrey, whose troops had defeated his and harried his borders, that Scotland was prosperous and secure, and James himself ready to ignore former humiliations.

He began by ordering his trousseau from Paris. Indoor gowns of black velvet trimmed with fur, a crimson jacket lined with cloth of gold, a wedding surcoat of white damask embroidered in gilt thread, and several pairs of scarlet hose were the principal items. As spade beards were coming into fashion, he decided to grow one. Then he had the Queen's crown remodelled. His presents to her included a gown valued at £160; and he seems to have paid for new clothes and jewelled chains for his courtiers and their wives.[2]

In the midst of these preparations he became alarmed at his rate of expenditure, replying evasively to King Henry's inquiry as to what salaries Margaret's ladies would receive. 'Dearest Father,' he wrote, ' ... It is not required that we should assign any such fees. Nevertheless, we ... will gladly ... give ... unto the said persons ... competent fees yearly, according to their qualities.'[3]

James's descent on Dalkeith had been carefully planned. Wearing the crimson jacket and accompanied by some sixty courtiers and their wives, he set off as if for hawking, on a black courser, his lure slung behind him. His beard, already 'something long', according to the English herald, caused comment; indeed, it must have looked odd in conjunction with the dark-red hair which still reached his shoulders. He rode at great speed, outstripping his suite, and thus emphasizing the romantic ardour of his approach.

Having received Margaret's portrait, he could not have expected to see a beauty, or even a pretty girl. In any case, his immediate object was his effect on her, and on the alert and critical English visitors, whose reports would be sent to King Henry, and thereafter circulated in the courts of Europe. It seems that he had determined first to reassure and then to charm her; no doubt he counted on his experience of women to succeed in doing both. And so, knowing the value set by the Tudors on reverential courtesy, he adapted his behaviour to that of a knight in an Arthurian legend.

There was no need for Margaret to hurry into a more elaborate gown when the news of his arrival reached her. Dressed for an informal yet semi-public meeting, she was waiting in the doorway of her presence-chamber when James rode into the courtyard, followed by his attendants. Of these, only his younger brother the Duke of Ross and a Hamilton cousin accompanied him through the ante-chambers.

Behind Margaret stood the Surreys and her ladies. As she and James faced one another he uncovered and she curtsied. Taking her hand, he kissed her cheek. He then welcomed the Surreys and made the round of the ladies, kissing each in turn.

The moment had now come for him to take Margaret aside for a private talk, and they conversed unheard for what seemed to the onlookers a long time. She appeared perfectly at ease. James, still bare-headed, was apparently complimenting her, for more bows and curtsies were noted. Presently supper was announced, followed by the ceremonious washing of hands. James stood back, so that Margaret might dip her fingers into the basin held by the kneeling official before he did, acknowledging her curtsy of thanks with another reverence. He then led her to the canopied dais, where they sat down at some distance from the rest of the company, while the musicians played and the dishes were presented, tasted and served.

So some three hours went by. When the cloth had been removed James conducted Margaret to the ballroom, where she danced before him with the Countess of Surrey. After a further series of courtesies he made his farewells and returned to Edinburgh, 'for it was late', says the English herald, 'and he went to his bed ... very well content with so fair a meeting'.[4]

Next day Margaret and her suite moved to the Castle of Newbattle to prepare for her entry into the capital. That night a fire broke out in the stables, and her three palfreys were burnt to death. At this sad and frightening omen, she broke down and would not be comforted. She was still in tears when James, accompanied by Surrey, who had ridden out to conduct him to the castle, heard what had happened and ordered replacements to be sent her. Then, 'flying as the bird seeks her prey', according to the herald, he hurried to comfort her as she sat at cards.

By this time, Margaret was sufficiently recovered to greet him with a kiss and to dance for him again. When wine and bread were served, James waited on her himself, drinking out of the same cup. He then played for her on the clavichord and the lute, and three of her gentlemen sang a ballad.[5]

During the next four days James came to Newbattle every evening, and listened kneeling while Margaret played for him. At supper, seeing her incommoded by the weight of her gown, he gave her his chair of state; as she accepted it hesitantly, he called to the Surreys to sit beside them. Then followed another little concert, more dancing and, with James's departure, his presentation of a courser, 'well appointed', in the Tudor white and green, to the Earl of Surrey.[6]

James, doing his utmost to please and impress, seems to have enjoyed the performance. Margaret remained passive, a show figure; perhaps she was beginning to feel rather dazed. On the fifth day, dressed in cloth of gold and heavily jewelled, she set off for Edinburgh in her litter, to be met by James and his nobles. Preceded by an usher carrying the sword of state, they approached the city, James talking to Margaret all the way along. As his courser became restive, he mounted another, placing her on the pillion. They then halted in a meadow, a little way from the gates, for a theatrical display. This reflected not only the taste of the age, but James's vision of himself as the monarch of chivalric legend.

A knight on horseback and a lady carrying a horn were waiting for them. A second knight appeared, seized the lady and blew the horn. Then came the dialogue.

'Wherefore hast thou this done?'

'What will you say thereto?'

'I say that I will prove upon thee that thou hast done outrage to me.'

'Art thou armed? Well then, prove a man and do thy devoir.'

So the joust began, first with spears, and then on foot with swords, followed by a call to surrender and a renewal of the combat. This was James's cue to cry 'Peace!' and, having summoned the performers before him, to ask the cause of their dispute. 'Sire, he hath taken from me my lady paramour, whereof I was in surety of her by her faith.' The other knight added, 'Sire, I shall defend me against him.' James told them to come to him again, 'for to agree you', and so concluded the scene.[7]

A white hart was then 'loosed', and, chased by a greyhound, offered to Margaret, who refused the first shot. As it disappeared a party of Greyfriars approached with a number of relics, which James would not kiss until she had done so. They finally came to the city gates, which were guarded by singing angels and the monks of St Giles carrying the arm of the saint; this was received with more kisses, to the sound of the *Te Deum*.

MARGARET TUDOR *(Mytens)*

At the centre of the town, bride and bridegroom drank wine from the fountain, pausing to meet Paris, Helen, Mercury and Venus, who were followed by the Angel Gabriel. This personage introduced the Virgin and St Joseph, whose marriage he celebrated in dumb-show. At their next stop, Justice, Force, Temperance and Prudence were waiting for them, each carrying emblems with which they defeated Nero, Sardanapalus and other tyrants. A confusion of red roses, greyhounds and drum-beating minstrels surrounded them to the Canongate, and then to the Church of the Holy Cross, where stood the precursor of the guillotine—known as the Maiden—which had been covered over, at a cost of 14s., by James's order. He had thought of everything.[8]

It becomes clear, if only from the herald's lack of comment on her behaviour, that Margaret was being outshone by James. Towering above her, he received the cheers of his people with a genial graciousness which made her the appendage to, rather than the participator in his triumph. His arm round her waist, he led her up the aisle of Holyrood Chapel to her stall, retreating to his own on the other side of the chancel. When they rejoined one another to kneel at the high altar, he indicated that they should do so simultaneously. After the service he again obscured her by 'holding of her body', till they reached the presence-chamber, where she was introduced to his courtiers. They separated for supper, and she was able to rest, while he entertained her suite in his own rooms.

It was an exhausting ordeal for a girl of fourteen; and from the point of view of the spectators, Margaret was thereby diminished. Her dress and jewels may not have set off her only assets, those of a delicate complexion and yellow hair, for she had neither the build nor the height to show them to advantage. Her progress from Richmond to Dalkeith had accustomed her to being the central figure. Now she was relegated; and no Tudor of either sex ever willingly accepted such a position. Her appearance—what could be seen of it—seems not to have disappointed the townsfolk, because the show itself and their magnificent King sufficed.

Next day, Margaret's share in the gorgeous intricacies of the marriage ceremony was smoothly sustained. Crowned, anointed, and once more encircled by her husband's arm, she walked through rows of courtiers to the banqueting hall, to be faced by some forty dishes and an outpouring of French wine, while James kept up and improved upon his *amour courtois* manners. He was more than ever admired as King, bridegroom and host. Gay and gallant, he dominated every scene.

After supper they rejoined one another in the great hall. Here the public had been admitted to receive the largesse 'cried' for them both by the heralds ('Do not cry mine', James told them, 'it suffices to cry hers.'), followed by dancing and mock duels. James then went alone to Evensong, returning to dismiss the company. 'Therefore,' says Young, 'each one withdrew to his lodging for to take his rest, and the King had the Queen apart, and they went together. God by His Grace will hold them in long prosperity.' All that night the bonfires blazed, and the streets were full of dancing and singing people.[9]

Next day James gave a reception, and then went to Mass in 'a rich robe of cloth of gold, black hose, a black bonnet, a pair of gold beads hanging at his girdle', and, with the Earl of Surrey, dined in public. 'Touching the Queen,' the herald adds, 'I say nothing, for that same day I saw her not.' This was disturbing; presently he heard that she was well.[10]

Two days went by before her next appearance, which was at High Mass. Forty-one gentlemen were then knighted by James who, resuming his Arthurian role, said, 'Lady, these are your knights,' as he led her into their private apartments for dinner.[11]

By this time he and Surrey had become friends; they walked about arm-in-arm and talked alone together, when not attending jousts, morality plays, dances and concerts. Margaret watched these performances from a distance with her Scottish ladies, and went to Mass only once, in a gown of purple velvet trimmed with ermine, and a jewelled girdle.[12]

Then she spoke out: not agreeably. The King's beard was long — and harsh. She objected to it, appealing for support to the Countess of Surrey. James chose to take the criticism as a joke and, sending for some shears, asked Lady Surrey and her daughter Lady Grey to be his barbers. He then said that they must be rewarded, and gave them several lengths of gold cloth.[13]

Still Margaret would not accompany him to Mass every day. They danced and sang together; but she refused to appear when another knighting ceremony was announced, and so the presentation of these honours was postponed. That same evening she attended the morality play which concluded the festivities.

Her English escort now left, loaded with King James's gifts. The Surreys remained. And then at last Margaret had time to write to her father. The first part of her letter was dictated to a secretary; she added a postscript in her own hand.

James's little jokes, his courtesies, his considerate and tactful attentions, his daily presents of jewellery were not mentioned. 'Sir,' she began, 'as for news, I have none to send.' After this staggering dismissal of everything that had been done for her, she launched into a diatribe against her husband's frequentation of the Surreys. The Earl was 'always with the King here', and never with her. He and the Bishop of Moray 'ordereth everything ... to the King's pleasure', without consulting hers. Her Chamberlain would bear her out; if he did not, it would be because he went in terror of Surrey, 'who hath such words unto him that he dare speak no further'. In fact, all her servants were being harshly treated, and now she was afraid that she herself would be so used. She was very unhappy, desperately home-sick, and had no time to herself. Seizing the pen, she scrawled a last, almost illegible complaint. 'For God's sake, Sir, hold me excused that I write not myself to Your Grace, for I have no leisure ... With a wish I were with Your Grace, now and many times more ... Written with the hand of your humble daughter ... '[14]

---

## NOTES

1 J. Mackie, *James IV*, pp. 1–82.
2 Leland, vol. IV, p. 283.
3 Green, vol. IV, p. 71.
4 Leland, ibid.
5 Ibid.
6 Ibid.
7 Ibid.
8 Ibid.
9 Ibid.
10 Ibid.
11 Ibid.
12 Ibid.
13 Ibid.
14 Green, op. cit., p. 100.

# V

# *Married Life*

WITH the exception of Margaret Drummond, who was almost certainly a virgin when James became her lover, all his mistresses were married women. He had never had relations with a girl of his wife's age, nor with one who had been so strictly brought up. The princesses of that day were not ignorant: but they were scrupulously sheltered. Their confessors were the only men they saw alone until they married.

Margaret Tudor was neither stupid nor romantic. She thought of her husband as the principal figure in a political alliance, and as part-founder of an Anglo-Scots dynasty. She knew her duty: but her capacity for strong feeling was at odds with her position; and neither James's warmth of heart nor his grace and charm could at once overcome the resentment — perhaps partly caused by shock — shown in her first letter to her father.

At this time, she may not have known about his mistresses and his brood of illegitimate children. Her attendants, both Scottish and English, did, and might have enlightened her, for it was not James's habit to conceal their existence, although he kept them out of Margaret's way in the early months of their marriage, while continuing to care for and visit them. Eventually, she accepted this situation and grew fond of James; but she never fell in love with him, nor he with her. Indeed, neither of them could have reasonably expected this to happen.

The difference in their ages was a serious barrier. The spoilt child and the experienced man of the world had little in common. The only tastes they shared were those of sport, dancing and music. Margaret took no interest in her husband's scientific pursuits, nor in his hobbies — those of carpentry and smith's work — nor could she play any part in the government of the kingdom; she merely followed where he led, on ceaseless and exhausting journeys from one district to another. He had so much to do that he was absent all day; he did

44

not become a husband till night, when the administration of justice and the public appearances were over. Whether hunting, playing games or dancing, he and Margaret were never alone; they would not have had much to say to one another if they had been.

Though he indulged her — possibly more than was necessary or wise — he could not provide her with the setting and the comforts to which she was accustomed. The Scotland of the early sixteenth century produced splendid displays, wild beauty, fine literature and care for learning. The poetry of Dunbar, Gavin Douglas and David Lindsay was of a far higher standard than that of Skelton or the young Thomas More, and there were three universities to England's two. James, his father and some of their nobles had built many churches and palaces. None of these amenities could have impressed a materially minded girl brought up in that 'flower of cities all',[1] most of whose inhabitants lived in houses of brick and stone. Those of Edinburgh, once stripped of their wedding decorations, were seen to consist of thatched wood. The Palace of Holyrood was unfinished, and the castle on the heights had become an armoury.

Then there was the difficulty of language. Scots dialect, whether written or spoken, must have been almost incomprehensible to Margaret, although she learnt it in a very short time. Perhaps it was as well that her interests, judging by the few books she ordered, were not literary. She was never influenced by any aspect of the Arthurian saga, on whose heroes James had modelled himself. Able, energetic and advanced, he yet dwelt in a medieval past which existed only in poetry and legend. Margaret could not have fitted into this daydream — one that was eventually to destroy him — because, as his wife, she was not available for the part of lady-paramour. In any case, she had neither the talents nor the appearance of a Guinevere, a Nimue, a Morgan le Fay. No enchantress, but a realist — and a discontented one at that — she was passionate but unimaginative. James, the sophisticated descendant of kings, floated through life with his head in the clouds. Margaret, the crudely youthful product of an *arriviste* dynasty, had her feet on the ground.

She shared neither his piety nor his visions. While he treated her as the petted recipient of a generosity he delighted to exercise, she appeared ungrateful and disobliging — but then her share in the performance was rather a dull one.

The portrait of her painted shortly after their marriage illustrates her attitude very effectively. For the rich array so ecstatically described by John Young, a dark gown, a drab coif and a nun-like girdle have been substituted. It is as if Margaret, sickened of glitter and magnificence, had deliberately selected the plainest outfit in her wardrobe, the kind worn by a waiting-woman or a country-bred dowager. Sullen and uncompromising, she stares out of the canvas in obstinate endurance. Her expression is acute, and self-confident to the point of arrogance. Thence the point of view which was to complicate and darken her career begins to emerge.

Margaret Tudor thought of herself as the daughter of a great house of which Scotland was the vassal. Her Plantagenet ancestors had nearly conquered and more than once crushed the kingdom she saw as inferior in every respect. In her opinion, one of the objects of the alliance was the subordination of the weaker to the more powerful country. Her husband's plan of independence became, to her, the absurd fancy of an idealist. In the first years of her marriage this conviction was not formulated, perhaps not even realized, by herself. Her later conduct reveals its inherent strength.

Meanwhile, James continued his courtship. When the Surreys returned to England he spent the evenings playing cards with her; he never forgot to reward her musicians; and his presents arrived almost daily—a velvet riding-dress, a golden image of the Virgin, a ruby ring. Like the rest of her family, Margaret was acquisitive; although she might not care always to wear rich gowns and valuable jewellery, she liked to possess them; and very soon her wardrobe so increased that when she travelled it filled some twenty carts.[2]

She now began to get over her homesickness, and made efforts to respond to James's attentions. She embroidered a purse for him, and became the patroness of his favourite poets, William Dunbar and Gavin Douglas. Dunbar replied with his famous allegorical tribute, 'The Thistle and the Rose', in which Margaret appeared as 'the fresh Rose, of colour red and white ... So full of virtue, pleasure and delight, So full of blissful, angelic beauty, Imperial birth, honour and dignity', and was greeted by 'birdies with voice on high' as their Queen and sovereign.

As her spirits revived, James took her on a tour of the midlands, stopping at Linlithgow and Stirling. They went on to Falkland, Perth, Elgin and Aberdeen, with all their train, sometimes staying at monasteries and convents. By the end of November they were back in Edinburgh, and a few weeks later the Christmas festivities began, with more presents of jewellery for Margaret and her ladies. Every night there was dancing and singing, till the death of James's brother put an end to gaiety.

Early in 1504 James left the capital to administer justice, returning in March for Margaret's coronation. The lands of Kilmarnock were then bestowed on her by Parliament, and Henry VII sent three commissioners to Scotland with the first instalment of her dowry.

So all seemed to be going smoothly. Yet there was no sign of an heir, and James had renewed his relationship with Janet Kennedy, now Lady Bothwell, whom he visited during his frequent absences. He seldom remained in one place for more than a few days together; and Margaret went with him on many of these journeys. The effect on her health was very nearly fatal in respect of child-bearing.

Some five years before her marriage her father had reported her as delicate, and small for her age. Although there is no record of her falling ill during her first eighteen months in Scotland, this constant travelling about the country in all weathers must have been taxing for a luxuriously brought up girl. Many of James's castles dated from the thirteenth century and were half ruined; and the accommodation provided by monks and nuns was not much better. Yet none of Margaret's attendants, nor her husband, that amateur of medicine, then connected these conditions with her failure to conceive. She seemed well and made no complaints; still the hunting, dancing and travelling continued. She appeared tireless, and was becoming almost as restless as her husband.

The death of his brother had increased James's difficulties, for if he himself died leaving no direct heir civil war was inevitable. As the months went by and Margaret showed no signs of pregnancy, his pilgrimages and retreats became more frequent. These were not outwardly penitential. He would set off accompanied by musicians and huntsmen, pausing to hawk or to inspect his buildings, hearing petitions, relieving the unfortunate. He was superbly generous: and so no King of Scotland had ever been more beloved. He was enjoying family life with Alexander, his twelve-year-old son by Mary Boyd, and also with Margaret Drummond's daughter, when his wife joined him at Stirling. She insisted on the children's removal, and he sent them to St Andrews.[3]

At about this time he took another mistress, listed in the Treasury accounts as 'the Lady of A'. His discretion was rewarded by Margaret's compliance. She was now in great spirits, riding, shooting at the butts and running races with her attendants. She seems to have made no objection when James left for a six months' tour in the south, rejoining her for the Christmas festivities of 1505.

These were more than usually hilarious. The Abbot of Unreason and the Lord of Misrule were allowed unlimited licence. Mock services, wild horseplay and elaborate practical jokes reached a climax when the King of the Bean sprang on the dais and drank from James's cup, refusing to leave until given a gold piece. Dancing was followed by an acrobatic display and a concert; then the story-tellers took the floor. Next day Margaret's nose bled so profusely that she stayed in bed.[4]

In the spring of 1506 James left to put down a revolt in Eskdale. Some of the leaders were executed on the spot, others sent to Dumfries for trial. He had now obtained supremacy within his kingdom, and beyond it the support of his father-in-law. Yet this did not suffice. He planned to make Scotland a European power through a military alliance with France. This was the first in a series of errors which led to the holocaust of Flodden.

A single adjective, the product of his own people, fits James to a hair. He was fey.* His ability combined with his arrogance to drive him to disaster. Reaching for greater fame, he acquired hubris, and the revenge of those gods who allow their favourites just so much triumph, and no more.

His original agreement with Louis XII had been commercially profitable; his marriage, even without children, was a safeguard. Now, hiring out a poor kingdom to a rich one, he got nothing in return but the enmity of Henry VII, who saw in this bargain a further menace from England's ancient foe: for if the French attacked, the Scots would arm and cross the Border. When Henry objected, James took no heed; and Louis blandly accepted the offers of his obliging young friend, while assuring Henry of his goodwill. The Scottish nobles' encouragement of the new alliance was an added anxiety; but when James sent troops and money to the Irish rebels all Henry could do was to arrest and imprison Lord Arran, now potential heir-presumptive, who had been travelling in England without a passport.

So James's vision of himself as a paladin masked the writing on the wall. In his thirty-fifth year, he looked upon his work, and saw that it was good. He had effected the final submission of the Western Islands, the restoration of his castles and, perhaps most important of all, the

* 'Doomed, fated soon to die, marked by extravagantly high spirits' (Chambers's *Twentieth Century Dictionary*).

establishment of a firm of printers in Edinburgh. Now those of his subjects who had libraries would no longer need to send for books from England and the Continent. Chapman and Millar's list contained several titles which reflected their patron's taste: *The Knightly Tale of Galagros and Gawaine, Sir Eglamour of Artoys* and *The Complaint of the Black Knight.*[5]

In the second week of May 1506 James's prayers were answered: Margaret was pregnant. Still she journeyed with him—on a sailing expedition, then to Linlithgow, then to Stirling, and so back to Edinburgh. She took to her chamber in the second week of February 1507, and on the 21st of that month their child, a boy, was born. Carried on an ermine cushion and robed in white silk, he was christened James in the chapel of Holyroodhouse, and proclaimed Prince of Scotland and the Isles. But the King could not rejoice, for Margaret was desperately ill. This, says a contemporary, 'gave him so great grief that, yielding himself up to anguish, he would not be soothed by any human consolation'.[6] Then he remembered St Ninian, and hurried to his shrine in Galloway. The saint was kind: James returned to find his wife out of danger.

A year later, his son was dead. Then plague swept over Scotland. And Dunbar was writing his 'Lament for the Makers':

> Our pleasance here is all vainglory,
> This false world is but transitory,
> The flesh is bruckle, the Fiend is slee—
> *Timor Mortis conturbat me.*

---

## NOTES

1 W. Dunbar, *Works.*
2 Green, vol. IV, p. 113.
3 Op. cit., p. 112.
4 Ibid.
5 Mackie, p. 170.
6 Lesley, p. 80.

4

# VI

## Scotland and France

THE spring of 1507 had been a time of gaiety and hope for the King and Queen of Scots. Their son then seemed healthy; and Margaret, now in her eighteenth year, might well expect another pregnancy before long. Agreement between her husband and father had been effected by Henry VII's clever young secretary, Thomas Wolsey, who visited Edinburgh in January; and Henry's disapproval of James's approach to Louis XII was silenced by Julius II's announcement of his Holy League. This was part of a scheme to drive French troops out of Italy, and resulted in war between France and the Curia. The Pope, who eventually headed his soldiers in person, now sent an embassy to Edinburgh. His legate presented James with a wreath of gold and a jewelled sword.*

In June Margaret arranged a tournament to celebrate her son's birth and her own recovery. She organized a semi-comic display centring on two Negro girls, a present from Admiral Robert Barton. He had brought them—with a red-tailed horse, a musk cat and several other exotic specimens—from Portugal in the preceding year, and they had been christened Margaret and Ellen. The Queen was especially fond of Ellen, of whom Dunbar wrote, 'When she is clad in rich apparel, She shines as bright as ane tar-barrel.'

It was given out that an unknown, 'wild' knight would defend Ellen against all comers, and the lists were set up in the courtyard of Edinburgh Castle. The decorations consisted of metal trees hung with artificial fruits and winged beasts. Black Ellen was then announced by the heralds. In a gown of gold damask trimmed with green-and-yellow taffeta, she appeared on a triumphal car, attended by knights and ladies. Her champion, whose followers were dressed as savages, in goats' skins, entered the arena and overthrew all his opponents. Desired to reveal himself, he raised his visor, and was greeted with a

* The sword now hangs in Edinburgh Castle.

burst of cheering. Black Ellen's champion was King James himself.[1] 'And how she shines like any soap,' noted Dunbar, 'the lady with the muckle lips.'

In order to ensure her own and her son's well-being, Margaret then made a pilgrimage to St Ninian's shrine, with her minstrels and a train of seventeen horses for her luggage. During her tour she spent some time with the baby Prince at Stirling. In October James returned from a separate pilgrimage to find her pregnant.

They and their courtiers then attended a display organized by Abbot Damian, who had manufactured a pair of wings with which he proposed to fly. Careless of danger, he took off in great style; then, amidst peals of laughter, his invention collapsed. He survived, only to be brought down again by two lampoons from Dunbar, whose mockery was unsparing.[2]

James now entered lists for which he had no qualifications: those of European politics. He took up the cause of the Duke of Gueldres — a second cousin twice removed — whose kingdom was being threatened by England and Spain. In courteous expostulation he wrote to Henry VII that, if he persisted in attacking the Duke, 'I, who believe that in war justice will prevail over wrong' (as in the *Morte d'Arthur*?) 'shall be sorrowfully compelled to esteem you, my illustrious father, as an enemy, and shall be constrained to oppose your troops.'[3]

Fortunately for James, this scheme of invasion was abandoned. He then sent ships and men to help his uncle, King John of Denmark, against his rebellious subjects. For such expeditions James had to give his admirals, the three Barton brothers, a free hand; as their methods were piratical and undiscriminating, he sometimes found himself at war with his own allies. Of these, Louis XII was the most powerful; and in January 1508 James marked the value of their connection by magnificent entertainments for the French envoys. He received them in state; and a banquet of the Round Table, in which they were honoured as his knights, concluded the festivities.[4]

In February the Prince of Scotland died at Stirling. Supported by the thought of Margaret's pregnancy, his parents rallied from the blow. James was quite sure that this next child would be a boy; he should call it Arthur, naturally. (For him, the name had no omens; six years had passed since the death of Margaret's elder brother.) He now made ready to receive his father-in-law's embassy, headed by Dean West; but when the envoy arrived, he was told that His Majesty was too busy with a new scheme for making gunpowder to see him. Margaret promised the Dean an early interview; a week went by before this took place.[5]

During that time, Margaret, West and Forman Bishop of Moray conferred daily; and so West became aware, not only that the Queen might influence her husband, but that her policy was pro-English, and that she did not approve of the new French alliance. Her common sense and her grasp of the situation were those of a much older person, and typical of her family. While James shone in the lists, the presence-chamber and on progress, talking to his foreign guests in Italian, French, Spanish and Latin, Margaret had been studying the relations between her own country and the backward colony—as she saw it—of which she was Vicereine. She did not then, or at any time, attempt to understand the fierce pride of the Scottish nobles who, although ready to betray their master, yet longed to defeat and humiliate those who had ravaged their lands in the days of her Plantagenet ancestors.

Margaret's outlook was coldly practical. Except for trade, nothing could be gained from France, and everything from agreement with England. Forman, who had just returned from his embassy in London, shared this view, and West had been instructed by Henry VII to destroy, or at least to weaken, French influence in Scotland. The Bishop, knowing which of his countrymen were for sale, believed that he could persuade James to loosen his continental ties; and he counted on a few of the King's advisers to support him in this scheme.

So while James 'shot the great guns', and discussed culverins and casting with Abbot Damian and other inventors, his wife was openly undermining his plans. Inexperienced, lonely, and carrying a child whose birth might kill her, she remained indomitably clear-sighted. That James's too skilful ally might plunge Scotland into a losing war became obvious when the King left his experiments to complain of his father-in-law's treatment of Arran. He regarded Henry's imprisonment of this cousin as an insult—and a challenge. The Earl must be released unconditionally, and at once. When West suggested that he should be set free after swearing allegiance to Henry, James flared up. 'If he takes any such oath, he shall be hung as soon as he arrives in Scotland,' he said, adding more gently that if Henry proved himself a truly loving father, he would live and die with him, and that his French commitments need not estrange them.[6]

James's Council, most of whom were in Louis XII's pay, supported his defiance of Henry, and so worked up the national hatred of

England that West felt himself not only unwelcome but in danger, and asked to be recalled. An elderly Stuart cousin, Lord d'Aubigny, then arrived; he had been living in France for many years, and was now Louis's ambassador. James gave him a splendid reception, in which Black Ellen and his performance as her champion were repeated.[7]

In July of that year Margaret retired to Holyroodhouse for the birth of a daughter who survived only a few hours. Once more, she herself was seriously ill, and James took her to Falkland to recover. They did not return to Edinburgh till January 1509, by which time she was pregnant again.

Like most of her contemporaries, Margaret did not expect more than three infants in every half-dozen to survive. Regular pregnancies were part of her profession, whatever the result. Every other year she faced an agonizing death, and therefore had neither time nor inclination to brood over her losses. The observers' accounts of their respective attitudes indicate that James, who had leisure to grieve, did so, when not pleading with saints to approach the Deity on his behalf. Margaret merely set herself to endure the next ordeal. Outwardly subscribing to her husband's piety, she was a practising Catholic, but not, as it later appeared, a devout one. She never felt the hand of her Creator in all her doings and thus did not fear, as her husband did, divine wrath and punishment.

At this time Margaret was ignorant and courageous enough to accept disappointment more or less philosophically. Her mother had lost five out of nine children; and she herself, regaining fertility after each confinement, saw these recoveries as her doctors did — part of a process which would eventually result in a healthy family. The squalor and filth of her surroundings had no connection in their minds, any more than in hers, with the deaths of her children. As far as that was concerned, everything that could be done, was done. Removal to another district at certain times ensured the 'sweetening' of each palace in rotation, according to the standards of the age, which in Scotland were much lower than those of her own country.

So Margaret took for granted huge, draughty rooms, airless private apartments, stinking moats, open privies, streets piled with excrement, gutters running blood and urine, and the mingled stench of stale spices, smoking chimneys and rotting woodwork. In winter no fires, however vast, could heat the outer spaces of banqueting-halls, throne rooms and galleries; no walls, however thick, prevented icy moisture forming on tapestries and hangings, while in summer the miasmas became denser and state garments more burdensome.

No heed was paid to these conditions, no thought given to possible improvements. The days were far too short for all that had to be done; the routine of private amusements and public appearances left no leisure for contemplation, and not much for anxiety. The pace was — sometimes literally — killing. The future could be visualized only in flashes, usually against a background of violent death. In such an existence, time rushes its victims from one crisis to another.

The pattern of James's diplomacy changed again with the death of Henry VII in April 1509; for it was necessary, if only from courtesy, to confirm his alliance with the new King, whose marriage to Katherine of Aragon was followed by the death of his grandmother, at the age of sixty-nine. As the executrix of his father's will, Margaret of Richmond had had some jurisdiction over Henry VIII's actions. Now he was supreme.

Forman's counsels and the Queen's influence resulted in James assuring Henry that he had no intention of making war on England; but at seventeen, that monarch saw the issues far more clearly than the brother-in-law twice his age; he realized that Louis XII would have no difficulty in making use of James's ambitions. He therefore arranged a Franco-English peace treaty which was signed in 1510.

Meanwhile, Louis's request for 4,000 Scottish men-at-arms was not complied with; for James had evolved a more sensational scheme — that of personally leading a crusade against the Turks, with the Venetians. For this he must have more ships, and so the building of the *Lion*, the *Margaret* and the *Jenny Pirwin* was set in hand. Naturally James counted on the Pope's support in this venture; but Julius, determined to destroy the power of France, was not interested in the rescue of the Holy Sepulchre. He declared Louis schismatic, and made an alliance with England against him, adding that if James insisted on supporting the French King, he would be excommunicated.

James then tried to intervene in Europe as a general peacemaker. These efforts were ignored; but Scottish prospects brightened with the birth of his second son in October 1509. He was christened Arthur, and seemed to thrive. Although Margaret was again very ill, she recovered more quickly than after her last confinement. Twenty-one months went by before her next pregnancy; this interval may have saved her life.

James's offer of leading a Scots-Venetian crusade was finally refused by the Doges, who gave the command of their flotilla to a Mantuan nobleman, and in the spring of 1510 joined Julius II in his war against France. Whatever chagrin James may have felt was over-shadowed by the death of Prince Arthur — at the age of nine months — in July of that year.

It seems that James now ascribed the deaths of these three children to God's vengeance for his share in the murder of his father.[8] He therefore decided to make a pilgrimage to Jerusalem, but at the last moment found it impossible to leave. Trouble on the Border had been renewed, his navy must be seen to and his efforts to reconcile France and the Vatican could not be abandoned. His plans for a crusade continued, so that, as he wrote to Henry VIII, 'one army drawn from all nations may be turned against the enemies of Christ'.[9] Henry, more concerned with his own adversaries, replied non-committally.

As Margaret had not conceived for more than a year, James decided that she should make a pilgrimage to the shrine of Saint Duthake, visiting Aberdeen on the way, where she was received with a series of 'moralities'. Scenes from the New Testament and a presentation of Adam and Eve were followed by the appearance of Robert the Bruce and other Scottish kings, accompanied by girls singing and playing, 'with hair de-tressed as threads of gold', accord-ing to Dunbar, and 'with white hats embroidered'. The Aberdonians gave her a gold cup filled with money, and Saint Duthake was gracious. Two months after her return she began her fourth pregnancy.[10]

In the summer of 1511 hopes of permanent peace with England were destroyed by the piracy of James's admirals. Sir Andrew Barton plundered a Portuguese ship carrying English goods — in English waters. The King of Portugal appealed to Henry VIII, who ordered his admirals, Edward and Thomas Howard, to chase and attack the *Lion*. Called upon to strike his colours, Barton refused. According to the ballad:

> 'Fight on, my men,' says Sir Andrew Barton,
> 'These English dogs they fight so low;
> Fight on for Scotland and Saint Andrew,
> Till you hear my whistle blow.'

So the battle continued until, with his crew, Barton was captured, dying of his wounds. Howard then pursued and took over the *Jenny Pirwin*, returning with both ships to Blackwall.

# 56 MARGARET TUDOR

Furiously raging, James accused Henry VIII of breaking the treaty of 1509, and desired him to bring the Howards to trial. Henry replied by sending one of his bishops to tell the Scottish prisoners that unless they acknowledged their guilt, they would all be hanged for piracy. 'My lord,' cried their chaplain, 'we appeal from the King's justice to his mercy.' 'You shall find the King's mercy above his justice,' was the answer, and they were ordered to leave the country within twenty days. Henry then coolly informed James that it did not become one prince to accuse another of breaking a treaty simply because a thief had been punished. 'If I had shown justice instead of mercy,' he added, 'Barton's men would have been as dead as Barton himself.'[11]

The clouds were thickening. Now surely, war must follow. Only so could Scottish pride be avenged.

## NOTES

1 Green, vol. IV, p. 127.
2 C. Lewis, *English Literature in the Sixteenth Century*, p. 66.
3 Green, op. cit., p. 131.
4 Strickland, *English Princesses*, vol. I, p. 70.
5 Green, ibid.
6 Op. cit., p. 135.
7 Ibid.
8 W. Drummond, *History of Scotland*, p. 136.
9 *L. & P. Henry VIII*, vol. I, p. 598.
10 Green, op. cit., p. 142.
11 Hall, p. 525.

# VII

## *The Road to Flodden*

THE summer of 1511 brought disappointment to those of James's subjects who had been hoping to invade England. Both he and Henry VIII were bent on agreement for the sake of their continental commitments; but their respective aims were opposed. James's alliance with Louis XII ensured, as he believed, that monarch's help in his crusade; Henry's alliance with his father-in-law, Ferdinand of Aragon, had involved him in plans for preventing Louis from further encroachment in Italy. Henry, Pope Julius and Ferdinand, seeing the power of France as a serious danger, had agreed to invade, and were therefore anxious to remain on friendly terms with Scotland; and Louis, still urging James to send him men and ships, counted on his support.

So James was given the impression, not only that his friendship was eagerly sought, but that he himself was now the head of a great power able to dictate terms to England, France and Spain. He therefore desired Margaret to write and tell Ferdinand that her husband was arranging for peace in Europe, and 'inviting to the same' the French and English kings.[1]

James and Margaret then received Henry's ambassadors, with whom terms were agreed, and continued their usual round of pilgrimages and visits in the neighbourhood of Linlithgow, where Margaret was to lie in for her fourth confinement in the spring of 1512. James spent much time at Leith, inspecting his largest ships, the *Great Michael* and the *James*. Here Margaret joined him, and they stayed for several nights on board the half-finished vessels, returning to Holyrood for a quiet Christmas.

James was very anxious. If this child died, neither a crusade nor a pilgrimage to Jerusalem was likely to atone for his sins and bring him an heir. He sent Margaret to pray for a happy deliverance at all the nearest shrines, and himself consulted 'Liddell the prophet', who saw him alone and bound him to secrecy.[2] Meanwhile, the Palace of Linlithgow was cleaned and repaired. In March James and Margaret moved in, and one of the most efficacious relics in Europe—the girdle of Our Lady—was lent them by the Abbot of Westminster and placed in the state bedchamber. This object had not, so far, been known to fail expectant queens; nor did it now. On April 11th, 1512, a son was born and christened James. In the same month Margaret began her fifth pregnancy.

As this prince did not seem any stronger than the children who had died, it occurred to the physicians that his wet-nurse might be unhealthy, and they engaged another. Still the baby pined; he grew weaker, and they brought in a third attendant, with no result. He was on the point of death when the milk of a fourth, an Irishwoman, had effect, and he survived; but he remained delicate, and it seems that his father did not think he would live, for he hurried on with his plans for a crusade. Then, once more, Scottish prospects improved with the defeat of the English in their attempted invasion of France. This failure, which disgraced the arms of England, and brought Henry VIII to shame in the eyes of Europe, assured James of Scotland's superior strength.

Margaret did not share his confidence. She knew little or nothing of the European situation, but she was unalterably convinced that Scotland must remain on friendly terms with the neighbouring kingdom. Although she and Henry had not seen one another since he was in his eleventh year, she believed in his abilities and in the efficiency of his forces, in spite of the disaster of 1512.

In June of that year Henry's armies had been shipped to Spain in order to invade through the Pyrenees. Waiting for the Spanish to join them, they were decimated by various diseases, and their numbers halved. This did not affect Ferdinand's main object, which was the conquest of Navarre. Before he achieved it, the English soldiers mutinied, and their commander, the Marquess of Dorset, had no choice but to put them on board and return, miserably, to his master. Bitterly enraged, Henry decided to execute him, with his subordinates and those of the mutineers who had survived. Such wholesale slaughter was not practicable; advised by Wolsey, he tried to hush up the scandal, and remained on superficially good terms with his treacherous ally and father-in-law. Wolsey was entrusted with the training of a new expeditionary force which, headed by Henry himself, was to invade Northern France in the summer of 1513. Henry then sent a second embassy into Scotland, led by Lord Dacre and Dean West, from whom James demanded a number of jewels, originally

Prince Arthur's, left to Margaret in her father's will, and still in Henry's possession.

Henry might have parted with this treasure, if he had not suspected that James intended to sell it in order to buy arms against himself. Approached by a Scots envoy on this point, he replied, 'Make your memorials [of the jewels] and you shall have them, on condition the King of Scots will keep his oath to me ... that none of us shall invade the other,' adding irritably, 'For Almighty God's sake! he should sit at home and mind his own cheer.'[3] But James, now conferring with the French Ambassador, de la Mothe, could not break off his relations with Louis, who was urging him to invade. He promised Dacre and West that he would not do so, and continued to write courteously formal letters to his brother-in-law. He then told Dacre that his wife's legacy was being withheld 'out of malice' to himself, and tactlessly remarked that as Henry and Katherine had no family (their first child, a boy, had died in 1510) Margaret was heiress-presumptive to the English throne.[4]

When the English Ambassadors left Scotland James asked Henry to receive the Bishop of Moray, and to give him a safe-conduct so that he might proceed into France. He was deeply insulted by Henry's refusal. During the summer and autumn of 1512 their relationship deteriorated, while that of James with Louis became closer and, from the English point of view, more suspect; for it was reported to Henry that the *Great Michael* would soon be sent to a French port, and that James was increasing his armaments on land.

By the beginning of November James's anxiety about his son's health had lightened, for he was much stronger and growing fast. Then, in the second week of that month, Margaret gave birth, prematurely, to a daughter who died in a few hours. This disaster increased James's eagerness for a crusade, and in January 1513 he made a secret pact, through de la Mothe, to send further supplies to Louis in return for the cost of his pilgrimage to Jerusalem. When Henry's spies told him of these arrangements, he sent Dean West back to Scotland with orders to warn his brother-in-law not to proceed on these lines.

In February 1513 Julius II died. His successor, Leo X, carried out his last instructions, of which one was the excommunication of James. Meanwhile, Margaret, who had again been seriously ill, had not grasped the full extent of her husband's French commitments. When West arrived, James was making a retreat for the purpose of prayer and fasting, so she interviewed the Dean in the chapel of Stirling Castle. After Mass she remained in her stall and, summoning him to speak to her, asked for news of her brother. What did he look like now? How tall was he? West described his master's 'stature and goodly personage', and presented Henry's letter. Before Margaret came to the end she exclaimed, 'If I were in my great sickness again, this were enough to make me whole!' West seems to have replied with some criticisms of James's actions, for she put in, 'I trust my brother will not cast me away?' The Dean answered reassuringly, and they parted.[5]

On April 1st, 1513, James came out of his retreat and began talks with West. He was now in a position which made it impossible for him to deal straightforwardly with Louis, Henry, or his own Council. His ministers were supporting the French alliance, and a number of them believed that the moment had come to invade England. Henry, whose Anglo-Spanish alliance had been joined by the Emperor Maximilian, was still trying to keep James to the agreement of 1509; and Louis's demands for men and ships were urgent and insatiable. So James was beginning to feel hard pressed, and even, at times, doubtful of success in all these ventures, although his vision of himself as a continental power still prevailed.

Distressed by his excommunication, he declared that the English envoys to the Vatican had influenced Julius II against him. West denied this, and James went on defiantly, 'I will never do obedience to the Pope, if he condemns me unheard.' West made no reply, and James announced that he was now in a position to make war on England, if he chose. 'But,' he said, 'I will not do it without ample warning by herald, the Pope shall not stop me.'

As next day was Sunday, James would not discuss business, and Margaret sent for West to her private apartments. She sat down, thus indicating that they were to talk at length. When West told her that Henry was going to France, she sank into gloomy silence. 'I pray Your Grace,' he said, 'use all means to preserve a good understanding between the two crowns.' Margaret then spoke of her legacy. 'I will pay it', West replied, 'if the King keeps the peace — not otherwise.' 'And not else?' Margaret persisted. Before West could answer James came in, and they talked of other things.

On Monday, West saw James alone, and began, 'Will Your Grace keep the peace in His Majesty's absence?' 'I will, if the King will do me justice,' James replied. When West offered him a sum of money instead of the jewels, he burst out, 'I have no need of your money, I will not sell my gear [rights],' and continued to hold forth so confusedly that the Dean decided to remain silent in the face of what he later described to Henry as 'void communications'. At last he interrupted James's threats and demands with, 'I will pay the legacy [of jewels] if you keep the peace. Otherwise, England will both withhold it, and take from you the best towns you have.' 'The Queen shall lose nothing for my sake!' James exclaimed. 'I will pay for her myself —' adding angrily, 'The sum is greater than that you mentioned.' He then said that Henry had removed Margaret from the succession. West denied this, and was dismissed. (Thirty-four years later, Henry cut out of his will Margaret's granddaughter, the five-year-old Mary Queen of Scots.)

During their next talk, James produced several letters from Louis XII containing promises of help and an assurance of payment for the crusade. West, knowing that these were unlikely to materialize, said nothing, and James explained, 'Now you see wherefore I favour the French King, and wherefore I am loath to lose him, for if I do, I shall never be able to perform my journey.' 'France has made you fair promises,' said West, 'but will never perform them,' and again asked for James's guarantee not to invade. The King did not speak for a little while; then he said, 'You know my mind well enough. I will keep the peace, if the King will do me justice.' 'Write it down,' the Dean suggested. 'You shall have no letter of mine,' James retorted, 'nor no new bond to show in France, whereby I might lose the [French] King.' 'My King', West persisted, 'only desires to know how you will behave in his absence.' James replied that Henry's 'absence or presence' mattered nothing to him. 'If you do not make a clearer answer,' West pointed out, 'the King will value it as a negative.' 'You know my mind,' James repeated.

West then lost his temper. 'I know neither you nor your mind,' he said coldly, upon which James began to shout abuse, striding up and down. At last he said, 'If you will put the demands in writing, I will answer them in writing,' to which West made a non-committal reply. A few days later, he saw Margaret, who began plaintively, 'Although my brother is unkind to me, I will do my best for peace,' and West left her to interview James's Council.

They supported their master's claims more aggressively. 'No answer can be given', West was told, 'till we know what justice we shall receive from England, for the King.' 'He will not consent to abolition,' one put in, meaning that James would make no assurance of neutrality. As this amounted to an unofficial declaration of war, West decided to pin them down. 'Is this the King's determinate answer?' he asked. 'Yes.' 'I marvel,' said West after a pause, 'for it is not an answer to my charge,' adding that James was therefore about to break the treaty of 1509. As the Council began to defend their master, he interrupted them with, 'You do but trifle with me, I could spend a twelvemonth in this way.' While they were protesting James came in, and said haughtily, 'I need make no new promises, being bound by the treaty.' West, aware that this was a prevarication, said so as soon as he and James were alone, upon which the King tried to placate him. He had had to speak 'sharply', he said, before the Council, or they would report him to Louis XII. 'I shall lose the French King if I show too much friendliness to England,' he naively explained.

West then asked James to promise that he would not supply France with ships, and suggested the sale or loan of the *Great Michael* to England. As James shook his head, he went on, 'I trust the French will not have her?' 'I wist not,' was the reply, and West realized that the vessel was already Louis's property.[6]

By this time, Dean West had come to the conclusion that these repetitive and increasingly hostile discussions were pointless, if not harmful, and begged to be recalled. Henry refused.

The Tudor King's plan, which he did not fully reveal to his envoy ('If my cap knew what I was thinking,' he said, many years later, 'I would throw it in the fire') was so to manoeuvre his brother-in-law as to expose his treachery, and then proclaim it, thus putting himself in the position of the injured party. The way to do this was to extract from James some kind of promise not to invade, so that when he did — and it had become obvious that this was his intention — he would appear as a liar, an aggressor and a fool. Henry's defences were strong enough for him to plan his French campaign without too much anxiety. Katherine and Surrey were to be in charge at home; she as Regent, and the Earl, now in his seventy-first year, as commander-in-chief of the home forces. While Surrey moved his men up to the Border Katherine was to follow with a supporting army, which would remain at York. Thus, if the Scots did overrun Northumberland — where, in fact, Surrey eventually met them — they would move on to find themselves faced, and possibly encircled, by the Queen's troops.

This form of warfare, the result of Wolsey's and Surrey's planning, was not only unknown to James and his advisers—whose armaments were plentiful, although not of the newest type—but never even visualized by them. Their method was simply that of attack; they discounted the strength of an enemy who waited for them to advance and then withdrew in order to spring. And James himself shared his nobles' contempt for the English soldiery who, a year before, had slunk home after a disastrous campaign.

James then continued to bluster and prevaricate in his talks with West, either complaining of Henry's 'unkindness' to himself and Margaret, or boasting of his new ships and the invincible powers of his French ally. When West said, 'The strength of England is more important, for without it you cannot perform your great voyage,' he replied, 'It would be dishonourable in England to prevent me,' with a perverse and almost pathetic disregard of the real issue, in which 'honour' had no place.[7]

West then warned him that if he insisted on fighting Henry on Louis's behalf, the English might invade Scotland, upon which James adopted a furiously satiric tone. 'Yea, my brother shall do right wisely!' he exclaimed. 'Sith he hath enterprised so great a matter as to make war upon France,' adding that Henry was not in a position to fight on two fronts—nor even on one. Still West persisted. 'If you break with England,' he said, 'it may something trouble the King's intended voyage, but will not prevent it.' Bursting with rage, James then became so incoherent that an attendant minister took West by the arm and led him from the room.

So the Dean's mission ended. A little later, James received him courteously, and suggested that he should visit Margaret, who, with her son, was at Linlithgow. West did so, found the Prince 'a right fair child, and large of his age', and made one last effort to obtain Margaret's support. When he told her of his reply to James's threats, she said mournfully, 'I am sorry it is not more favourable,' and made no further reference to her jewels. She then gave him presents for Henry, Katherine, and her sister Mary. Meanwhile, James was writing to Henry on behalf of 'our dearest fellow, the Queen', about her legacy. When West came to take leave, he said that he desired peace above all things—'But,' he added, 'if the King does not oblige me, I shall declare war.'

Then at last West was able to tell his master that the King of Scots had committed himself. Yet the jaws of the trap had not quite closed: for James's declaration was not in writing; nor had it been announced by his heralds. He allowed Margaret to make a final appeal. Irritated by West's commiseration, and his criticisms of her husband, she decided to stand up for James, while putting her own case to the brother on whose support she still relied. Surely family feeling must count for something. 'Right excellent, right high and mighty prince, our dearest and best beloved brother,' her letter began ... 'We cannot think that of your mind, or by your command, we are so fremdly [strangely] dealt with,' and again put forward a request for her jewels. 'We are ashamed therewith, and would God had never word been thereof,' she went on. 'It is not worth such estimation as is in your diverse letters ... and we lack nothing; our husband is ever the better the longer to us ... Your loving sister.'[8] To this letter there was no reply.

---

## NOTES

1 Green, vol. IV, p. 142.
2 Op. cit., p. 145.
3 R. Lindsay, *History and Chronicles of Scotland*, vol. I, p. 260.
4 Green, op. cit., p. 151.
5 *L. & P.*, vol. I, pt. 1, p. 791.
6 Op. cit., pp. 791–5.
7 Ibid.
8 Ibid.

KING JAMES IV *(artist unknown)*

# VIII

## *Nemesis*

IN APRIL 1513 Ferdinand of Aragon wrote to Louis XII suggesting a truce. Before terms could be considered, de la Mothe arrived in Edinburgh with Louis's final demands, all of which were granted by James, against the advice of a number of his ministers. He agreed to send Louis his fleet — it consisted of four ill-equipped vessels with skeleton crews — in return for 50,000 francs and armaments to be supplied on arrival. Through de la Mothe, Louis urged James to declare war on Henry at once, and to invade as soon as the English reached Calais. The crown of England, he added, would then fall to James; and he himself would not make peace with Henry until he had James's consent.[1]

Suddenly, James had doubts, and tried to withdraw from the conflict. On May 24th he wrote to Henry, suggesting that they should come to terms with Louis. Determined to avenge the disaster of 1512, Henry refused, on the grounds that he could not consider a truce of which he had received no official information.

Under Arran's command, the Scottish fleet sailed from Leith just as an Irish chieftain, O'Donnell, reached Edinburgh with offers of help against England which never materialized. Then Louis, fearing that James might yet fail him, concocted a scheme with his wife, Anne of Brittany, to ensure the invasion of England. The resultant appeal, which would have been contemptuously ignored — or greeted with shouts of laughter — by any other ruler, was entirely successful, for it invested James with the mantle of medieval chivalry.

Queen Anne, whom James had never met, was plain, middle-aged, and as acute a diplomat as her husband. Remembering James's self-identification with the fellowship of the Round Table, she and Louis decided to stage a drama in which legend became reality. By special envoy, Anne sent James her tokens — a glove and a turquoise ring — imploring him to rescue her, a distressed damsel, from the machinations of those evil men, Maximilian, Ferdinand and Henry VIII. He was her knight. Surely the prevailing rumours that he shrank from combat were false—would he not prove them so by doing battle on her behalf? 'For my sake,' she concluded, 'march forth, were it only but three feet, on to English ground.' With a second letter, she sent him 14,000 crowns for expenses.[2]

The effect of these communications might have been described by any admirer of the *Morte d'Arthur* as literally magical. James's hesitations, the disapproval of his ministers, the enraged and tearful appeals of his wife, the warnings of his brother-in-law—all these vanished before the glittering image of himself in armoured glory, riding to the rescue of a queen. He prepared to declare war on Henry VIII, who had embarked from Dover on June 25th.

That monarch also liked to see himself, every now and then, as an Arthurian figure. But Henry's rather vulgar romanticism never for a moment obscured his political ambitions. While set on re-creating the conquests of his Plantagenet forebears, he took no unnecessary risks. Before going aboard his flagship, he turned to Surrey, and giving him his hand to kiss said, 'My lord, I trust not the Scots—I pray you, therefore, be not negligent.' Surrey, who had been hoping that at the last moment Henry might change his mind and give him a command in France, was on the verge of an outburst. He managed to reply, 'I shall so do my duty that Your Grace will find me diligent—and to fulfil your will shall be my gladness.' Then, turning away, he choked down his chagrin. As he and his gentlemen stood watching the fleet set sail, he said to them, 'Sorry may I see him [James] or I die, that is cause of my abiding behind, and if ever he and I meet, I shall do what in me lieth to make him as sorry as I can.'[3]

While James was composing his last letter to Henry and instructing Lyon-King-at-Arms about his declaration of war, Margaret decided to withstand him on his own level. She came to him in tears, describing herself as insulted and outraged by his response to Anne of Brittany—that rival queen, twelve years her senior—accused him of unfaithfulness to his marriage vows (her own acceptance of Lady Bothwell, Mary Boyd and the mysterious Lady of A. was thus ignored) and implored him to revoke his call to arms. It was not yet too late. 'What a folly, what a blindness,' she exclaimed, 'to make this war yours! Keep your promise to England, and enjoy peace at home.' As for Anne of Brittany—'Should her letters prove more powerful than the cries of your little son?'[4]

James ignored this rather uninspiring rhetoric, and proceeded with his letter to Henry, whom he addressed as 'Right excellent, right high and mighty Prince, our dearest brother and cousin,' going on to outline his own grievances and to explain his defence of Louis XII. He added that Henry had 'wronged' Margaret, and made peace impossible, concluding, 'We require you ... to desist from further invasion and the utter destruction of your brother the most Christian King [of France] ... We will do what thing we trust may cause you to desist.'[5] By the time this letter reached Henry's camp at Thérouanne, Margaret had begun her sixth pregnancy—and her husband and brother were irrevocably committed to war.

The contrasting behaviour of James and Henry illustrates the Gothic as opposed to the Renaissance attitude, in spite of certain resemblances. Both kings had the common or democratic touch, and so were as beloved by their humbler subjects as by their intimates. Both were fearless, pious, highly intelligent and unusually accomplished. As was then the case with most monarchs, both were semi-divine in the eyes of their people.

Yet the difference in their actions represents their respective ages. While Henry, the 'new man' of an upstart dynasty, made deliberate and skilful use of his assets, James took his for granted, as became the descendant of many kings. In the leisurely fashion of an earlier day, he was still mustering his troops, while Henry, advancing from Calais beyond Ardres, had already reached his first objective; there his soldiers, beset by storms and struggling through the mud, began to lose heart; so at odd hours—on one occasion at three o'clock in the morning—Henry went round the camp, chatting to the men on guard. A young officer, who kept a diary of the campaign, long remembered his saying, 'Well, comrades, now that we have suffered in the beginning, fortune promises us better things, God willing'—and the shade of that other Henry, he of Agincourt, suddenly rises.[6]

James addressed his armies only once, in a grandly heroic strain, and spent his spare time at the shrines of his favourite saints. Henry relied on St George, and, while daily attending Mass, appealed to the Deity in the manner of one potentate addressing another. At twenty-two, he was superbly confident of divine support, and sure that, although he still had no heir (Mary, Katherine's fifth and only surviving child, was born in 1516) he would soon have a son. James, at thirty-six, attributed the deaths of his children to God's displeasure, and could not be certain of his successor's survival.

Their wives' behaviour was equally dissimilar. While Margaret did her utmost to persuade James to withdraw, Katherine was 'horribly busy', as she put it in one of her letters, making preparations to defend the home front. Finally, James's commanding officers, although recklessly brave, were too much at odds with one another to provide a solid resistance. Surrey, a cunning and ruthless dictator, moving inexorably from one vantage point to the next, had learnt the bitter lesson of defeat as a boy of fourteen—on Bosworth Field.

Whatever doubts James still had were suppressed when he composed the declaration which Sir William Comyn, Lyon-King-at-Arms, delivered to Henry on July 25th in his tent before Thérouanne. As that town had not yet fallen, the Tudor King was temporarily at a disadvantage; but nothing in his setting or in his demeanour gave that impression. James's herald was considerably taken aback when, ushered in by Garter-King-at-Arms, he faced the monarch he had to defy.[7]

Henry was more than six feet tall, and had then the figure of an athlete. His brilliantly clear skin and close-cropped auburn hair contrasted with a tight mouth, small grey eyes, and arched, delicately feminine eyebrows which gave him a look of cold surprise—now enhanced as, with what an onlooker called 'a sober countenance', he stood surrounded by his splendidly attired staff, himself the most splendid of all, in jewelled armour and a purple velvet cloak, his hand on the hilt of his sword.[8]

The Scots emissary presented his master's letter, bowed and stood back. It seems that Henry did not read it at once, for the herald, desired to speak, began, 'Having now besieged Thérouanne two months, without being fought with, Your Grace should return home, without making further war.'

After a pause Henry said, 'Have ye now your tale at an end?' 'Nay,' was the answer. 'Say forth, then.' 'Sire,' Comyn replied, 'My King summoneth Your Grace to be at home in your realm, on the defence.'

The huge, golden figure remained motionless and silent for a moment or two. Then, quietly at first, and with studied formality, Henry answered, 'Ye have well done your message. Yet it ill becometh a Scot to summon a king of England. And tell your master that I distrust not so the realm of England but he shall have enough to do, whenever he beginneth.' After dwelling on his mistrust of James and his own preparations, Henry's tone changed. 'And he, to summon me, now being here for my right and inheritance!' he exclaimed. 'He knew well, before my coming hither, that hither would I come. Tell him, there shall never Scot cause me to return my face!' He then referred to his sister's marriage as an unappreciated condescension, adding, 'Recommend me to your master, and tell him, if he be so hardy as to invade my realm—or cause to enter one foot of my ground—I shall make him as weary of his part as ever man was.' He went on to warn his brother-in-law's messenger, 'on the word of a king, and by the faith that I have to the crown of England', that there would be no peace till the Scots were utterly defeated.[9]

The herald, considerably 'dismayed', according to the onlookers, referred Henry to James's letter. Having read it, Henry said, 'Now we perceive that the King of Scots, our brother-in-law and your master, be the same person as we ever took him to be—for as we never esteemed him to be of any truth, so now we have found it.' He then touched on James's broken oath, and the 'great dishonour and infamy', shown by his waiting to invade until he himself was away. 'Therefore,' he continued, 'tell thy master I have left an earl in my realm at home which shall be able to defend [withstand] him, and all his power.' He added, 'This say to thy master, that I am the very owner of Scotland, and he holdeth it of me by homage. He, being my vassal, doth rebel against me—and with God's help, I shall, at my return, repulse him from his realm. And so tell him.'[10]

By this time, Comyn was emboldened to protest. 'Sire,' he began, 'I am his natural subject, and he my natural lord—and that [which] he commandeth me to say, I may boldly say, with favour. But the commandments of other[s] I may not, nor dare not.' He then suggested that Henry should reply in writing, and was greeted with a broadside. 'Wherefore came you hither? Will you receive no answer?' Upon which Comyn retorted, 'Yes—your answer requireth doing, and no writing, that is, that immediately you should return home.' 'Well,' Henry told him, with ominous calm, 'I *will* return—at your damage, to my pleasure—and not at thy master's summoning.'[11]

Then followed an argument about Queen Margaret. 'Moreover— fellow!' Henry burst out, 'I care for nothing but his mistreating of my sister. [Presumably he was referring to James's mistresses.] Would God she were in England, on condition she cost the Scottish King not a penny!' 'If Your Grace gave your whole realm,' replied the herald firmly, 'she would not forsake it, to be entreated as she is.' 'I know the contrary,' Henry declared, 'and know what all this matter meaneth,' adding that Louis XII had so misled James as to destroy him. As the envoy began a further protest, Henry turned to Garter-King-at-Arms. 'Take him to your tent, and make him good cheer,' he said. The English herald then reassured his guest, to whom Henry sent the usual fee on his departure.[12]

Henry's answering letter roused Margaret to further efforts for peace; it incited James to a wild defiance. 'We cannot marvel,' it began, 'considering the ancient and accustomable manners of your progenitors, which never kept longer faith and promise than pleased them ... at your dishonourable demeanour. Remembering the brittleness of your promise ... we thought it necessary to put our said realm in readiness ... having firm trust in our Lord God, and the righteousness of our cause.' James was then reminded of the fate of the King of Navarre, and of Louis XII's habit of betraying his allies. Henry concluded by saying that he should continue to 'persecute' the French King, 'by the help of Our Lord, and our patron saint, St George'.[13]

This letter arrived in the second week of August, when James was on the point of departure. As he intended to lead his troops in person, he made arrangements for a regency, headed by Margaret; and she, knowing his now desperate position and fatalistic disregard of his own safety, again besought him to try for a last-minute settlement. She slept little, and when she did her dreams took an appropriate form. She lost no time in describing them to James, who seemed at first to waver, as she told him of her necklaces and brooches melting into pearls, and of many other 'affrightments of her sleep'.[14] When he brushed these omens aside, she went on, 'It is no dream that ye have but one son, and him a weakling. If otherwise than well happen to you —' and so continued. As she tactlessly added, 'It is no dream that ye are to fight a mighty people,' his determination stiffened, and she tried another form of persuasion. 'If ye will go,' she implored, 'suffer me to accompany you. It may be my countrymen will prove more kind to me than they are to you,' and suggested that she and Katherine of Aragon might, between them, avert the worst. 'If we shall meet, who knows what God, by our means, may bring to pass?'[15]

That a woman should meddle with the business of war could not be considered. James was now ready to depart — from Linlithgow. Margaret had one last hope. Seeing him in deep depression, as one expecting death, and constantly in prayer, she devised a scheme suited to his mood.

He was on his knees in the chapel, when he became aware of someone standing over him, and looked up to see a strange figure. It was that of a man in blue draperies, with long hair and beard. He made no reverence and, kneeling beside James, abruptly began, 'Sir King, my mother has sent me to thee, desiring thee not to go where thou art purposed—which, if thou do, thou shalt not fare well in thy journey, nor none that is with thee. Further, she forbade thee to meddle, nor to use the counsel of women—which, if thou do, thou shalt be confounded and brought to shame.' This visitant then vanished, 'as if he had been a blink of the sun, or a wisp of the whirlwind', while the King and his attendants stared at one another.[16]

If by 'my mother' the seer meant the Queen of Heaven, or some saint, and whether 'counsel of women' was a hit at Anne of Brittany, no one could determine, James least of all. Plunged into deeper gloom, he was yet more firmly resolved. Then Margaret turned on him again. 'I have but one son by you,' she repeated, 'which is over weak a warrant to the realm of Scotland. It is over soon to you to pass into battle leaving so few successors behind you—' and begged him to stay a little, if only till she was confined. This plea was as useless as all the rest.[17]

James started his march on August 13th. When he reached the Border, he heard that Arran, pausing to raid the Irish coast, had returned to Ayrshire with his plunder, and so indefinitely delayed the help promised to Louis XII. Eventually the fleet, under another command, reached France, where the greater part of it remained. By the time the Scots forces were disembarked. Thérouanne had fallen (it was the first town taken by the English since the days of Joan of Arc) and the war between Henry and Louis was over.

On August 22nd James and his army crossed the Tweed. His first objective was the fortress of Norham Castle, which he besieged for six days before it surrendered. He then moved on to Ford, held by the beautiful Lady Heron, whose husband was a prisoner in Edinburgh. Here he remained for a week, having advanced only six miles into England, after a fortnight's marching and halting. So Surrey and Katherine were given more time than they had hoped for, and could proceed in better conditions.

Contemporary and other historians have accused James of lingering at Ford in order to become the lover of Elizabeth Heron, who then reported his plans to Surrey. This seems unlikely, for he was apt rather to dash forward than to hang back in any campaign. In fact, his advance was delayed by the condition of his troops: some had deserted, and others were either sick (for the plague had followed them

from Edinburgh) or unwilling to fight. James's only hope therefore
was to give those that were left a rest and to make the castle, which he
destroyed on departure, his headquarters.

This pause gave Surrey his opportunity, not to fall upon the Scots,
whose forces still equalled his, but to lure James into an advance
which would draw him further away from his base; for the last thing
the Earl wanted was to invade Scottish territory, where he would be
at a great, possibly an overwhelming, disadvantage. So he followed
the example of James's French allies and sent him a challenge, in the
medieval manner, asking him to appoint the day and hour of battle.
For if the rumour that James intended to retreat was true, Surrey
might have to postpone his plan of attack until such time as the Scots
forces had recovered.

Surrey's herald reached James on September 6th, and they agreed
to fight on the 9th.[18] James then advanced towards the Cheviots,
reaching the outer ridge on the 7th. Here, above a slope of some five
hundred feet, known as Flodden Hill, he encamped. The terrain was
such as to form a natural and, from the English point of view, an
almost impregnable fortress. Surrey, seeing that to storm it would be
dangerously rash, again employed Arthurian tactics. On the 8th he
sent his herald to James with another challenge, requiring him to
come down into the plain on the following afternoon, where he himself would await him from midday till three o'clock.[19]

Enraged by this insolence, James replied that he would 'hold his
ground at his own pleasure', and accused Surrey of witchcraft. The
Earl, he said, was insisting on that particular battlefield because he
had ensured its safety through the black art.[20]

By this time Surrey had taken the Stuart King's measure. He
guessed that, having agreed to fight on the 9th, James would not attack
before then; to do so would be to defy the laws of chivalry. As the
Till lay between his army and the Scots encampment, he decided to
move his troops across one of its tributaries in the dawn of that day.

On the evening of the 8th James addressed his chieftains, some of
whom were threatening to desert, in a furious appeal. He promised
them — as it then seemed, not unreasonably — a great victory, adding,
'My lords, I shall fight this day with England. Although ye would
leave me, and flee, and shame yourselves, ye shall not shame me.'
His rage had effect, and they agreed to remain.[21]

At five o'clock the next morning James's sentries reported the
movement of the enemy towards the ford, and the King, joining his

master gunner, saw them filing slowly across a narrow bridge. As that officer prepared to fire, James intervened. He forbade him, on pain of death, to take the advantage. He intended to meet the foe on open ground and equal terms, as became his honour. Bursting into tears, the master gunner knelt and implored King Arthur's disciple to change his mind—and was sternly desired to hold his peace.[22] So Surrey's only gamble succeeded. Having moved his main force to face Flodden Hill, he deployed his supporting troops behind the ridge. By midday he was ready to attack from all sides.

Yet even now James had the advantage. He could set his sights on the English from above: and he gave the order to fire. His cannon, recently reinforced, were new and plentiful. As they roared out, the English commanders gave the same order. Then, to their amazement, they saw their troops unhurt, and moving forward. The Scots had fired over their heads. They continued to do so, wasting more than half their ammunition.

James at once gave the order to strike tents, to set fire to the masses of ordure—thus causing 'a great and marvellous smoke', in fact, a sixteenth-century version of a gas attack—which obscured his movements from the English. He now prepared to ride down the ridge at the head of his army. His horrified nobles begged him to take a protected position. He refused. 'Your presence is worth ten thousand men,' he was told. Drawing his sword, he brushed them aside. It was not thus that the most famous of all kings had achieved imperishable glory at the battle of Barham Down.[23]

So the armies met, as he had wished, on equal terms; each numbered, roughly, some 20,000 men. But for hand-to-hand encounters the English had the deadlier arms. Not only were they more skilled in archery; they used the eight-foot halberd, or 'brown bill'. The Scots fought with fifteen-foot spears, and so their guards were of little use against the shorter and lighter weapon. Yet their desperate ferocity, and the knowledge that the King was fighting with them, strengthened their attack. For some time, it seemed that the English were being repulsed. Then, as the halberds got the better of the spears, and thousands of arrows found their mark, Surrey's forces began to split up their ranks. In driving mist and rain, the Earl, who up to now had directed operations from the rear, was within a few yards of James, his bastard son Alexander, and their group of nobles.

At this point, Lord Huntly, who was standing above the central conflict, saw James's red-and-gold standard fall, and suggested to the

Earl of Hume that they should try to save him. Hume replied, 'He does well that does for himself,' and presently managed to escape. Huntly attempted a rescue, failed, and also got away.[24]

As Surrey and his bodyguard came nearer, James dismounted, ordering his nobles to do the same. This sudden change to fiercer in-fighting had effect, until Surrey's men began to hack their way through. The chieftains resolved to die first (presumably in the hope of James being taken prisoner) and made a ring about him.

He and Surrey were now within a few feet of one another; then only a spear's length divided them. The grim old warrior and the brilliant king, who had gamed and danced and feasted together, were almost face to face. So James, the more accomplished swordsman, might yet have lived, like the fabled Sir Eger, to remember how— 'I strake him while that I might stand, While there came blood through the steel.' As Surrey drew nearer, a cannon-ball crashed on to James's helmet, and an arrow pierced his armour. And the English swept on, over the bodies of his nobles ...

The Scots on the right flank saw a way out, and began to retreat; but Surrey's men were waiting for them, and closed in. No prisoners were taken. The English right wing did not rejoin the main body until every Scot of that section lay dead or wounded on the bloody grass. By seven o'clock all was over.

And then the Highlanders, who had formed their own battalion, descended from the ridge to plunder their dead and dying comrades. Nothing Surrey had achieved could have been a better proof of defeat and shame. He let the thieves take all they could carry, and told his officers to find the King.

Several had seen him fall; and at last they came upon him, still wrapped in his cloak, among the heaped corpses of his nobles; the young Alexander lay beside him. There was some dispute as to his identity—for his face was a face no longer. Two days later, Lord Dacre, with James's Sergeant-Porter and one of his Councillors agreed in recognizing him through 'the privy tokens' of his body.[25]

Of the Scottish army, two bishops, two abbots, twenty-six nobles and some 9,000 men had fallen. The English reckoned their losses at 1,500. It was said that King James had killed five of Surrey's body-guard before his sword broke in his hand. 'O!' exclaimed Hall, writing twenty years later, 'What a noble and triumphant courage was this, for a king to fight in a battle as a mean soldier! ... He was able, as he thought, to have vanquished that day the greatest prince of the world ... But God gave the stroke, and he was no more regarded.'[26]

So James completed his saga in the Arthurian manner. As at Barham Down, 'the battle was cruel, none spared other'. And there were further parallels. As the King of Britain fell by the hand of his incestuously conceived son, so the death of James IV may have appeased, according to current beliefs, the angry ghost of James III. Sauchieburn was avenged. On the afternoon of September 9th, 1513, a seventeen-month-old child became James V.

<hr />

## NOTES

1 M. Wood, *Flodden Papers*, p. 80.
2 Drummond, p. 71.
3 Hall, p. 555.
4 Drummond, p. 136.
5 Hall, p. 545.
6 A. F. Pollard, *Henry VIII*, p. 51.
7 *L. & P.*, vol. I, pt. 1, p. 972.
8 Ibid.
9 *L. & P.*, ibid; Hall, pp. 547-9.
10 Ibid.
11 Ibid.
12 Ibid.
13 *L. & P.*, ibid.
14 Hall, ibid.
15 Drummond, ibid.
16 Lindsay, vol. I, p. 260.
17 Op. cit., p. 273.
18 Drummond, ibid.
19 Hall, p. 560.
20 Society of Antiquaries of Scotland, vol. VII, p. 146.
21 Ibid.
22 Lindsay, op. cit., p. 276.
23 Society of Antiquaries of Scotland, ibid.
24 Hall, p. 561.
25 Lindsay, ibid.
26 Hall, p. 564.

# IX

## *Queen-Regent*

A HUNDRED and forty miles of wild and mountainous country lay between Flodden and the Palace of Linlithgow, where Queen Margaret was waiting. She heard nothing definite until five or six days after the battle, for many of those who escaped had fled before it was over, when her husband was still alive. The full tale of disaster reached Edinburgh first; from there, messengers were sent to Linlithgow. Margaret then moved, with the infant King, to Stirling, and prepared for a siege. The English were expected to pursue their victory, and either occupy or destroy the capital; for there were no means of defending it. The Scots cannon had been captured, and the rout of leaderless soldiers, pausing to plunder and lay waste the Border, had taken refuge where they could. More than a week went by before it became clear that Surrey was on his way home.

A complete and, as it seems, determined silence has been maintained, from that day to this, as to Margaret's reception of the news. While the battle was going on she wrote to Lady Dacre, asking for her prayers.[1] Nothing more is recorded until, from Stirling, she summoned the Regency Council to meet her. On September 21st — twelve days after the death of James IV — his son was crowned at Scone. In the same week, Margaret wrote to Henry VIII asking for leniency, and begging him not to invade. A month later, she wrote to Katherine of Aragon thanking her for her sympathy 'in the blow that has fallen upon me', with a further appeal, in his nephew's name, to Henry's family feeling. He replied that he would not invade, unless the Scots rose against him.[2]

Margaret made no inquiry about the fate of her husband's body, nor any suggestion that it should be returned to Scotland for burial. She never spoke of him, except formally, again. Far from being stunned by his death and the annihilation of his army, she was roused to speedy and efficient action. It seems that she had made her plans as soon as he left her.

So the conclusion must be drawn that Margaret's affection for James—if, indeed, it ever existed—had been destroyed by his persistent and irremediable folly. If she had succumbed to private paroxysms of grief, or appeared in public as a Niobe, her state would have been sympathetically reported. No such descriptions exist. His people continued to mourn James, recording their loss and the horrors of Flodden in ballads and songs, some of great beauty. In no way did Margaret contribute to these outpourings. She occupied herself, to the exclusion of all other business, with the safety and establishment of her son, and with the assurance of her brother's support.

When it was said by a number of people that James's body had not been correctly identified—that he had escaped to go on a pilgrimage, and would eventually return—she took no steps to verify or confute these rumours. It is as if she was certain, from the moment of their parting, that he would be killed. The disposal of his remains did not concern her. She made no efforts to resolve the mystery surrounding them, which so increased as to enhance belief in his survival. He was dead; she took his place. From her point of view—the Tudor point of view—he had brought needless disaster on her and his successor. He had been unfaithful, misguided and headstrong. Freed from his romantic vanity, she could now conduct her life according to her own judgment, and try to restore the fortunes of the kingdom he had ruined. He was best forgotten. When his plaid cloak, embroidered with the royal arms, was presented to Katherine of Aragon, no one thought of sending it to his widow. Her sister-in-law reported its arrival to Henry in a triumphant letter.[3]

So it was that when some of James's captured attendants were allowed to see his corpse at Berwick, disagreement about his identity rose to fury. Some maintained that it could not be he, because the iron chain he always wore about his waist was missing. Others replied that he would never have carried it into battle. Others again recalled that many of the nobles who died with him wore the same armour as himself, and that any one of them, his face similarly battered in, might now be lying, uncoffined and neglected, before them. Someone else declared that this was not the King's body, but that of Lord Elphinstone, who had been killed at the same time, and was very like him.[4]

No prayers were said, no watch kept over the corpse (which was reported as 'showing great dignity in death') because James had died under sentence of excommunication. His neck, it presently transpired, was 'opened to the midst by a wide wound', and his left hand hung by a piece of skin.[5]

At Berwick the body was embalmed, enclosed in lead and taken to the chapel of Richmond Palace. When the King returned from France, it was suggested that James's funeral should take place in St Paul's. Henry, that most correct of Catholics, asked the Pope's permission for the ceremony to be performed, and after a delay of several months was told that this might not be, in view of the Scottish King's excommunication. 'It is a due punishment for one who hath perjurously broken his league,' Henry said, and gave no further orders about his brother-in-law's corpse, which, still uncoffined, was removed from the palace to the neighbouring monastery, where it remained until 1538, when that establishment was dissolved. It was then placed in a lumber room.[6]

Some years after the accession of Queen Elizabeth, a glazier, repairing the windows, smelt the spices and reported the matter to the local authorities. No official notice was taken, although several people, including Stow the historian, came to look at the lead-wrapped figure. The glazier severed the head from the body, and took it home; then he carried them both to the church of St Michael in the City. There, the rotting fragments were coffined and interred. In the 1750s, a skeleton enclosed in ox-hide, with an iron chain about the waist, was discovered at Hume Castle. But there is no reason to suppose that it was that of James IV, although it was claimed to be.[7]

For more than a century after Flodden the people of Scotland told one another that the Queen of Elfland had rescued their hero and taken him away to her kingdom. So he could not be dead; nor, now, would he ever die, for she had made him immortal; one day he would return in triumph.

The seed of these fantasies was already sown when Margaret met the Council at Stirling. After the arrangements for her rule and for the coronation had been agreed, certain details of the late King's generalship were disclosed. His gunners had continued to fire over the heads of the enemy, because he had sent his skilled German mercenaries to France — where they remained, in the pay of Louis XII and his successor — together with his newest cannon, christened by him the Seven Sisters. (Henry VIII, more orthodox, had named his best guns after the Twelve Apostles.)*

* Some of these can be seen in the armoury of the Tower.

That most of the Scottish chieftains had perished—in many families no males survived—was the result of James's desperate advance into the fatal plain. It was considered that the reports of his actions would create a disastrous impression on Scotland's potential allies; so a letter was presently composed and sent to the King of Denmark, as from James V, to explain—they could not be excused—his father's errors. 'Our army', the child King was made to say, 'was not handled with sufficient care ... The English, intent on deceit, took care not to fight at the prearranged time or place ... Our dearest father, made impatient ... rushed too boldly upon them ... and threw away his own life and those of most of his nobles.'[8]

It was then said that Lord Hume, who, with his troops, had stood aside from the mêlée, had not only betrayed his master but murdered him, and had been heard to say, 'I have assisted in teaching a Scottish king that he was mortal.'[9] No immediate decision was made about following up this rumour, for there were many more urgent problems to be dealt with than Hume's possible treachery, the most vital being the safety of James V. Removing him from Stirling to the holy precincts of Scone for his coronation was a risk, but it had to be taken; in no other way could his reign be established. Surrounded by officials and nobles in deepest mourning, he sat on his governess's lap, was anointed and touched the regalia. When the crown was held over his head, and Archbishop Beaton desired the congregation to accept him as their sovereign, the baby King was greeted with an outburst of weeping. Then, under a strong guard, he was taken back to Stirling.

Yet in some ways James was fortunate. At his birth his parents had put him in charge of the poet Sir David Lindsay, who remained with him as Vice-Chamberlain of his household till his majority. Lindsay had been told never to leave James's side. 'When you slept, he later reminded him, 'it was nightly close to my cheek ... I bore Your Grace on my back, even as a packman.' The child's first recorded utterance was 'Pa, Da Lyné'—'Play, Davy Lindsay'—and when he began to walk he would staggeringly dance to Lindsay's playing on the lute, 'with many a bend and beck', according to that gentleman, who recalled that 'Ginkerton', an ancient Scottish melody, was his young master's favourite tune. He would ask for it incessantly —'From play thou'st never let me rest.'[10]

James's health and liveliness were apparently sustained by this companionship; he was a handsome child, and showed great intelligence. When Margaret described him to Henry 'very small and tender', she was not referring to his physique, but to his helplessness. A few weeks after he was crowned his uncle replied to this appeal by telling Lord Dacre, now Warden of the Eastern Marches, to command Margaret to send the boy to England. Dacre informed her that James must be 'ordered and ruled by the King's Grace', who was 'his natural guardian', adding that on no account were the Scots nobles to remove him to some island, 'where he shall be in further danger, and more difficult for the King to attain'.[11]

This rather ogrish concern was ignored. Owing to the expenses of his French expedition, Henry was not in a position either to invade Scotland or to kidnap his nephew. He told Dacre to harry and burn the Border, so as to demonstrate English power, while Surrey disbanded his forces. Then, after some correspondence with Margaret, Henry evolved a more practical and less costly scheme which exactly suited her plans. She had been accepted as supreme Regent, according to the terms of her husband's will, and was solely and entirely responsible for her son. Her authority was officially unquestioned, as is shown in her proclamations, which were prefaced with, 'James, by God's Grace, King of the Scots, and Margaret, Queen of Scotland and testamentary tutrix of the same.' This enabled her to concur with most of Henry's policies.[12]

So the brother and sister dominated what much later came to be known as Great Britain. It was well for Scotland that they did; but this aspect of their situation infuriated the younger chieftains, especially those whose fathers had been killed at Flodden, and who cared only to avenge their deaths. The prosperity of Scotland was as nothing; the vendetta their one desire. More bloodshed, further devastation—this time on the other side of the Border—obsessed them. As the response of their followers was slow and feeble, they looked abroad for allies against the hated English, approaching in turn France, Denmark and Austria. Thus Scotland was again divided. Parliament could not agree, either on foreign or internal policy.

Somehow Margaret, now in the fourth month of her pregnancy, kept the balance. She was perfectly self-possessed, and determined to fit in with Henry's plans. She had already made a private alliance with Dacre, through his wife, and corresponded regularly with Wolsey, Surrey and Katherine of Aragon, who all admired her energy and grasp of the situation. This made her unpopular with and distrusted by a number of Scottish nobles; she did not care for that, as long as she could keep the peace. The common people pitied and supported her, as did the burgesses and most of the higher clergy.

The mistake she made was that of regarding herself as her brother's Vicereine. Outwardly, she conformed to Scottish notions; she used Scots dialect in some of her letters, but not always in her conversations, and, in the first year of her regency, governed responsibly and with courage; for she knew that certain groups of nobles, one of which was headed by the Humes, might imprison and murder her if she took any risks. Also, she had to plan for her son's future in the event of her death in childbirth. Her first action was to seize and secrete all the bullion from the Treasury. Contemporary and later historians have accused her of plundering the state to enrich herself; in fact, she was preparing her defence against civil war; and unless she held on to the pay of the royal troops, her enemies in Parliament and the Council—who had already rejected Henry's offer of a truce— might embark on another invasion. At all costs, that must be avoided.

Meanwhile, the question of her marrying again was being discussed. Louis XII, who knew that his wife could not live, was considering an offer; and Henry, among others, thought it might be advisable for her to marry the Emperor Maximilian.[13] Margaret herself had no plans or wishes: she was too busy; in any case, she must remain single until after her confinement. When, at last, she did begin to think on these lines, the result was fatal—partly because she hardly thought at all.

Having secured herself financially, Margaret decided to fill the vacancies on the Council with those bishops who would support the English alliance. As was then the custom, she applied to the Pope for their appointment through her secretary, Painter, who reported her to the other Councillors. When they accused her of acting behind their backs, she appeased them by dismissing him. They then employed him to spy on her, and continued to negotiate with Louis XII for a renewal of the French subsidies, in order to invade England in the spring. He promised them men, arms and money; and in November, his envoy, escorted by Arran, Lord Fleming and Sir James Ogilvie, arrived in Scotland. This gentleman, the Sieur de la Bastie, was the representative of the Duke of Albany, James V's first cousin once removed. When the Duke's entry into Scottish politics came under discussion, and Margaret realized that the Council had written to him without telling her, she was appalled, and at once

6

informed Henry VIII. Albany's position had always been anomalous. Now it became extremely awkward.

John Stuart Duke of Albany was the only son of Duke Alexander, the brother of James III who had plotted against that monarch and been exiled to France, where he died in 1481. Duke John was therefore heir-presumptive to James V, for his claim preceded Arran's. When the infant King came to the throne Albany, now in his thirty-fourth year, was one of the greatest nobles in France and high in the favour of Louis XII, for whom he had fought in Italy, Spain and Greece. He had no designs on the crown of Scotland, and no wish to leave France, where he was honoured (he held the post of Lord High Admiral), popular and successful. His mother was French; he had been married for eight years to an heiress of the House of de la Tour d'Auvergne, and, apart from the fact that they seemed unlikely to have any children—for the Duchess was delicate—was both rich and happy. In fact, Albany was ideally placed. Now the Scottish Council wanted him to leave his wife and country to share the Regency with Margaret, in the hope that he would rule her and seal the French alliance. It was his duty to do so, they said, adding that if she died in childbirth, Albany, as head of the government, would organize the invasion she was trying to prevent.

That the Duke spoke no English and had lived all his life as a Frenchman did not concern those who were bent on destroying the Tudor domination; some of them knew so little of his circumstances that they were planning a marriage between him and Margaret. When they heard that the Duchess was still alive, they began to consider a divorce; in the meantime, they urged him, through de la Bastie, to 'come home'. As Louis XII did not want him to leave, Albany replied evasively to these offers, in the hope that they would not be renewed. At the same time he wrote Margaret a letter of condolence and offered her his personal support, as did Louis XII, who was increasingly alarmed by the reports of an Anglo-Scots truce.

For this, it was necessary to send a Scottish embassy into England; but all Margaret's suggestions were met with excuses from the Council. While Henry warned her not to accept Albany in any capacity, they made it clear that unless she consented to receive him they would not begin to discuss terms with the English. The wrangle continued throughout the last months of 1513; then Margaret gave her consent to Albany's arrival at some distant date, and the truce was fixed for February 1514. These arrangements were confirmed by the

Parliament of March 20th, which Margaret, who was to be confined in April, could not attend. Angry disagreements went on between the elder and the younger chieftains; those who had not fought at Flodden were especially anxious to invade. Although Scotland was re-arming, no decision was reached. As a precaution, Dacre continued to lay waste the Border, and to encourage discord between the nobles—an easy matter.

Margaret then retired, with James V, to Stirling, and on April 12th, 1514, gave birth to a son, who was christened Alexander and given the title of Duke of Ross. In May, attended by the faithful Dunbar, who celebrated her recovery in a long poem, she was publicly churched and gave a reception for the Council, so that they might pay homage to her sons. Louis XII, now a widower, asked for her hand; so did the Emperor Maximilian; both proposals were received with non-committal courtesy.

Urged by Dunbar to be 'glad in heart and expel heaviness', and described as 'a bright star … pleasant, young and fair', Margaret appeared in excellent spirits—and almost beautiful. Her charm of manner was particularly effective, and several formerly hostile nobles came over to her side. They were joined by the great Douglas clan, which included Lord Drummond, the father of James IV's dead mistress; he brought with him his grandson, Archibald Earl of Angus, a handsome youth of nineteen, whose father had been killed at Flodden.

It was then arranged that a convocation to discuss general policy should be held at Edinburgh. Margaret desired all the nobles to attend; they agreed to do so, and to abandon, temporarily at least, their private feuds. She could not be sure that they would keep their word; but they did—and on July 10th she presided over them with tactful authority. Her gracious suavity and persuasive address—and perhaps also her looks— were much admired.

Fear and hatred of England were revived by Henry's offer of adopting his nephews. He temptingly added that, as he still had no children, he would acknowledge James V as his heir—'and of this', he concluded, 'shall come more good and well to both England and Scotland than tongue can tell.'[14] This suggestion was ignored; but Henry's announcement that he had not the least desire to invade reassured the older Councillors—indeed, why should he trouble to acquire a kingdom ruled by his elder sister?

The Scots nobles now began, rather unwillingly, to think of internal unity, and promised to keep the peace with one another. When Margaret asked for an oath of loyalty, they gave it, as being 'content to stand in one mind and will ... to the pleasure of the King's Grace, Your Grace, and for the common weal.'[15] Yet Tudor caution prevailed; Margaret remained wary. 'Blood', she wrote to Henry, 'will never turn to water.' Albany might suddenly arrive, in which case she and her sons would need her brother's protection. The general view was that she had nothing to fear from her subjects. 'The Scots', reported the Venetian ambassador, 'are always defeated by the English, who are brave men and experienced soldiers.'[16]

With her children, Margaret left for Perth. Here she held court for the rest of the summer — and here Lord Drummond and the Earl of Angus were in constant attendance. No one suspected what plans the old lord had made, nor what his hopes were. His grandson, a childless widower, had recently been betrothed to Lady Jane Stuart of Traquair, with whom he appeared to be deeply in love, and the announcement of their marriage was expected shortly.

There was some surprise when Margaret gave Angus's uncle, the bishop-poet Gavin Douglas, the see of Dunkeld, and, later, the Archbishopric of St Andrews, without consulting the Council. It was thought that Douglas's description of the fairy queen in his *Palace of Honour* was a tribute to her. The poem had appeared in 1501 — but the author may have presented it to her as a new effort, so that she might read of herself as 'a lily sweetly fair', carrying 'a sceptre of delight'.

The Bishop's verses were reasonably applicable. For the first time since her arrival in Scotland ten years earlier, Margaret was well, happy and triumphant. The kingdom was at peace; her sons were healthy; Albany's arrival had been postponed; and she had conquered, it seemed, the hearts of her nobles. Of her own ... she was not so sure. A contemporary, describing Angus as 'most lusty in the Queen's sight', noted his beauty, his accomplished grace and gay address.[17] More important still — he was always there.

On August 4th, 1514, Margaret and Angus were privately married in the church of Kinnoul by a Douglas cousin. The witnesses were sworn to secrecy. Three weeks went by before any announcement was made.

## NOTES

1 *L. & P.*, vol. I, pt. 2, p. 1009.
2 Hall, p. 395.
3 *L. & P.*, op. cit., p. 1061.
4 Green, vol. IV, p. 167.
5 P. Vergil, *Anglica Historia*, pp. 221–2. F. Godwin, *Annals of England*, p. 13.
6 J. Stow, *Annals*, p. 494. Godwin, p. 14. *Venetian State Papers*, vol. II, p. 146.
7 F. Grose, *Antiquities of Scotland*, vol. II, p. 232.

8 Mackie, p. 273.
9 Drummond, p. 274.
10 Strickland, *Queens of Scotland*, vol. I, p. 79.
11 *L. & P.*, op. cit., p. 1040.
12 Ibid.
13 Op. cit., p. 1019.
14 Lesley, p. 63.
15 Green, op. cit., p. 184.
16 *Ven. S. P.*, vol. II, p. 189.
17 Lindsay, vol. II, p. 284.

# X

## *Angus and Albany*

IN THE sixteenth century the riches acquired by a subject marrying a royal personage were even greater than those received by such aspirants today. But as then the monarchy was also the fountain of political power, the position of the successful climber became extremely dangerous. Caution, tact, courage and skill were required to a degree equalling the profits of the union; failure in the exercise of these qualities might cause, not only the loss of everything gained, but the ruin, and perhaps the death, of the aspirant.

Angus, that handsome young cavalier, had not yet acquired the talents necessary for his new status, except the ability to please. He had what is now called a way with him, but he lacked foresight.[1] His situation was further complicated by the fact that a Queen five years his senior was so enamoured of him that everything he did, all he was, appeared wonderful in her eyes. At twenty-four, Margaret had fallen in love for the first time; and so Angus, complacently accepting the worship of a woman whose deprivations had been constant and galling, was blinded by his own triumph. He saw himself as a potentate whom none dared attack, and who had only to command.

Lord Drummond should have been able to curb his grandson's haughty disregard of the circumstances. He did not do so, because his own arrogance was more besotted, his ambition greedier than those of his pupil. His view was that they were both above law, custom and tradition. The Queen granted all their requests; no one else need be considered. In any case, Drummond, as Lord Justiciary of Scotland, and the father of that other Margaret whom the late King might have secretly married, was more naturally overbearing — and far less good-tempered — than the younger man. Determined to regain his former greatness, and intoxicated by his success in manoeuvring this splendid alliance, he became maniacally belligerent, counting — rightly, as it turned out — on the Queen's support. Margaret came to rely on him as on the father she had parted from when she was still a child. She continued to be fond of the Earl; and he made easy use of her affection.

The people of Scotland received the news of Margaret's second marriage with surprise, but not disapproval; it mattered little to them which clan gained the upper hand as long as they themselves were left in peace; and the Douglases were no more brutal and corrupt than their rivals. The general view was that she and her sons needed a protector; and Angus, backed by his grandfather, seemed a suitable choice.

The rage of the Council at finding themselves outstripped by old Drummond and his hitherto negligible grandson was such that gang warfare appeared imminent. Then, secretly, the nobles began to take sides, some for and some against the Douglases, while agreeing that Margaret had forfeited her regency by marrying without their consent. She replied to this decision by naming Angus as co-regent; she added that the late King's will had not limited her regency to the period of her widowhood, and that therefore she was still entitled to that and to the guardianship of her children. But the situation was more complicated than either she or the Council would admit. Neither claim was paramount.

James IV and his advisers had no doubt assumed that, in the event of his death, Margaret ought to take another husband, both for the increase of the dynasty and the safety of the realm—but that when she did so, she would marry a person of her own rank, preferably one whose powers would protect Scotland's independence. According to the Council, her marriage with Angus was a betrayal of her trust, for which she must be punished by the loss of her position. When Margaret pointed out that, in the terms of the will, she could marry whom she liked, they replied that James IV had no right to bequeathe the government unconditionally; it now devolved upon themselves, and they proposed to hand it over to Albany. They reminded her that in Scottish law any woman marrying again forfeited the guardianship of her children. (But Margaret was not 'any' woman; she was Queen-Regent by Act of Parliament and their endorsement of the will.) Margaret then again referred them to this document, as making no embargo on her authority in the event of a second marriage, no matter with whom.[2] So the problem of her rights must remain in abeyance until James V reached his majority—and for the next thirteen years there could be no solution.

There were many who rejoiced over this new confusion in Scottish affairs. Henry VIII perceived in Angus's elevation a means of strengthening his own hold on that country; the less powerful nobles could now resume their favourite pursuit of clan war; and the Douglases saw a prospect of acquiring greater wealth and scoring off their enemies.

On August 26th, 1514, the Council informed Margaret that Albany had replaced her. They followed up this announcement by sending Sir William Comyn as Lyon King-at-Arms to summon Angus before them on the charge of marrying the Queen-Regent without their consent, thus ignoring the fact that this consent could only come from James V — i.e. from Margaret herself.

That Margaret had behaved rashly, if no worse, in marrying Angus did not then occur to her, because she was sure of retaining the regency and the guardianship of her sons. According to her interpretation of the will, she was in the right, and she prepared to defend that right without compromise or hesitation. She knew that not only the Douglases but also their adherents were gathering behind her. More important still, she counted on her brother's support and Dacre's assistance in subduing those she thought of as rebels. Yet she intended to use gentle and persuasive tactics to get her own way, thus rather undermining than crushing those she hoped to win over. She also knew that if civil war broke out, she could appeal to the people as the widow of their adored King and the mother of his children; they would defend the royal family — possibly even to the point of allying themselves with the English — against any attack. Finally, she seems to have thought that although she might not be able to prevent Albany coming to Scotland, she had cancelled his regency by giving Angus the position.

Margaret left Perth for Holyroodhouse so as to receive Sir William Comyn formally. Standing between Angus and Drummond, she bade him deliver his message. His opening phrase indicated the Council's defiance. Instead of addressing her as Queen-Regent by the Grace of God, he began, 'My Lady Queen, mother to His Grace our King.'

Before he could proceed, Lord Drummond stepped forward and struck him on the mouth. There followed a scene of confusion, and the herald left without delivering his summons to Angus.[3]

Exaggerated reports of this incident eventually reached Henry VIII (presumably through Dacre's spies) and Margaret hastened to reassure the brother who had alarmed that same herald a year earlier;

for she knew that Henry was strict about etiquette — at least, as far as others' behaviour was concerned. Drummond had not boxed Comyn's ears, she wrote, but had merely 'waved his sleeve' at him; she felt bound to add that Sir William had been 'pushed on the breast', by the Earl: but that was all.[4]

Margaret then told Angus to take the Great Seal of Scotland from the Lord Chancellor, Archbishop Beaton, who refused to part with it. Angus removed it by force, upon which the Council told the Treasury authorities to withhold Margaret's dower rents. As this crippled all her activities, she decided to take up a more submissive attitude. This meant sending for Albany; and she and Angus declared themselves willing to do so.[5]

Margaret arranged to meet the Council and preside over the Parliament of September 12th. Entering Edinburgh in state, she was wildly cheered by the people. This triumph resulted in several nobles going over to her side; but when she realized that her party was far outnumbered by those who were pressing for Albany's regency, she returned to Stirling. There she and her children remained, entrenched against a siege and protected by Douglas men-at-arms. She then asked the Council for the guardianship of James V. They replied that she had lost the office of tutrix, and must no longer meddle with 'matters pertaining to the crown'.[6]

Margaret decided to ignore these resolutions, and summoned Parliament to meet her at Perth. The Council forbade the members, on their allegiance, to attend, and required her to give up the Great Seal, which she did. Meanwhile, as they had heard nothing from Albany, they sent over Sir William Comyn to fetch him, and suggested a meeting with the Queen's Commissioners. Their discussions were fruitless, and all through October and the first half of November an armed truce prevailed between her party and theirs. The Council, knowing that Margaret had asked Henry to send troops, remained inactive and rather nervous. When it was announced that Comyn had been shipwrecked, Margaret wrote triumphantly to Henry that this showed God to be 'of my party'.[7] (He always had been a Tudor partisan: they both knew it.) And then at last the Council received Albany's answer. It was not what they had expected.

Albany began by announcing that he was not going to accept the regency until certain conditions had been agreed between himself and the Council, which de la Bastie would put before them. They must restore his ancestral rights, of which one was the fortress of Dunbar

and the other the earldom of March. Also, they must revoke the
sentence of treason passed upon his father by James III. He added
that he would not undertake the government unless the nobles 'offered
all good ways' to the Queen and her husband. In other words, he
refused to join in a civil war, or in one against England. He was
empowered, however, to bring French support if Scotland was
invaded.[8]

Discussion of these terms began in January 1515. Then Louis XII
died and was succeeded by Francis I, who seemed more likely to
support the violently anti-English group than his predecessor.
Rightly, Henry and Margaret both thought that Francis was planning
to use Scotland to get back the French fortresses and cities taken by
Henry in 1513, and that Albany would therefore appear as the agent
of a hostile country, undermining English power from within the
Border. The truce made between England and France had been
renewed on the accession of Francis; but that would not prevent his
helping Scotland to prey on her neighbour while he prepared for war
on the other side of the Channel.

Henry felt the situation to be extremely dangerous, and urged
Margaret to prevent Albany's arrival. As she and Angus had already
been besieged by Arran's troops and were still being threatened, she
replied that she could not go back on her word; her tactics must
remain conciliatory—as those of the Council now were, owing to
Albany's influence. Meanwhile, she wrote to the Pope asking him to
intercede with them for the return of the crown jewels and the
guardianship of her children.[9]

When Henry realized that Margaret was without money—for the
bullion she had taken from the Treasury had been spent—and that her
rents and jewels were being withheld, he threatened to invade. She
then told him that the Council might seize Stirling and kidnap her
sons. The nobles had already 'deposed' her; she was pawning such
valuables as she had left, and her stores of food were running low.
'The enemy', she added, 'look to the coming of Albany, and behave
as if they were kings.' Henry must come to the rescue, by sea and
land. 'The bairns', she concluded, 'are well and life-like, thanks to
Almighty God.'[10]

Throughout this indeterminate conflict, Henry, Albany, Margaret
and most of the older chieftains all desired to avoid war; but without
it, they were bound to be frustrated. Henry and Margaret wanted to
colonize Scotland through her regency; the Scots Parliament were

set on complete independence and the control of the Border. The more powerful nobles—Arran, Argyll, Lennox and Hume—were hoping to obtain supremacy out of the general confusion, and ready to change sides at any moment. (Huntly, who had a feud with Arran, came over to Margaret in January 1515.) Albany's plan was to establish peace in Scotland, cement the French alliance and, having installed a competent deputy, end his days in France.

Meanwhile, the increasing arrogance of the Douglases was having a bad effect on Margaret's cause. She was still personally popular; when the Council accused her of betraying Scotland to the English, she pointed out that she was neither sending her sons to England, nor planning to join her brother herself, unless they forced her to do so. She then suggested to Henry that he should write 'counterfeit' letters to the Council, to which she would have a key, while he prepared to invade. She added that any letters signed by her 'Margaret R.' would have been dictated by the lords; those ending 'your loving sister' were to be accepted as her own.[11] (This was disingenuous, to say the least, but she was now desperately afraid for herself and her children.) Advised by Wolsey, Henry decided to confine himself to threats—for the present—and renewed his offers of adopting his nephews. He agreed that Margaret, who was pregnant, could not leave Scotland immediately; so he advised her to move to the Marches, thus coming under Dacre's protection. He added that, having made James V his heir, he would acknowledge the little Duke of Ross as King of Scotland.[12] He had, of course, no intention of keeping these promises.

Henry then instructed his ambassadors in Paris to prevent Francis sending over Albany as Regent—for, he explained, 'He is the most suspect person that might be sent, for the surety of the two young princes, because he aims at the crown of Scotland.' To these protests Francis replied that he vouched for Albany's integrity, and that, to oblige his 'good brother and cousin' he would postpone the Duke's departure till May.[13]

By this time, Dacre gleefully reported, 'There was never so much disorder in Scotland as there is now—pray God it continue.'[14] But Margaret's position had improved, for Hume had joined her, and was in touch with Dacre. This encouraged her in her pacific attitude, and she agreed to preside over the 'rebel' Parliament of March 1515. The people, Gavin Douglas informed Dacre, had become so weary of the ceaseless petty skirmishes between the clans that they would agree to be ruled 'by the Grand Turk' for the sake of peace, and were more than ever attached to the Queen, in spite of their dislike of the Douglases.

It seemed that there could be no settlement, either between Margaret and Parliament, or between the rival lords, until Albany arrived. In the second week of May 1515 his squadron was sighted off the coast of Ayrshire by the English fleet, which had been sent to take him. It was evaded, and on the 15th the Duke landed at Dumbarton with a train of a thousand followers. He then proceeded to Edinburgh, where Margaret and Angus received him. Their meeting was courteous and formal.

Almost at once a relationship was established which surprised Margaret, for it was so pleasant as to be reassuring. The agent of Francis I and the enemy of the Tudors was a stout, rosy, middle-aged gentleman, whose gallant manners and distinguished bearing were those of a man of the world. Albany, richly dressed and lavishly attended, had the high-bred ease and agreeable approach of a sophisticated courtier; the contrast between his behaviour and that of the Scots nobles must have been rather painful. In his first talks with Margaret he showed his goodwill by promising the renewal of her dower rents—provided they were not used against himself—and added that he had no designs on the crown or on the safety of her children. He aimed at peace; but the punishment of law-breakers— among whom he included Gavin Douglas and Lord Drummond— must come first. He required her acknowledgment of his authority; then he would see to it that she lacked for nothing.

The enthusiasm with which Albany was received—a ceremonious investiture, banquets, pageantry, all the tributes given to a reigning sovereign—exacerbated many of the nobles and gave him the impression that he had only to give orders to set everything to rights. Later, he realized that he had fallen into a nest of criminals, who intended to use him while defeating one another. Albany, the only man of honour in a circle of scoundrels, was soon forced to take sides —not always wisely—and to treat as enemies many who might have helped him; among these was the Queen he had replaced. To her, he became a tyrant and a bully; yet he had intended to use her as became his chivalry and her honour.

Albany, that vigorous and well-meaning administrator, was neither ruthless nor unscrupulous. He knew nothing of the Scots, and never attempted to learn their language or to defeat their villainy. Desiring peace, he found a sword thrust into his hand.

Meanwhile, Margaret appeared to him as a potential ally (if only he could separate her from her brother's policy) and as a woman in need of help. Surely they could share, instead of quarrelling over, their respective duties—especially as Francis I had now announced that he would be responsible for the care of her sons.

When news of what seemed like agreement between Margaret and the Duke reached Dacre, he was much alarmed. Having communicated with Henry VIII, he wrote to warn her against French scheming and the machinations of the new Regent, adding that she and her children were in great danger. Albany might be a fool (Wolsey, who knew him, thought so) but he was certainly a rogue. Margaret knew that he was neither; but when he set about the destruction of the Douglas power she felt him to be hostile, and guessed that he might separate her from her children. Their first breach was caused by his summoning Gavin Douglas before the Council in her presence on the charge of having obtained the see of Dunkeld through English influence. The Bishop had done this— with Margaret's connivance. When he denied the accusation, Albany said to Margaret, 'Madam, I have made you understand this deed, which touches the King your son and my sovereign lord, which is the thing you should hold most tender.' Margaret replied, 'My lord, be ye right sure that no person in the world desires so much the good of my bairns as I do, and I will not sustain no man that would do against the right and privilege of my son's crown.' She then solemnly declared that the charge was false. Albany said that he would maintain the rights of James V (in other words, the anti-English cause) with his life, and adjourned the meeting. A few weeks later Gavin Douglas's correspondence with England fell into his hands, revealing the Bishop as an English agent and Margaret as the instrument of her brother's ambitions, and Douglas was imprisoned. Lord Drummond was the next culprit. Margaret's defence, that Sir William Comyn had provoked the Earl's attack through his insolence to herself, was dismissed; Drummond was deprived of his honours, and sent into custody.[15]

As Margaret saw her principal allies being removed, she was appalled, and rushed to Albany to plead for them. In tears, she begged him to release them. He could not do so. She and Angus then left Edinburgh for Stirling, and set a strong guard about the children. But she was much impoverished; and Henry, watching upon events, had sent her nothing: nor had he written to her. In an agony, she

appealed to Dacre, whose spies reported that her distress might bring
on a miscarriage, and so kill her.

Her state was deplorable. She faced death for herself, her unborn
child and her sons from those nobles who might seize and dispatch
them all in the resultant struggle. She had no money left to pay her
own guard of the Douglas men-at-arms. She was within three
months of a confinement which must, at best, temporarily remove
her from the care of her family, if it did not end her life or turn her
into a permanent invalid; and she had married a young man who,
while doing what he could for her, was of little use compared to those
two older members of his clan now in the hands of her enemies. Her
brother, having promised to help her, had apparently withdrawn. And
Dacre, on whom she seems most to have relied, made her feel that
all she did was wrong. He pointed out that her circumstances could
not, now, be worse. It was useless to imagine that she would be able to
keep her children out of Albany's clutches; and when, through their
murder, he became King of Scotland (she should recall the fate of the
Princes in the Tower) what hope was left for them and her husband?
'They will fall into his hands,' he declared, 'to their utter destruction.'[16] When Stirling fell, which was inevitable, it would be impossible to effect a rescue. The nobles who had joined her would desert;
not one person in her employ could be trusted — and she was surrounded by spies. (Dacre did not add that many of these persons
were of his own faction.)

It was at this point in Margaret Tudor's life that the metamorphosis
which has given her the reputation of a predatory, violent and menac-
ing figure began. Her strength of purpose did not weaken; but, for
the next decade, it was forced out of one channel into another. Living
in scenes of terror, suspense and shock, and in danger, not only from
those she had always known were her enemies, but from persons on
whom she must depend, she was whirled into a maelstrom. Finally,
this turmoil was heightened by the fact that, at a comparatively late
age, she had fallen in love. She could not concentrate on the welfare
of her sons, because she was obsessed by the risks Angus had to face.
She had raised him high; if he fell, she would be to blame.

So it was that this once over-indulged, passionate and now
frustrated creature became, not so much the victim of the tempest, as
the tempest itself. That she continued sane is remarkable; and
indeed, there were times when her behaviour changed so abruptly,
veering from one extreme to another, that in retrospect her tempera-

ment appears unbalanced. To her contemporaries, whether they supported her or not, she seemed capricious, hysterical, monstrously selfish, and impossible to deal with or to understand.

It occurred to no one that Margaret had more to endure — including the delusions of triumph — than falls to the lot of most young women. In her day, such disasters as the loss of four out of five children, the death of a husband in battle, and the threats to her life and the lives of those she loved were looked on as a corollary to greatness and power. That she might be forcibly deprived of both was a possibility a queen must accept. But Margaret could not do so; she fought against that eventuality with all her might: struggling on, beyond exhaustion, she would not admit defeat or despair. Never for an instant submissive or resigned, she became, in the eyes of most historians, a fiend: the evil woman of Scottish legend, the treacherous instrument of English policy.

And yet there were those — her elder son among them — who loved her, and could not tear themselves away from her fortunes: the fortunes of one who should have been utterly crushed, but who survived, although scarred and broken; she remained resolute, her wits and common sense once more in command. She achieved, at last, victory over herself. Standing above the battle, she acquired indifference — the only anaesthetic then available.

---

## NOTES

1 L. & P., vol. II, pt. 1, p. 290.
2 Green, vol. IV, p. 186.
3 Strickland, *Queens of Scotland*, p. 108.
4 L. & P., op. cit., p. 520.
5 Wood, p. 93.
6 Green, op. cit., p. 189.
7 L. & P., op. cit., p. 1453.
8 Green, op. cit., p. 190.

9 L. & P., vol. I, pt. 2, p. 1030.
10 Op. cit., p. 1453.
11 Op. cit., p. 1477.
12 Ibid.
13 *Ven. S. P.*, vol. II, p. 230.
14 Green, op. cit., p. 199.
15 Op. cit., p. 206.
16 L. & P., op. cit., p. 187.

# XI

## *Flight*

HUME had been one of the first chieftains to welcome Albany.
Shortly after the Duke's arrival he showed him a battered corpse with
an iron chain round its waist; this, he said, was that of the late King,
for whose death he had been responsible. He then seems to have
hinted that the murder of James V and his brother would ensure
Albany's succession, and went on to speak of his own influence and
power. Assuming that Hume knew no Latin, Albany made a mocking
remark in that language to one of his gentlemen about the Earl's
ridiculous appearance. But Hume understood the drift of the jest,
and so had left the Regent's party for that of the Douglases. There
could be no more dangerous ally; yet Margaret and Angus now had
to accept anyone with a large following.[1]

As Margaret had once more taken refuge in the Castle of Stirling,
she did not attend the memorial service for James IV, which Albany
commanded to be held in Edinburgh. Although his plans for her and
the children were both practical and humane, she realized, as he did
not, that he was in the hands of those who had schemes of their own,
and that they might act before he could stop them. Her intention now
was to escape with Angus and the children into England; meanwhile,
she must appear to co-operate with Albany.

The Duke and the Council then decided that she should have
access to, but not charge of, her sons. Eight guardians, of whom she
was to choose four, would be responsible for them; and a deputation
set off for Stirling to take them from her. Warned of their coming,
Margaret decided to make a stand which would advertise the cruelty
of this plan, so that when she escaped it would become clear that she
had been forced into breaking her word. She came out of the castle
with Angus and their attendants, holding the three-year-old King by
the hand; behind her stood a nurse, carrying his brother. As soon as
the deputation was within hearing, she called out, 'Drop the portcullis!' As the iron gates crashed down she came forward, and went

on, 'Stand! Declare the cause of your coming, before you draw nearer to your sovereigns.' 'We are deputed,' said the foremost official, 'by the Parliament now sitting, to demand and receive our King and his brother.' 'This castle', Margaret replied, 'is my enfeoffment, given to me by the late King my husband, of whose children I am the protectrix. Therefore I can in no wise deliver them to any person. But,' she added, with characteristic diplomacy, 'I respect the Parliament, and I require six days to consider their mandate—for my councillors, alas, are few.'[2]

This combination of audacity and common sense was effective, and the deputation withdrew. Angus and Margaret then decided that he should placate the lords by saying that he had advised her to do whatever they wanted. This would prevent, or at least delay, his arrest on the charge of high treason, while he collected his forces.

Albany then ordered Hume, who was Provost of Edinburgh, to arrest Angus's younger brother, George Douglas. Hume replied that he could not do so without Parliament's consent, and, with Douglas, made off for the Border. Meanwhile Angus left Stirling to call up his followers, and returned with sixty horse to find the castle surrounded by Albany's soldiers—some five hundred men-at-arms—whose commander ordered him to join them in storming it. Again, Angus appeared to comply; he then managed to enter the castle by an underground passage. He and Margaret had a hurried consultation, and agreed that she should make a further appeal for the custody of her sons, while he set about collecting a larger following. After he left, she was told that Albany himself, at the head of 7,000 men, was advancing on Stirling.

Angus was seen leaving the castle, and sixteen of his party were killed; he managed to escape. Margaret, alone but for her servants and five ladies-in-waiting, came out into the courtyard, with her children, to await the Duke. The little King was now wearing his crown and carrying a sceptre; thus, if he were forcibly removed, Albany would be in the position of a rebel who had laid hands on the sacred person of his sovereign. But the Duke was no fool; he behaved with great circumspection. In any case, his intentions were honourable and kindly.

Margaret had been carrying the huge keys of the castle. She now gave them to James, and they waited for Albany to approach. He did so unattended, and knelt and kissed the boy's hand, declaring his allegiance. The bewildered child, who did not understand French, looked up at his mother. Smiling and serene, she told him to give

7

Albany the keys. The Duke received them humbly, and told Margaret that she could remain with her children as long as she pleased, but that she must accept their guardianship as ordered by Parliament, and was not to leave the castle without his permission. He did not add that the lords now had the right to remove her sons from her in the event of an attempted rescue by their stepfather. Margaret asked for leniency for Angus. Albany replied, 'I can have no dealings with a traitor.'[3]

For some days Margaret remained in Stirling. She was then told that she must leave her sons with their new guardians and return to Edinburgh. Whatever this parting may have cost her, she obeyed without protest. Her plan was to placate Albany and the lords, while arranging with Dacre, through Hume and Angus, for her escape. She could only do this by appearing to accept Albany's decrees; and if she saw him every day, she might persuade him to let her rejoin the children. (She may not have known that he had not wanted to separate her from them, and that this decision had been forced on him by the Council.) On August 10th, 1515, she was established in the Castle of Edinburgh, and thus within easy access of the Duke at Holyroodhouse.

Margaret then wrote to Dacre telling him that Albany had seized her children — what should she do? In the same week Albany informed that nobleman that she was 'quite content' with the arrangements made for her, and she confirmed this in a letter signed 'Margaret R.' A fortnight later, she wrote to Wolsey describing the real state of affairs. 'Do not believe', she began, 'that Albany is kind. I am in much woe and pain.' She added that her supposed letters of agreement were forged, that Henry's to her were being withheld, that she was without friends or money, and that she had been accused of having smuggled James V into England and replacing him with a substitute.[4]

As if uneasy, Albany again wrote to Dacre, describing his good intentions towards the Queen and her children. Dacre replied that to separate them was needlessly cruel, and in a long letter to Margaret told her to leave Edinburgh — how, he did not explain — for Blacater, just outside Berwick; from there he would convey her, Angus and the children into England.

Margaret did not waste time describing her difficulties. She asked leave of Albany to retire to Linlithgow for the birth of her child. It was now September; she would remain there till October and then return to the capital. Permission granted, she, Angus and Hume

moved in to Linlithgow, where they stayed for forty-eight hours. At
midnight on September 13th they escaped to Tantallon, a Douglas
stronghold, and went on to Blacater the next day. Now only a few
miles separated them from the Border and Dacre's territory. At some
point in this journey they had approached Stirling in the hope of
collecting the children, but found that any attempt to do so must end
in their all being captured; this would result in Hume's and Angus's
execution. Forced to choose between her sons and her husband,
Margaret decided to save Angus from the vengeance of the lords, and
to negotiate with Albany from a distance.

Albany, amazed and horrified at the trick she had played on him,
sent messengers to Blacater begging her to return: when his letters
were ignored, he asked the French ambassador, Du Plains, to persuade her to come back, and again promised access to her children
and the renewal of her rents. As soon as Dacre heard of these approaches, he sent Margaret a letter of warning. Albany, he said, was
about to besiege Blacater with 40,000 men. (This was not true.) She
must therefore leave at once for the nunnery of Coldstream. She did
so, he waited on her, and they discussed her next move. A few days
later Dacre decided that she would be safer under his own roof, and
they set off for Morpeth Castle, his official residence. When they
reached the fortress of Harbottle, a few miles away, her pains began,
and there, on October 7th, she gave birth to a daughter, who seemed
healthy and was christened after her. Margaret herself had suffered
for forty-eight hours, and was very ill indeed.

On October 13th she roused herself to consult Dacre, and, with
him, to dictate a letter to Albany and the Council. She began by
announcing the 'delivery of a Christian soul, being a young lady', and
demanded the immediate restoration of the regency and the 'whole
rule and governance' of her sons. She added that she had escaped
from Scotland in peril of her life, and made it clear that she had now
abandoned her conciliatory attitude. She was in her own country,
and, although some hundreds of miles from her brother's court, under
his protection. Thus she could enforce her desires through invasion,
devastation and all the miseries of Flodden.[5]

The unfortunate Albany was now being censured by the Council,
threatened by the English and criticized by the French. It had never
occurred to him that a woman so near her time would — or could —
embark on flight; nor had he imagined that Margaret might lie to him.
He dared not cross the Border and seize her; and he was beset by the

angry disagreements of the lords, his anxiety for the welfare of his little
cousins and the indignation of the common people. His martyrdom
did not end there. Within a few days of Margaret's arrival at Harbottle she wrote to the Venetian Ambassadors in London, to the Pope
and to Francis I describing her despair and Albany's monstrous
brutality. A pregnant woman – a mother torn from her little ones – a
wife whose husband was accused of treason simply because he had
protected her from her enemies – an anointed Queen deprived of her
rights by an interloping villain; in all the courts of Europe, except
that of France, Margaret's lot was discussed with indignant pity,
which rose to horror when Wolsey and Henry VIII added their
comments. The minister's bursts of chivalrous rage were particularly
effective, for at this time he was more histrionically gifted than his
master. It was shameful, he cried, that His Grace's royal sister should
be so used; she might die of her sufferings. Her handwriting had been
forged and her clothes and jewels stolen – poor, helpless lady! Albany
should be sent packing, and England have charge of those innocent
babes. And for this hideous cruelty Francis I, that false friend, was
responsible – but he would regret his treachery when Scotland was
invaded. The English King only desired peace; but if the insensate
and bloody-minded Scots insisted on war, they should have it – and
France too, should this beastliness continue. At a meeting with the
Venetian envoy the Cardinal started up and, 'speaking with great
passion', exclaimed, 'Never hath such a thing been done, as violence
against a Queen! Believe me, His Majesty and the kingdom will not
brook such an outrage!' Meanwhile, Henry was writing to Francis,
'Beware, lest the affairs of Scotland injure our friendship.'[6]

Poor Albany wrote pathetically to Margaret begging her to 'listen
to reason'. If she did not, he would – how best to phrase it? – 'resort
to sterner measures, to prevent disunion between Scotland and
France'. Margaret replied with a long list of grievances – kidnapped
children, stolen jewels, broken promises, forged letters and general
persecution. She longed for her sons – but how could she venture into
a country ruled by tyrants in the pay of foreigners who were ruining
the people? (In fact the Scots, who had hoped to bleed their wealthy
guests, were beginning to realize that, far from spending money, the
French were living on them, at vast cost. Albany's first bills for food
and drink had come to £700 a month.) So the accusations and
defences and protests multiplied, while Margaret, undefeated, lay in
great pain with what Dacre thought was sciatica.

Poor Dacre—his importunate charge appeared to have taken root. She was in need of medicaments, and her daughter required baby-clothes he could not provide—at least, not of the kind suited to a princess of the blood; and he dared not begin preparations for her journey until he had her brother's instructions. It was winter; when he did hear from London, Her Grace might not be able to travel—and he had hoped to get rid of her before Christmas. Also, she was now making a series of scenes with him about Henry's neglect, Albany's sinister designs, the lords' malicious spite, her own miseries—and the ineptitude of the local physicians. He was not to blame for any of these mishaps. When—when—would she get well and go? But Dacre was of a tougher breed than Albany, whose nerves were beginning to give way; now, if crossed or found fault with, the Duke would tear off his jewelled cap and throw it into the fire, to the contemptuous amusement of the Scottish nobles.[7]

Du Plains tried to defend Albany by denying all Margaret's charges. She had been in no danger from the nobles, or anyone else, he wrote to Wolsey, and had simply left Scotland in a temper because the Duke had become more popular than she was. Her sons were perfectly safe in the care of 'the ancient lords' she herself had chosen as their guardians. He added that Hume had persuaded Angus—whom he described as 'young and good-natured'—that he and the Queen ought to escape. In fact, a great to-do was being made about nothing by a capricious woman and her foolish husband, whom the King of England was using as the tools of his anti-French policy. The whole problem could be solved by sending the children to France. Wolsey ignored this letter.[8]

Angus and Hume, who had remained at Coldstream, then tried to induce Arran to join them and Margaret against Albany. He consented, and took an oath of loyalty to her, but reverted to his former allegiance when he heard that a warrant for his arrest and the confiscation of his lands had been issued. Angus, who was in the same position, with the additional charge of high treason against him, began to feel uneasy. He came to Harbottle every now and then, to see his daughter, and spent the rest of his time in hiding, on the other side of the Border—or so it was thought.

By the end of November Margaret was well enough to be carried in a litter to Cartington and thence, after a short rest, to Morpeth, where Dacre had made elaborate preparations to receive her. The walls were hung with new tapestries, a quantity of gold and silver plate was provided, and, he complacently reported, 'the best wild fowl and victual to put in them that can be gotten for money'.[9]

Then, at last, the couriers arrived from London, with affectionate letters from Henry—he would receive his sister and her husband as soon as she could travel—and, better still, coffers of dresses and jewels. Joined by Hume, Angus and other Scottish nobles, Margaret gave daily receptions. Propped up in her state bed, the little Lady Margaret Douglas lying beside her, she delighted to show off these proofs of Tudor splendour and her brother's kindness. Presently she was carried in a chair to the presence-chamber; then Henry's gifts— twenty-two magnificent gowns, several lengths of gold and silver tissue, satin petticoats and ermine trimmings—would be laid out, and her supporters admitted to gaze on the display. 'So, my lord,' she would say, 'here you may see that the King my brother hath not forgotten me, and that he would not I should die for lack of clothes.' Dacre's second-in-command, Sir Christopher Gurney, much admired her indomitable spirit—'but,' he wrote to Wolsey, 'I think her one of the lowest brought ladies, with her great pain of sickness ... When Her Grace is removed, it would pity any man's heart to hear the shrieks and cries that Her Grace giveth ... and yet, for all that, Her Grace hath a marvellous mind upon her apparel.'[10]

These receptions overtaxed such strength as Margaret had regained, and she returned to bed, much to Dacre's distress. She now became more difficult than ever. 'Please it Your Noble Grace,' he wrote to Henry, ' ...We do not see any recovery,' going on to explain that his master's 'dearest sister' refused the attendance of the local physicians and insisted on that of Henry's own doctors. 'We beseech Your Highness for the sending of the said physician and surgeon,' Dacre continued, hastily adding, 'We do not suspect any danger to life.' Having implied that her obstinacy partly accounted for Margaret's lack of improvement ('her sickness is only in the great joint ... and specially the great and intolerable ache in her right leg') he complained of her rejection of all food but roast meats and jellies. She would not touch the broths, minced beef and almond milk prescribed. Her only pleasure lay in the contemplation of her new gowns; she would send to have them 'holden before her' twice a day, and was now writing to her Edinburgh tailor for some of purple and crimson velvet lined with cloth of gold. 'If only to be warm were gorgeous ... ' But Margaret, shivering in the vast rooms of a medieval fortress, was neither, for she could not get up and dress. She pre-

ferred Gurney's company to Dacre's, and would talk to him of her
sons. The eighteen-month-old Alexander was her favourite—'a
goodly child', she told this new friend. 'She praiseth him more', Sir
Christopher reported, 'than she doth the King.'[11]

In the second week of December Dacre was informed that
Alexander had died after a few days' illness. He and Gurney decided
to keep the news from Margaret for as long as possible. 'I think verily',
Gurney wrote to Henry, 'that Her Grace would take his death unto
her great heaviness.' In Christmas week the rumour reached her that
the baby had fallen ill; and on the morning of December 28th she
knew that he was dead. She collapsed; her life was despaired of—and
the London physicians had not arrived.

Some years later, it was suggested that Albany had poisoned the
little prince; Margaret rejected the notion. The Duke had been cruel
to her: but he was incapable of murder; and she would not use her
child's death as a weapon against him. She believed—she changed
her mind later—that James V was in safe hands. (She and Albany
were in regular correspondence about his education.) The Regent
had now released Gavin Douglas, and was still begging her to return.
If she had told him that it was not himself but his party she feared, he
would not have believed her. The lords drove him to distraction
sometimes; but he was sure of their loyalty, and did not perceive that
they were using him against Margaret. Meanwhile, he continued to
do his best, although he was increasingly homesick, and longed for his
wife, his friends and all he had given up—he hoped temporarily—
for the cause of a country he was beginning to dislike.

By the end of January 1516 Margaret had begun to recover,
although slowly, and was able to discuss with Dacre and Du Plains the
terms of a truce between England and Scotland which would be the
basis of a permanent peace. As her status was one of the principal
items in the treaty, she decided not to return to Scotland until her
position was clearly defined; on this point she and Henry diverged.
His intention was so to blacken Albany's character in the eyes of
Scotland and Europe as to force him out of the regency; thus Henry
would break up the Franco-Scottish alliance and remove all danger
of an invasion. Dacre therefore made out what he described as 'a
perfect book', setting forth Albany's 'attempts and injuries' against
the Queen and her sons, 'with accumulation and such aggravations ...
as we can add'.[12] One of these was the murder of Alexander.

When Du Plains arrived at Morpeth he saw this document, and

then perceived in what respect Margaret's attitude differed from her brother's. She still required the charge of James V, a say in the affairs of the kingdom, the renewal of her rents and a pardon for her husband and his relatives; but she did not assume Albany's intentions to be evil, and was ready to come to an agreement with him — although not with Francis I—provided Henry approved. While Dacre and Henry were presenting Albany as the reincarnation of Richard III, Margaret was hoping to make him accept second place in the government; she had had time, by now, to see that he might be valuable to her, if she could separate him from the pro-French party in the lords, and persuade him to support her authority. She would not recognize the fact that the Duke's loyalty to Francis I made this impossible: or rather, she meant to entice him away from that connection by suggesting a series of compromises.

There was no personal enmity between Margaret and Albany; she was beginning to realize that his measures against the Douglases had been forced on him. So she disregarded Dacre's charges, and in reply to the Duke's letters of reassurance wrote to him in a judiciously amicable manner. 'Cousin,' she began, 'the true experience of perfect love and favour is the due execution of deeds ... All causes in controversy between you and me and other my friends be now towards the way of good treaty, for the profit of all parties.' She then stated her conditions, pointing out that so far Albany had not fulfilled his promises, adding, 'If you had, it would have put me in more trust.'[13]

Dacre saw and passed this letter; but it convinced him of what he had suspected—Margaret and Albany were becoming too friendly, and that would, in the end, strengthen Francis I's hold on Scotland. She must therefore be removed from the influence of Du Plains, and placed under her brother's and Wolsey's jurisdiction. Once in London, she would do whatever they wanted, for she had promised Dacre that she would be entirely guided by Henry—and he believed her. Dacre was as sure of her co-operation with her brother as Albany had been of her alignment with himself. Dacre's immediate duty, as he saw it, was to keep Margaret in a good temper until she was ready to travel. But she could not be parted from her daughter; so her journey must be postponed until the spring.

Dacre then became aware that Margaret was concealing certain matters from him. While placing herself in his hands in the attitude of a helpless and persecuted female, she was corresponding with 'Scottish personages' of whom he did not approve. 'At times,' he told

Henry, 'Her Grace ... hath not made us privy to everything,' although she continued to declare that 'she will do nothing without the consent of Your Highness.' He had therefore, without her knowledge, re-phrased some of her letters to Albany, so that 'there should grow no further ... favour between them.' If it suited Henry's 'gracious pleasure', she should be detached from her proximity to the Duke as soon as possible.[14] As for Angus—he was negligible.

During February and March Angus's visits to Morpeth became less frequent, and Margaret realized that they were made rather for their daughter's sake than for her own. As the niece of one King and the half-sister of another, this child was one to be proud of, while Angus's relationship with her mother had proved disappointing, for it had put a price on his head and driven him from his estates. He had received a personal and very gracious invitation from Henry, which he accepted; now—there were other considerations.

In his wanderings on the northern side of the Border Angus had seen a good deal of the lovely—and gentle—Lady Jane Stuart of Traquair. (Margaret's imperious temper combined with her suffer-ings to make her a rather taxing companion.) As he had once, not very long ago, been contracted to the Lady Jane, they were, in a sense, husband and wife. And husbands and wives—in short, the result was a daughter. Angus, 'plus simple qu'il n'est malicieux', according to Du Plains, was a susceptible young man. Also, his favourite proverb, one now curiously recurrent in his mind, was, 'Better hear the lark sing in the open country than the mouse cheep in a fortress.' If he did not take care for himself, no one else would; not even his English wife, although she had done her best. He consulted Hume—it seems that he could not make up his mind unaided—and they decided to come to terms with Albany.

In the last week of March Angus and Hume spent some days at Morpeth, where preparations for Margaret's journey were being made. Then it was discovered that both noblemen were missing. A few days later Dacre was informed that they were at Coldstream.

Margaret's despair so affected Dacre ('She makes great moan and lamentation', he reported to Henry) that he decided to fetch them back himself. When he reached Coldstream he tried every inducement —bribes, threats, remonstrances, appeals. It was useless. They would not abandon their plan of rejoining Albany. Returning with the news of this betrayal, Dacre tried to cheer Margaret by reminding her of Henry's power. His Grace had sworn to support and restore her; so she must triumph. 'Whatever ensue hereafter,' she replied, 'I will refuse all the world to come unto him, and be ordered by him in all my causes—for without his help, I know of no succour.' She was constantly in tears, crying out against the man for whom she had risked—and lost—so much. She repeated again and again that without Henry's protection both she and her son would be destroyed.[15]

On April 8th she set forth with all her train, in such luxury as Dacre and Henry had been able to provide, stopping for the usual receptions at Newcastle, Durham and York. She was about to leave the northern capital, when two visitors were announced—Gavin Douglas and her husband.

Angus seems to have implied that Hume had persuaded him to leave Morpeth against his will. His later actions show that he was playing a double game, or rather, that Margaret had agreed that he should do so, for he presently became her agent in Scotland. Either for this reason, or because he desired to placate Albany and thus be certain of the restoration of his estates, he did not suggest accompanying her to London, but asked if he might follow her there later on. He was anxious, as such young men generally are, to be on good terms with everybody: Margaret, Henry VIII, Albany, the lords— and also with Lady Jane Stuart, if possible. He therefore proposed that he and Gavin Douglas should join the embassy which Albany was sending into England to discuss the treaty. That he shoud appear to have deserted Margaret would create a very bad impression on her powerful brother; and he wanted—perhaps sincerely—to work for her: but without being punished for it. All he needed was her consent to this ingenious scheme. Did she approve?

NOTES

1 Green, vol. IV, p. 269.
2 Op. cit., p. 211.
3 P. Tytler, *History of Scotland*, vol. I, p. 97.
4 *L. & P.*, vol. II, pt. 1, pp. 252, 255.
5 Ibid.
6 Op. cit., pp. 252, 273-4, 296. *Ven S. P.*, vol. II, p. 262.
7 J. Pinkerton, *History of Scotland*, p. 135.
8 *L. & P.*, vol. II, pt. 2, p. 290.
9 Green, op. cit., p. 228.
10 *L. & P.*, vol. II, pt. 1, p. 365.
11 Ibid.
12 Green, op. cit., p. 232.
13 *L. & P.*, op. cit., p. 443.
14 Green, op. cit., p. 236.
15 *L. & P.*, op. cit., p. 498.

# XII

## *The English Visit*

MARGARET agreed to Angus's plan. She did not then know that the Scots embassy had overtaken her, and was already approaching London. Nor did she grasp the change in her husband's character. He was reverting to type.

When he became head of the largest and most powerful of the Scottish clans, Angus was ruled by his grandfather, whose influence gradually brought out his treacherous and grasping side. Having achieved the subjugation of the Queen, Angus did all that she required — until his properties were confiscated. Then his innate ruthlessness prevailed. That he should not only regain, but add to these lands became an obsession; he was prepared to go to any lengths to effect that supremacy. Also, it may be that his marriage had enhanced his desire to dominate, while circumventing or deceiving anyone who stood in his way. By the time he and Margaret met in York this apparently simple young man had become as cunning and predatory as any other Scottish chieftain.

Meanwhile, Margaret's anxieties vanished with her return; it was as if she had been homesick for thirteen years. She seems to have felt that, somehow, Henry and Wolsey between them would ensure her regaining all she had lost — jewels, rents, the regency and the guardianship of her son. She intended to remain in England until this rehabilitation had been accomplished. No doubt she knew that Henry would use her; she was willing to be used, because she identified her interests with his. It did not occur to her that they might diverge.

From Stony Stratford she wrote ecstatically to her 'dearest Brother' that, next to God, her only trust was in him; she enclosed a letter from her son's ambassadors with drafts of two replies from herself, asking him to decide which she should send. In radiant health and spirits she reached Enfield on May 3rd, 1516, and stayed the night. She then proceeded to Tottenham, where Henry was waiting for her. While they were on their way to Cheapside for her state entry into the City, he asked for Angus, and received her answer with a single comment — 'Done like a Scot!' After that, the Earl of Anguish, as they called him, was not mentioned again.[1]

Escorted by Henry and his courtiers, and riding a white palfrey, Margaret left Cheapside at six o'clock in the evening for Baynard's Castle, a Gothic palace overlooking the Thames. The splendour of the procession and the Londoners' welcome re-created the triumphs of her childhood. She and Henry, united in the enjoyment of that acclaim, temporarily postponed discussion and gave themselves up to amusement. The King made a pet of the little Marget, as he called his niece, and was eager to show off his first surviving child, the Lady Mary, now three months old. That she preceded Margaret as heiress to the English throne did not really matter; for her father still planned — so he told his sister — to make James V his heir if he had no son; and he was thinking of arranging a marriage between the cousins.

The family life of which Margaret had been deprived since her fifteenth year was enriched by Henry's high spirits, Queen Katherine's affectionate ways and the grace and sweetness of the sister she had left in the nursery. When Mary Tudor's three months' marriage with Louis XII ended in widowhood she had become the wife of Suffolk, Henry's closest friend.* The young Queen-Duchess seems to have outshone Margaret on most occasions; but the elder sister was incapable of jealousy where any member of her family was concerned. The three Queens spent much time together; and so Margaret, hitherto surrounded by women in whom she could not confide, found a new happiness, apart from her pleasure in the jousts, banquets and balls provided by Henry and the Cardinal.

Meanwhile, the Scots embassy waited to be received; but Henry would not see them until Margaret had done so. When she did, they were informed that her brother had made an alliance with the Emperor Maximilian, and was no longer interested in the peace treaty with Francis I. Next day, Henry, 'speaking with great passion', told them that their treatment of his sister had been intolerable, and that he would invade unless Albany was dismissed.[2]

Albany then suggested visiting England on his way to France; he believed that an interview with the King would result in a satisfactory agreement. Henry consented, and a rather sinister welcome was planned. If the Regent came to London, he might find it difficult,

* See p. 185.

if not impossible, to leave; and then Margaret would expect to return
with full powers. At the last moment, Albany put off his departure —
unwillingly, for his wife was ill, and he so detested life in Scotland
that only his loyalty to Francis kept him there.

A few weeks later Margaret heard that her son was ill, then that his
life was in danger. Henry blamed Albany, and at a Council meeting
he and Margaret told the Scots envoys that the Duke should be
dismissed, Henry wrote to warn the Scottish Parliament that if his
nephew died, Albany would be held responsible, and should therefore
'purge him of the said ... suspicions by translating himself to other
countries'.[3] He then ordered one of his agents to report on the child's
health, and was told that he need not fear: James V was 'a right fair
young Prince'.[4]

Margaret's next concern was for her jewels and dresses. The
twenty-two gowns sent by Henry must be supplemented from the
wardrobe she had left in Scotland, if she were to appear as became
her station. The Council in Edinburgh submitted a list of goods 'to be
delivered in all haste', and eventually she received a collection of
pearls, rubies, jewelled rosaries and head-dresses, silver statues,
gold chains, ermine dressing-gowns — and 'the King of France's
great diamond set in a red hat'. This item was valued at 8,000
crowns.[5]

Henry then drew attention to her status by moving her from
Baynard's Castle to the Palace of Scotland Yard, formerly the London
residence of James IV's ancestors. There she entertained and was
feasted by him in great splendour; but her rents had not been paid,
and she began to worry about her Christmas presents. Finally she
wrote to Wolsey, suggesting that, 'for the King my brother's honour
and mine', he should lend her £200, adding, 'I beseech you heartily
that I may have it tomorrow night at the farthest.'[6]

Wolsey advanced this sum, and Margaret made no more demands
until, with the end of the Twelfth Night festivities, she began to think
of her husband. Her suggestion that he should join her was well
received by Albany; but Dacre advised his remaining in Scotland
until the terms of the new truce could be agreed. The conditions of
Margaret's return were discussed, and Albany promised that 'Her
Grace shall be right heartily welcome', and should have full access to
her son, but stipulated that her entourage must be confined to
twenty-four persons: for the Scots Council suspected her of arriving
with an army, seizing the five-year-old King and taking him back to

England. They added that she would be established in Stirling, while James remained in Edinburgh.

Correspondence between Margaret, Wolsey and Albany on these points continued throughout the spring of 1517. By this time she was anxious to return, not to what she thought of as home – that could only be England – but to the renewal of her career as Henry's Vicereine and the charge of her son; her departure was fixed for May 18th. On the 9th she, Katherine and Mary were involved in the crushing of the 'evil May Day' insurrection of the London apprentices, thirteen of whom were hanged, while preparation for the dispatch of four hundred more was set in hand.

On this occasion Wolsey had arranged for Henry's appearance as a stern but kindly sovereign. The condemned youths, with halters round their necks, knelt before him; he refused to commute sentence of death. The three Queens then flung themselves at his feet, imploring him to exercise his prerogative of mercy. After some minutes' consideration, he consented, was wildly cheered and returned to Windsor to hunt.[7] From there he conducted Margaret on the first stages of her journey north.

It had been a wonderful visit; the contrast between that carefree family life and the lonely existence ahead may have been partly the cause of Margaret's falling ill at Doncaster. She was returning to rule over a set of treacherous, insolent and uncouth nobles, to a husband she had begun to mistrust and to a child from whom she had been forcibly estranged, in the hideous discomfort of a savage country. Her only consolation was the news of Albany's departure for France, and she delayed her entry into Edinburgh until his ship had sailed.

Angus met her outside Berwick with a force of 3,000 borderers, and on June 17th they entered the capital together. Loaded with presents for her boy, Margaret hurried to the castle – and was refused admission to his apartments. Too broken to protest, she returned to Holyroodhouse.

A fortnight later James was moved to Craigmillar, and there she visited him. Within a few hours of their meeting she was accused of planning to remove him to England, and the castle was fortified as if for a siege. Margaret's common sense prevailed, and she retired to her manor of Newark in Ettrick Forest, where she was joined by Angus and those of the Humes who had escaped execution for the murder of Albany's deputy, de la Bastie.

So the regency had fallen vacant. Arran was preparing to seize it;

but before he could collect his forces Margaret proposed that she and
Angus should have joint rule. At this time she knew nothing of his
relationship with Jane Stuart of Traquair, and they were on amicable
terms.

The lords rejected Angus in favour of Arran, but offered the former
a place on the regency council, which he refused; so a feud between
these two chieftains was added to the murderous rivalries Albany had
managed to keep in check. The Island nobles invaded, the Arran-
Hamilton and Douglas clans set upon one another and Parliament
was, as ever, divided against itself. In fact, it was obvious to all but
themselves that the Scots were incapable of rule, and that only
conquest and colonization could bring them peace and prosperity.
Preferring to wallow in their own degradation, they rejected any
constructive policy, whether from within or from abroad.

Margaret was under the impression that Albany would return in
January 1518. Later on she realized that Henry had given back
Tournai to Francis I on the understanding that the Duke stayed
away indefinitely. The secret was well kept; Francis observed his side
of the bargain for the next four years. While rejoicing in Albany's
absence, Margaret did not at first grasp its effect on her own position.
Left to themselves, the Council broke all the conditions of her return.
She was almost penniless, and access to her son became increasingly
difficult. The lords were not aware that when she did see him, Margaret re-created their relationship; the child's love for and dependence
on his mother grew with each stolen visit. His infrequent contacts with
his stepfather had the opposite effect. James's secretive instinct,
eventually turning to slyness and deceit, was thus early fostered, and
no one, not even Margaret, observed this development. His health
and education were the only concern of those who looked after him.

Margaret's disgust with the lords did not prevent her approaching
them tactfully. She told Dacre that they still feared Henry's vengeance
on her behalf — Flodden was not easily forgotten — and that while '*he*
may get reason of Scotland, so may not I ... There is neither kindness
nor truth in them,' she added. 'Wherefore I had liever be dead than I
should live my life among them.'[8] She had come to the conclusion
that unless they treated her better, she, with James, should return to
England in order to invade, and so bring the Council to their senses;
and indeed, this cauterization would have been the best remedy for
Scottish ills. But neither Henry nor Wolsey wanted to spend money
on another war; they preferred intrigue; thus Margaret found herself

ground between the millstones of Scottish Anglophobia and English caution. She refused to give in, and throughout the spring of 1518 appeared daily before the Council, hoping to wear them down by the reiteration of her wrongs.

Meanwhile, Angus did nothing—or so it seemed. Margaret was at Tantallon when she heard that he had seized the rents of Methven and Ettrick Forest, her most valuable properties. She appealed to Arran, who managed to extract some of the moneys due to her, and ordered Angus to leave Newark, where he had established himself as lord of the manor. Margaret received £2,000 of the £9,000 owed her; still Angus remained at Newark, ignoring the summons of the Council. In the course of 1518 he and Margaret met in anger; sometimes he was able to persuade her of his goodwill—he was working for her brother, he said—and soothe her bitterness. Then the reason of his absences was revealed. He was living—on her land and at her expense—with Lady Jane Stuart, and their daughter, known as Janet Douglas, whom he had apparently made his heir.

Margaret showed considerable restraint. For many months pride prevented an outburst, and appearances were maintained. Then rumours of a break began to spread. In the courts of Europe it was said that the Queen of Scots and her husband 'were not in very good accord'.[9] Still she did not speak of this final outrage. At last, in April 1519, she wrote to Henry of her financial problems, begging him not to heed the 'fair words' of the Council. Angus had stolen her rents, they had not met for six months and she was 'much troubled' by his behaviour. 'He loves me not,' she went on, added that she was sending Henry a confidential agent to explain the whole matter, and implored him 'to be kind' on a point to be raised by her messenger. She concluded, '*I will not marry but where you wish.*'[10]

In short, Margaret had had enough, and was contemplating divorce. Such matters were often arranged—and she believed that the Vatican would support her. For precedent was not lacking. In 1499 the Pope had annulled Louis XII's marriage so that he might marry Anne of Brittany; and Suffolk had procured the annulment of three marriages before he became the husband of Mary Tudor.* So Margaret must have felt herself in a strong position when she suggested to her brother that she should divorce Angus for adultery.

Henry VIII was incredulous—appalled—disgusted. Divorce—! For some time he could not bring himself to consider such an impious

* See p. 167.

notion, or to answer Margaret's letter. He consulted Katherine (the wife he later described as 'beyond comparison') who was equally horrified, and suggested sending an Observant friar, Father Chadworth, to lecture and reason with her sister-in-law. Henry then recovered sufficiently to write to Margaret reminding her of 'the divine ordinance of *inseparable* matrimony, first instituted in Paradise', and desired her to 'return to God's word and the lively doctrines of Jesus Christ'. All this disagreement was evil, and she and Angus should be re-united without delay. He concluded with a quotation from St Paul to the Corinthians. 'For ye are yet carnal; for wherefore is there among you envying and strife and divisions, are ye not carnal?'[11]

Considerably taken aback, and unaware that Henry had considered divorcing Katherine in 1514, Margaret knew better than to argue; but the idea of divorce remained in her mind. She consulted Arran, who advised her against reconciliation; he knew that Angus had become an English agent, and wanted him out of the way. (In so employing his Scots brother-in-law Henry had shown less than his usual acumen.) Margaret wrote to Albany of her difficulties, and when he urged the Council to keep their promises to her began to realize that he might help her where everyone else had failed. Dacre's spies reported this correspondence, and he assured Henry that he was doing all he could to prevent the Duke's return.

In October 1519 Father Chadworth arrived and began to work on Margaret, who much resented his 'loud and sharp sentences'.[12] She was in no mood to be preached at by a common friar. He persevered, and after eight weeks was able to report progress, then triumph, to Henry and Katherine. (At this time, Henry was privately celebrating the birth of his son by Elizabeth Blount, whom he later created Duke of Richmond.) Margaret, arraigned by her brother of 'suspicious living', agreed to meet Angus and be publicly reconciled. She hated him: but as she could not afford to quarrel with Henry, this was not the moment to show her feelings; she would only get her own way by a parade of amiable compliance. And she could rely on Angus to behave with the gallant courtesy which had first attracted her.

Angus wrote gratefully and humbly to Henry, assuring him that this sad estrangement was over. Then, with an escort of four hundred cavaliers, he conducted Margaret to the Castle of Edinburgh to visit the seven-year-old King. Here they were greeted by the opposing parties in the Council. Those in favour of the reconciliation welcomed them with a salvo of cannon and the blare of trumpets; the others,

Arran's faction, stood sullenly apart. Margaret, who had again been ill, exercised all her charm, with the result that a few weeks later she regained possession of Ettrick Forest, and Angus left Newark. Lady Jane was established in one of his private properties, and he took up residence in Edinburgh with a vast concourse of followers. He then killed Arran's brother, Lord Patrick Hamilton, in a hand-to-hand skirmish, and very soon dominated the city.

Margaret retired to Stirling, where she received an embassy from Francis I. This alarmed Dacre, who wrote her long letters of warning and remonstrance. While remaining outwardly subservient to the wishes of the brother who had done nothing for her since she left England, she decided to bring about Albany's return. From the moment of his arrival in Scotland he had tried to help her; and she believed that if they made an alliance, of whatever kind, they might together eliminate Angus and rule the kingdom on Henry's behalf.

Although Margaret has been censured by contemporary and later historians for betraying first her subjects and then her brother, her actions at this time were neither treacherous nor foolish. She may have been too confident of Albany's power to help her, and mistaken in thinking that she could lure him away from his loyalty to Francis I. The fact remains that she and her son had no one else on whom to rely. She might have defended herself against Henry's accusations (as she did to Dacre) by replying that, after fifteen years in a country he had never entered, she knew what she was doing. His and Wolsey's tactics of alternating commands with threats only increased the Council's hatred of England — although they were unable to create the united front which would have brought them independence. The majority desired Albany's return, and detested Angus; therefore Margaret's desertion of the Douglas cause was now the sole means of regaining her position with their support. Henry's employment of Angus (supplemented by his reverence for the sacrament of marriage) was a wasted gesture; for that nobleman was only interested in defeating the Arran faction, and ruling Scotland through Margaret while continuing his relations with the Lady Jane. Meanwhile, Margaret's determination to regain power had been forced, through Henry's neglect, into a channel shared with Albany. But Henry, Wolsey and Dacre were still convinced that he was the dangerous and belligerent envoy of Francis I.

That monarch's attitude towards the Anglo-Scots imbroglio varied with the shifting currents of the continental situation. He suspected

Henry of planning to regain the territory taken by his Angevin and Plantagenet forebears; and Henry suspected him of allying himself with Austria and Spain in order to invade England; therefore a war with Scotland must be avoided. Finally, Dacre, the most active figure in this involute pattern, was mistaken in thinking that the Scots could be irrevocably subdued through his fostering of clan warfare. They had been weakened thereby, and the majority were ready to sell out to England; but invasion and conquest in the manner of Edward III — which Henry could not now afford — would alone have crushed such defences as still existed. Thus, threatening the Scots with another Flodden merely made Margaret's position impossible; yet her courage was unimpaired, and her efforts for the establishment and security of her son were stubbornly sustained.

In June 1520 Francis and Henry met on the Field of Cloth of Gold, where Albany was in attendance. Francis told Henry that the Duke's return to Scotland was James V's only safeguard, adding that Margaret would obtain greater power through Albany's support. When Henry replied that he was satisfied with the Duke's intentions, Francis turned to Albany and said, 'Remember that.'[13] He then sent him on a mission to Rome, where the Duke raised the question of Margaret's divorce. Wolsey, hearing of this, wrote to the Scots Council on her behalf — he did not want her to be driven into desperate measures — and sent her, so he told Dacre, 'a comfortable letter'.[14]

Dacre's methods were more direct. He wrote to Margaret in terms unbecoming a subject, accusing her of renewed hostility to Angus. 'Remember', he went on, 'of what family you are ... You took him for your husband without consent of His Grace ... and should go to him by the laws of God.' He added that unless she subscribed to these precepts she would receive no help from England.[15]

Rather disingenuously, Margaret replied that the lords had insisted on her recalling Albany, and that she was in their power. 'I pray you remember', she added, 'that an you were in another realm where you should live your life, ye would do that ye might to please them ... and so must I.'[16]

By this time, Francis I had come to the conclusion that Albany's return to Scotland would result in war between himself and Henry, and sent to the Council to tell them so. They then warned the Duke that if he did not resume the regency before August 1st, 1521, he would no longer be accepted as heir-presumptive. He promised to return, and desired them to supply Margaret with the moneys due to her. When Dacre told her that she was making a fatal mistake in trusting Albany and should return to her husband, she replied that if Angus had 'desired my company and my love, he would have shown him more kindly'. Aware that Angus had sent Gavin Douglas to the English Court to inform against her, she begged Dacre not to believe the Bishop's 'evil tales', and ignored his diatribes against Albany.[17]

In October 1521 Francis decided that Albany might safely return, and a month later the Duke arrived. Wolsey and Dacre then announced that he intended to divorce his wife in order to marry Margaret, and that he would enter Edinburgh at the head of a French army. While the Duke, unattended but for his suite, was making his way to Stirling, Margaret informed Dacre that she would not have sent for him if Henry had helped her. 'My lord Governor', she added, 'is come to this realm for the good of it, wherefore I trust the King my brother's mind to do the same.' She then accused Dacre of encouraging Angus and Gavin Douglas to malign her.[18]

From Stirling Albany and Margaret proceeded to Edinburgh Castle. When the captain presented Albany with the keys, he gave them to Margaret. Smiling, she returned them, and they entered James's apartments together.[19] A few weeks later he offered Margaret the regency, and suggested that she and Angus should make it up and resume married life. Once more she had recourse to the *suaviter in modo* tactics which had served her in the past, and appeared to agree. She and the Duke thus remained on the best possible terms.

In fact, Margaret was more than ever determined to divorce Angus —and to use Albany's influence at the Vatican to that end.

---

## NOTES

1 Hall, p. 584.
2 *Ven. S. P.*, vol. II, p. 307.
3 Green, Vol. IV, p. 242.
4 *L. & P.*, vol. II, pt. 1, p. 694.
5 Op. cit., p. 747.
6 Green, op. cit., p. 247.
7 Hall, p. 590.
8 Green, op. cit., p. 209.
9 *L. & P.*, vol. III, pt. 1, p. 60.
10 Op. cit., p. 61.
11 Op. cit., p. 168.
12 Pinkerton, p. 181.
13 *L. & P.*, op. cit., p. 300.
14 Ibid.
15 Op. cit., p. 786.
16 J. Brewer, *Reign of Henry VIII*, vol. I, p. 515.
17 Green, op. cit., p. 302.
18 Ibid.
19 Ibid.

# XIII

## *Albany Betrayed*

ALBANY began his renewal of the regency by accusing Angus and Gavin Douglas of high treason, with the result that the Earl went into hiding on the Border and the Bishop, safely established in London, combined with Dacre to assail Margaret's reputation by telling Henry that his sister and the Duke were lovers; and thenceforward a number of historians have assumed this to be the case. Tudor blood — no sense of religion — capricious egotism — such are the slogans.* Thus, Margaret's preference for young and handsome men and Albany's devotion to his wife have been ignored. She would have had no scruples about becoming the Regent's mistress if they had been attracted to one another; but the very openness of their relationship — 'they are always together, in the forenoon, *or after*', Douglas reported[1] — indicates that it was based on common interests and a goodwill which did not, eventually, survive disagreement about policy.

Margaret's disregard of formality and her resolve to make the Regent her ally were her only means of regaining the guardianship of James V. She seems to have realized that the Duke meant to leave Scotland as soon as possible, and concluded that the reins of government would then fall into her hands. Already Arran, heir-presumptive after Albany, was on her side; and she believed that the three of them might lead a party which would establish peace and, somehow, satisfy both Henry VIII and the Scottish Parliament.

Her assurances of the Duke's loyalty were ignored by Dacre, who continued to accuse him of plotting to murder James V (had he not poisoned Alexander?) and seize the crown. Dacre told Wolsey that Albany was and always would be, a dangerous enemy. For he had removed the King from Stirling to the 'windy and right unpleasant Castle and rock of Edinburgh', and concealed the boy's 'rich gowns ... and made clothing thereof to some of his pages'. The poor child 'lacked honest whole hosen and doublets', while the Duke's officers

* Andrew Lang, Agnes Strickland, *et al.*

had orders not to admit his tailors. Worst of all, Albany was encouraging Margaret to divorce Angus—why else had he gone to Rome?—and would become her husband as soon as he had obtained the annulment of his own marriage.[2]

While still unaware of these charges, Margaret wrote to Henry of Albany's good intentions—'all the honour and authority he makes me ... he does gladly'—and of his desire for a permanent peace. She drew up a document embodying the requisite conditions, and begged Henry to consider it.[3]

In the Christmas week of 1521 Dacre announced that Albany had threatened to kill him, that Margaret was bribing Angus to agree to a divorce (this was true) and that the understanding between her and the Duke was such that 'they care not who knows it, both by day and night.' He added that Angus must be supported and Francis I forced to recall the Regent. According to Dacre's spies, Albany had said to his Scots attendants, 'Who is this Dacre? Is there none of you borderers that can fall into an altercation with him, and do me a pleasure?'[4]

These reports reached Henry in January 1522, and he instructed Wolsey to organize general propaganda against Albany. The Cardinal therefore informed the Spanish envoys that the Duke had come to Scotland with an army, 'full of ill will and contrary to our treaties with France ... He has practised with the Queen', Wolsey went on, 'so that she hath been seduced from us.' Thus, he added, if Henry died leaving no son, Albany would marry Margaret and 'lay claim' to England. James V, he concluded, was in grave danger.[5]

Henry's accusation of his sister was brought to her with all the publicity then available by Clarencieux-King-at-Arms. He reached Edinburgh on February 22nd.

Margaret, who had been counting on her brother's co-operation over peace, listened eagerly to the opening sentences. 'His Grace', the herald then announced, 'hath no little marvel and grievance at your regard for the Duke of Albany, whose love to you is reported throughout Christendom, to Your Grace's reproach, and that of the noble house from which you spring. Your Grace may believe that the return of the said Duke may be advantageous to your son—others see it for your destruction.' Margaret was then accused of forwarding Albany's regency to satisfy her lust, and of insisting on the divorce. 'There can be no peace for Scotland', the herald concluded, 'so long as the Duke remaineth within its bounds.'

Appalled — 'marvellously abashed' — Margaret, struggling with her tears, was unable to speak at once. At last she said, 'I well perceive that the King's Highness hath me in great displeasure, through seditious and ill reports contrived against me by very false persons. I swear before God and all honest creatures that they are utterly false.' She repeated her reasons for summoning Albany, and concluded, 'The Duke hath never attempted, procured nor desired anything that might sound to my dishonour.' The herald then left to wait on Albany at Holyroodhouse.[6]

The Regent's answer to Henry's charges was more violent. 'I swear by the Sacrament', he exclaimed, 'that I might break my neck if ever I were minded to marry Her Grace, or do to her any shame or dishonour. I have enough with one wife. I greatly marvel that the King's Highness, upon light reports, would have the Queen his sister to be so openly slandered — as if I kept the said Queen as if she were my wife or my concubine! All my life, I will deny it.'[7]

A few days later Albany and Margaret interviewed the herald together. She reiterated her belief in the Regent's integrity. Albany said that he could not bring himself to answer Henry's letter, adding more calmly, 'The King of England need not misdoubt that I would attempt anything against his sister's honour. Compliments of mere courtesy in France', he explained, 'might [elsewhere] be surmised sometimes to be solicitations and suits of love.'[8]

The Scots Parliament supported Margaret in their statements to the herald (they would have been the first to accuse her of misconduct) and he reported to Dacre on his way home. Meanwhile, Albany offered Angus a pardon; that young man then gave his consent to the divorce, and abandoned the English cause. As both Scotland and England were now too hot to hold him, he took ship to France.

Margaret's reply to Henry's letter was indignant, pathetic and reproachful. (Rather foolishly, she said that she had given up the idea of divorce.) He ignored it, and a few months later informed Francis I that, as 'supreme lord' of Scotland, he must insist on Albany's recall, adding, 'he wants — damnably — to contract matrimony with the Queen'.[9]

This letter followed the Anglo-Spanish declaration of war against France, and in July 1522 Henry's troops crossed the Channel. Albany, commanded by Francis I to invade, found that the Scots Parliament did not wish to do so in force, preferring a tentative entry, which reached Carlisle. Here, his situation seemed to him and his advisers so hazardous that, through Margaret, he began secret negotiations with Dacre for a truce, and withdrew to the Castle of Milk, five miles from Berwick. He then interviewed Dacre, whose situation was in fact much more precarious, for the Scottish forces far outnumbered those left in England.

Escorted by two of Albany's gentlemen, Dacre found the Duke surrounded by his staff. He bowed, stepped back and began in a loud and threatening voice, 'My lord, what displeasure has my sovereign done unto you, that ye with this great army are come hither to invade this realm? I marvel', he went on, glaring round at the nobles, most of whom were in his pay, 'that all ye, my lords, will be aiding to this scheme, remembering the nighness and proximity of blood betwixt my sovereign and yours. I come here, not for treaty, but at the instance of my lord here present.' He then described what would happen if Albany insisted on war.[10]

A long discussion of terms followed, a truce was made and Albany returned to Edinburgh, having missed his only chance of a successful invasion. When Francis I heard of this failure, he was very angry. Albany, deciding to make his excuses in person, sailed for France on October 27th.

Margaret got all the credit for the success of Dacre's bluff, and received letters of praise and affection from Henry, who now offered peace for sixteen years and the hand of the Lady Mary for James V, on the understanding that the Franco-Scots alliance was abandoned. The lords refused to consider this suggestion, and hostilities were resumed.

Deserted by Albany and frustrated by Parliament, who made access to her son more difficult than before, Margaret decided that her only hope lay (after all!) with England. Albany had promised to return in August 1523 with a French army; but she no longer had any faith in his abilities. As James was now in his twelfth year and advanced for his age, she resolved to make him the figurehead of her policy. It was a bold move; yet she believed that he would behave as became a king, and that his co-operation would take the lords by surprise.

James admired and loved his mother, and disliked most of his guardians. A handsome, intelligent, disagreeable boy, he was eager to assume the authority she offered. She had convinced him that his uncle was the greatest king in Europe, and his circumstances inclined him towards the English alliance as the preliminary to freedom.

At this time, Sir David Lindsay was still in James's service. He entertained his charge by dressing up 'as a fiend or grisly ghost', and provided him with a menagerie of dogs, birds and monkeys. James's favourite pet was a green-and-yellow parrot, which he taught to perch on his wrist like a falcon. History, science and geography were instilled through Sir David's stories and poems, and James enjoyed his lessons.[11] 'Of his age,' Margaret informed the new Earl of Surrey in the summer of 1523, 'I trow there be not a wiser child, nor a better hearted ... He saith plainly that no good Scottish man will hold him in one house against his will.'[12] She did not mention her son's violent temper, nor that he had tried to kill the porter of Stirling Castle when that functionary refused to open the gates—for she had encouraged him to think of himself as wrongfully imprisoned.[13]

Margaret and Surrey (he had taken over his father's post of Captain-General) were planning her and James's escape to England. She declared that she would leave Scotland in her smock, if need be. At her suggestion, the young King wrote to the lords demanding his freedom and an alliance with Henry VIII. Meanwhile, Albany, now a month overdue, did not appear, and Surrey's forces arrived in Newcastle. A few weeks later his men laid waste the Border. 'There is left', Wolsey told the Spanish envoys, 'neither house, fortress, village, tree, castle, corn, or other succour for man ... Such is the punishment of Almighty God for disturbers of the peace.'[14]

The Scots lords did nothing. 'They laugh at the injuries done to poor people,' Margaret told Surrey, and implored him to march on Edinburgh. It was a startling change of front, but only so, now, could peace with England be effected—and that was still her principal aim. At a meeting with Parliament on August 31st, she desired the lords to act for 'the King's weal. As you will answer to God and your kingdom,' she concluded, 'be no longer abused with the fair words of France.' Parliament, divided between Francis's and Dacre's pensioners, did not trouble to reply when James told them that 'the same realm shall not contain myself and the Duke of Albany.'[15] Then news came that Albany had sailed. On September 24th, 1523, he landed at Dumbarton, and Surrey's troops were halted at Jedburgh.

One of Margaret's agents, the Prioress of Coldstream, was reporting her movements to the lords, while obtaining information about those of Albany, who had arrived with an army of French and German mercenaries with orders to invade.[16] He counted on the success of these highly trained troops, and planned to place them in front of his less reliable Scottish forces. But he had not grasped the real nature of his so-called supporters; nor was he aware that Margaret was corresponding with Surrey. Her accounts of Albany's powers alarmed the Earl, who told Wolsey that the Scots were certain to take over the northern counties and might reach the Midlands. Wolsey, assessing Scots resolution at its proper worth, advised him to stand on the defensive. He and Henry VIII were agreed in thinking that Margaret should stay where she was and pretend to support Albany; they ensured her doing so by cutting off supplies. She complained of her helplessness, but did what she was told.

Albany tried to win over James V by giving him presents and allowing him to ride freely about Stirling. 'Be blithe and merry,' he said, 'for I will spend my life in your service,' and wrote to Margaret, assuring her of his support and offering her a pension, which she at first refused.[17] Through her only trustworthy agent, Patrick Sinclair, she told Surrey that she no longer believed in the Duke's promises, and subjoined a detailed list of his armaments.

On October 11th she received Albany at Holyrood and attended a concert and dance given by his French entourage. She then joined the King at Linlithgow, while informing Surrey that in her official letters to him she would urge an alliance with France; he must disregard this proposal, as coming from Albany, whose advance to the Border was about to begin. 'I shall bide firm and stable at the King's Grace my brother against all other,' she concluded.[18]

On October 18th, 1523, Albany met the lords at Edinburgh, and in a fiery speech appealed to them to avenge the shame of Flodden. Falling on their knees, they swore to follow him to the death. Certain, at last, of victory, he set forth at the head of his trilingual army, leaving Margaret and James at Stirling. It was then easy for her to convince the boy that the Duke might carry him off to France, where he would remain a prisoner and never see her or Scotland again. On November 14th she wrote to Wolsey that she had had to do Albany's will and accept his money while working against him — could she and James now take refuge in England? She received no answer, and became increasingly alarmed for herself and her son. Then came wonderful news from the Border — so wonderful indeed, that she could not, at first, bring herself to believe it.

On November 1st Albany, with some 60,000 men, laid siege to Wark Castle, from the northern bank of the Tweed, and tried, unsuccessfully, to take it by bombardment. He then appealed to the nobles to join him in crossing the river. They refused. Flodden was still a hideous memory. They dared not move.

Hardly able to believe in this betrayal, Albany harangued them, passionately and at length, while the rain poured down and an icy wind tore at their cloaks. His speech had then to be translated into Scots; this took a considerable time.

The chieftains stayed where they were. Within the next hour they began to retreat. The foreign troops waited for Albany's orders.

Silently, the Duke mounted his horse and led them towards Teviotdale. Here he was halted by a group of nobles, who accused him of cowardice. 'Our Border is undone by the Earl of Surrey,' said one, and another added, 'We beseech you to abide and give him battle, as ye have promised.'

Then the Regent exploded. 'I will give him no battle!' he burst out, 'for I have no convenient company to do so —' and spurring his horse, galloped away. 'By God's Blood!' one chieftain shouted after him, 'we will never serve you more, nor never wear your badges again!' Tearing them off, his companions joined in his curses; one exclaimed, 'Would God we were all sworn English!'[19]

Albany was no coward; but he had had enough experience in war to know the uselessness of attacking without the support of the clans. This final treachery convinced him that the Scots were worthless poltroons, and that France would do better without them. (Apparently it did not occur to the Duke that another reason for their refusal to fight was the fear of losing their English pensions.) So the Scots lived on, to fall as miserably at Solway Moss in 1542 as their sons fell, nine years later, at Pinkie Cleugh. They were doomed to defeat and degradation at the hands of the English until, with the union of the kingdoms, they submitted to the rule of a better-organized country.

Returning to Edinburgh in furious disgust, Albany only desired to leave Scotland for ever. The lords would not allow this. They were so besotted as still to count on the French alliance. The Duke then tried to renew his friendship with Margaret, to be told, 'Considering how many false promises I have had from you before, I will thank you when your words and deeds are one,' When she consented to receive him, and he said he was sorry to have displeased her, she replied, 'I have cause for nothing else than displeasure, and this I can prove, before Your Grace, and the lords of the Council.'[20]

Margaret's distrust of Albany was genuine and well founded. She believed that, instructed by Francis I, he was planning to kidnap the King, who might, in the process, be murdered; and she knew that there were those among the Scottish nobles who would have set about either business without scruple. Still, as throughout all her deviations, her first thought was for James. He and she stood alone, surrounded by potential enemies – but she had now lost for ever what remained of her reputation. 'She is right fickle,' the Prioress of Coldstream informed Wolsey. 'Wherefore, take not too much of her credence.'[21]

In fact, Margaret had reached the point where she was prepared to lie to anyone – Albany, Henry, Dacre, the lords, her own agents – in her son's interests. So it came about that all those who wrote of her, whether in her own day or in the ensuing centuries, have described her as a treacherous termagant, an unwise mother and a faithless wife. That she had some cause to be all of these has not – so far – been considered.

On November 18th Parliament met, and having dismissed James's guardians, replaced them with the Earls of Moray, Cassilis, Fleming and Borthwick for a period of three months. They then announced that the King would be separated from Margaret, but gave her leave to visit him at stated times. She objected to this arrangement as 'strange and suspicious', adding that she feared for the boy's safety, and that if he was killed she would denounce the lords before the world. To Albany she wrote, 'It is force ... when I am put from the thing that I love best.'[22]

Three weeks later, Margaret and James received Albany and the lords at Stirling. Drawing the King aside, Albany asked him how he would prefer to be guarded. Instructed by his mother, he replied, 'I will be content with whatever is for my good,' thus showing that she had resisted the temptation to make an emotional appeal.[23] Now she could not be accused of influencing her son against Parliament and the Duke. This enabled her to speak more freely for James and herself.

She began by telling the lords that she knew Albany was planning to kidnap James. 'I will be a good Scotswoman', she went on, 'and accept whatever is for the good of my son. I have not one person to take my part. Why am I holden suspect, and not allowed to be with my son?' 'You might take him to England,' she was told. 'You are the King of England's sister, and he will do more for you than any other.' 'My deeds', Margaret retorted, 'have shown otherwise. I can prove your malice. My brother will see how much I suffer for his sake. He is much displeased that such things are laid to my charge. This', she went on, seizing the chance to score, 'will make the Governor flee for fear, and the lords fall from him, for he is in the greatest dread of

England—and dares not trust Scotchmen to fight for him, fearing they should betray him to the English.'[24]

To this too accurate prophecy, Albany replied that he had eight hundred men-at-arms, and might forcibly remove James from Stirling Castle. Margaret agreed to consider a change of guardians and appeared to yield on the other points. She then composed a statement which she sent to Henry VIII, pointing out that she had been made to agree, against her will, to the lords' arrangements for James. This caused Albany to mediate between them, and she remained with her son. She wrote to Dacre suggesting a truce; he replied that peace must last till James came of age.[25]

Albany now began a correspondence with Wolsey, which alarmed Margaret. Then she caught smallpox, and was incapacitated till the beginning of January 1524; yet at least, she informed Dacre, she and James were again together, and he was ready to do whatever she and his uncle suggested—but why was she no longer consulted by her brother? Had he forgotten her? Henry did not answer this appeal.[26]

In April Albany made a suggestion which softened Margaret's resentment. He was ready—as was Francis I—to help her with the divorce, in the event of Henry, 'or other evil disposed persons', trying to force Angus on her. He proposed a written agreement between himself and her to this effect, and drew one up for her signature. When this was discovered by Dacre, he accused Margaret of going over to the French interest, to Henry's 'great displeasure and dishonour'. She replied that she had not signed Albany's bond; her handwriting must have been forged. Dacre then resorted to bluff. 'Everyone knows', he wrote, 'that Your Grace and the Governor wrote the bond. There is no other way but battle.'[27]

Margaret was not so easy a prey to these tactics as Albany had been. She persisted in her denials, and Dacre had to apologize and withdraw the charge, adding that as she might have been forced to sign the agreement, it could be proved invalid.[28]

Then, to Margaret's unspeakable relief, Albany, who had been trying to leave Scotland for the last six months, sailed from Dumbarton on May 31st, 1524. Unaware that this was the end of a chapter— for although the Duke had promised to return in August, he never set foot in Scotland again—Margaret was now separated from James, but not, she believed, irrevocably. With Albany's departure, the regency was within her grasp.

At about this time it was observed, not only by Dacre's spies, but by several persons in Margaret's entourage, that a well set-up youth, Harry Stuart, the younger brother of Lord Avondale, had been appointed master-carver to her household. He was often in her company—although not more so than a number of other courtiers. As an influence, he was negligible; for neither he nor his wife had any affiliation with the more powerful clans. The fact remained that he was highly personable.

It is unlikely that this young man paused to look back on Margaret's variations with regard to Albany. If he had, he might have approached her less confidently. Between the first period of her regency and the Duke's final departure from Scotland—from September 1513 to May 1524—she had effected several changes of front. In 1513 she resisted Albany's arrival, but came over to him two years later, and then defied him by taking refuge in England. In June 1517 her attitude was neutral; in 1519 her split with Angus caused her to return to Albany for help over the divorce, and their agreement on policy lasted, with reservations, till October 1522, when she betrayed him to Henry VIII. In May 1524 he left Scotland on the understanding that she would support him. Although these fluctuations were less generated by caprice than by tactical ingenuity, their range and frequency might have served as a warning to Harry Stuart—but his ambition was not so easily halted.

## NOTES

1 *L. & P.*, vol. III, pt. 1, p. 809.
2 Green, vol. IV, p. 306.
3 Op. cit., p. 308.
4 Pinkerton, p. 190.
5 *Foreign State Papers* (Supplement), p. 18.
6 Green, op. cit., p. 309.
7 Op. cit., p. 311.
8 Op. cit., p. 312.
9 *L. & P.*, op. cit., p. 970.
10 Brewer, vol. I, p. 534.
11 Strickland, *Queens of Scotland*, p. 178.
12 *L. & P.*, vol. III, pt. 2, p. 1358.
13 Strickland, ibid.
14 Brewer, op. cit., p. 543.
15 Op. cit., p. 546.
16 *L. & P.*, op. cit., p. 1413.
17 Ibid.
18 Green, op. cit., p. 351.
19 Brewer, op. cit., p. 559.
20 *L. & P.*, op. cit., p. 1496.
21 Brewer, op. cit., p. 550.
22 Green, op. cit., p. 357.
23 *L. & P.*, op. cit., p. 1508.
24 Ibid.
25 Op. cit., vol. IV, pt. 1, p. 5.
26 Op. cit., p. 86.
27 Op. cit., p. 102.
28 Ibid.

# XIV

## *The Return of Angus*

MARGARET was now in her thirty-sixth year and, according to the standards of that day, well advanced in middle age. Recurrent illness had marred her fresh colouring, and traces of smallpox remained on one eyelid. Never having been a beauty, she was not affected by these flaws in her appearance. Confidence in her power to charm and persuade increased; as always, her courage rose to meet each crisis. While still tormented by fears for her son's safety, she was not so much in awe of those to whom she felt herself responsible. Her letters to Henry, Dacre, Wolsey and Surrey (he had now succeeded his father as Duke of Norfolk) were no longer subservient or timid; while retaining all the forms of courtesy, they were firmer in tone, less plaintive and more reasonable.

This crystallization of Margaret's attitude may be partly accounted for by Albany's departure, and also by the devotion of the common people. Like all the Tudors, she knew instinctively how to touch the hearts of those who saw her infrequently or from afar, and were themselves alternately used and discounted by the nobles. This loyalty to Margaret was combined with adherence to the chieftains, among whom Angus, unfortunately for her, was one of the most popular. He himself had long been aware of this asset; and so, within a few weeks of Albany's return to France, he appeared at the Court of Henry VIII, and once more blandly offered himself as agent for the Anglo-Scottish cause. He was accepted, on condition that he and Margaret were reunited. Angus replied that this was his dearest wish.

This reconciliation seemed to Dacre and Wolsey so obvious a basis for the new regime that they counted on Angus being received, both by his wife and by his rivals. As far as Margaret was concerned, Henry knew better; as aware of her capacity for violence as of his own — and of the uses to which it could be put — he at first prepared rather to tempt than to order her into renewing a relationship with a man she loathed and was determined never to see again. Henry did not grasp either Margaret's unconventionality—living apart from her husband did not trouble her in the least—or her impiety. Himself a deeply religious man, Henry had to square his conscience—the conscience which was to achieve European fame in three years' time—with his actions. In his sense, Margaret had none; she simply did what seemed to her expedient and pleasing to herself. Her resolution was even more obstinate than her brother's (while seldom changing her mind, she changed her tactics with the speed of light) and she was prepared to risk everything she had gained, except James's safety, rather than let Angus resume his position, either as her husband or as a Scottish potentate. Her hatred of him was enhanced by her increasing dependence on Harry Stuart of Avondale.

At about this time, or a little later, there appeared a portrait of Margaret standing between two men who look like brothers. (Here her predilection for a particular physical type is unconsciously demonstrated by the unknown artist.) To one she hands a purse and some papers—in September 1524 Harry Stuart was made Treasurer to her household—while turning away from the other, who points at his rival in indignant accusation. The man pointing from a shadowy background—Angus, presumably—is ignored by her. And the richly clad courtier receiving the insignia of authority is subordinated. She dominates this oddly intimate scene.*

With the same cool assurance, Margaret ignored Angus's first letters to her—she may not even have opened them—and Dacre's suggestions that he should return. She was as determined as ever to consolidate her position as Henry's Vicereine, but she would not, in any circumstances, share it with Angus; nor would she consider his re-entry into Scotland. (In this she had Arran's and several other nobles' support.)

Henry, seeing the situation more clearly than his advisers, wrote to her in mild and affectionate terms, pointing out the improvement in Angus's character, and assuring her of his own and that nobleman's support of her son's authority. The twelve-year-old King's personal rule—i.e. Margaret's autocracy—must be effected at once; and no one was better able to bring about this happy solution than the head of the most powerful clan in Scotland. Angus, Henry rather rashly added, would now become Margaret's 'loving and faithful husband'.

* This picture, now in the possession of the Scottish National Portrait Gallery, is described as representing Albany and Angus. Neither of the men resembles the other portraits of the Duke.

MARGARET TUDOR AND THE EARL OF ANGUS
*(artist unknown)*

The young man longed, he told her, to be reconciled; so he was sending him to her 'to deliver your countrymen from war'. He had instructed Angus to cross the Border in order to set James at liberty, in other words, to place the boy under Margaret's jurisdiction. The Earl, Henry concluded, was 'greatly amended'.[1] Writing to Dacre on the same lines, Henry told him to find out if Margaret would agree to these proposals; if she did not, 'other practices' (war?) might be considered. The first necessity was an Anglo-Scots conference presided over by Margaret, Angus and the English ambassadors. Finally, Albany must be prevented, by whatever means, from returning.[2]

Margaret's reply to Henry was restrained and reasonable. Angus, she wrote, was a mischief-maker and a tale-bearer, and therefore worse than useless. Also, he was so detested by the majority in the Council that civil war would result if he reappeared. Her letters to Dacre on this point were more vehement—so much so, that that iron character agreed, temporarily, to prevent Angus from crossing the Border.[3]

This was Angus's second metamorphosis. The first, created by his grandfather's manipulation of his marriage to Margaret, although a slower process, had shown him as deceitful and greedy, but rather crude in his methods. Now, his status as Henry's agent united with his newly acquired sophistication to give him a subtler approach, and a conscious use of his assets. His appearance had always been admired —today, the combination of a long beard with incipient baldness would not be so regarded—and in France he had learnt a courtesy and polish which concealed the brutish cunning of his real nature. Now he knew how to assume a modesty he did not possess. Only Margaret realized his potentialities—and may well have felt that the improvement in his manners was a very dangerous sign. Yet to convince Henry of her fear and hatred of this Iago-like figure was not feasible, once her brother had made up his mind.

Henry now began to appease Margaret by flattering and cajoling James V. He wrote to the boy, not only as one monarch to another, but as to a grown person, praising his 'fresh wit and great towardness of wisdom'. Henry added that he himself was much concerned for his nephew's 'royal dignity' and the danger of Albany trying to kill him. He promised James his full support against the Regent's party, and was sending Norfolk to advise him.[4]

To Margaret's next letters of objection Henry replied with

reassurances and a firmer announcement of his intentions. He had decided on Angus's return; but she should bear rule, and her husband would not be allowed to 'meddle'. He then told Dacre to promise her that she should 'have her pleasure' on these points. But Angus must, sooner or later, be received.[5] These promises were, of course, deceptive. Soon after Norfolk arrived in Scotland he was told by Wolsey that it was 'right to use the Queen of Scots in this manner, but not so as all shall depend on her. I mistrust', he added, 'threads wrought by women's fingers.'[6]

Margaret replied by calling on Arran's party to support her in rejecting Angus, and telling Dacre that, although she might not be able to prevent his arrival, she would neither see him nor write to him nor receive his emissaries; thus nothing would be achieved by his presence.

There were many who would have joined her in arranging for Angus's capture and imprisonment, or even his murder. But this, she knew, would cause the rising of his clan and bring about civil war, with further risk to her son's life. Margaret's attitude was so consistently sustained that Wolsey advised Dacre to prevent Angus entering Scotland — without Margaret's co-operation it would be of little use — adding that he might set about kidnapping Arran, so as to weaken the power of Angus's rivals.[7] This scheme was abandoned.

On August 19th James V, having entered Edinburgh in triumph, opened Parliament at the Tolbooth and was enthroned. His mother sat on one side of him, Arran, who had arrived with 4,000 men, on the other. The principal object of this meeting was to cancel Albany's governorship, and to subdue his following, now headed by the Chancellor, Archbishop Beaton. When called upon to take the oath of allegiance, Beaton replied that, having done so at the coronation, there was no need for him to reassert his loyalty. Margaret ordered him and his party to swear; he said that he was, and always would be, ready to serve the King. Margaret said, 'You have made a bond with the Governor which the King wishes and commands you to break.' This was James's cue to add, 'I require you, under penalty of treason, to deprive the Duke of Albany of his government.'

'Sire,' Beaton replied, 'there is no man in your kingdom unwilling to obey you — but I entreat you to take better counsel, for your own good and honour.' He added that the Franco-Scots alliance should be maintained.

Margaret then burst into angry speech, and was seconded by

Arran, who announced that anyone disobeying the King's orders would be punished. At some length he described the misery caused by the Scots being forced to pull French chestnuts out of the fire. He added that James's marriage with the Lady Mary would result in his being proclaimed Prince of England. Eventually the lords were forced to cancel Albany's governorship, and next day Beaton and some half-dozen of his supporters were imprisoned. Margaret wrote to Norfolk and Henry of her triumph, but still refused to admit Angus.[8]

A month later, the tide began to turn against her. Albany had been very popular, and the Council's fear of England militated against the marriage of James and Mary. Their much vaunted hatred was expressed in hysterical bluster: but it affected the people. They now complained, Norfolk told Wolsey, that the Queen had taken too much upon herself (women should not rule men), was indulging in 'ungodly living' with Harry Stuart, and ought not to keep her husband out of Scotland.[9]

It was at this point that Margaret made the gravest mistake of her career. If she could have brought herself to accept a reunion, however superficial, with Angus, she might have kept the regency (and perhaps even continued her relationship with Harry Stuart) with the support of the Douglas clan. She was unable to do so; and she believed that her will must prevail. She was determined, not only to divorce Angus, but to marry her lover.

Yet Margaret was in the right, in the sense that Angus's designs were entirely predatory. He intended to seize the government of Scotland and the guardianship of James until the King reached his majority. When that time came ... something might be arranged: a sudden illness, an accident. Margaret, aware of this possibility, was fighting for her son's life when she continued to forbid Angus's return. (She went so far as to threaten Wolsey with an appeal to Albany, in the event of Henry's forcing her to receive her husband.)[10] She would have done better to meet and win over Angus, and so control his activities. This could only have been effected by the temporary dismissal of Harry Stuart, whom she loved and trusted. She had no one else to trust, for Arran, as heir-presumptive, was serving her and James for his own ends.

Margaret finally succeeded in convincing Wolsey of Angus's worthlessness. Henry was not so persuaded, and continued his flattery of James by sending him the Garter and a guard of honour.

When Norfolk told Henry that Angus was not to be relied on—that his reappearance might result in gang warfare, the rule of the Douglases and even a return to the French alliance—Henry still urged Margaret to be reconciled to him. Angus then wrote to her, from Newcastle, declaring his loyalty.[11] His letter was excellently phrased, and would have deceived anyone but a wife.

The period of what amounted to Margaret's dictatorship lasted till the first week of November 1524, when Henry's emissaries (they were not given ambassadorial rank), Archdeacon Magnus and Roger Ratcliffe of the Privy Chamber, arrived with letters and presents for his nephew. They were ushered into Holyroodhouse to the sound of trumpets, and escorted to the chapel, where James and Margaret were attending Mass. Henry's letters were then presented to the King. He looked through them, with the help of his new tutor, Gavin Dunbar, Archbishop of Glasgow, who had replaced Sir David Lindsay. (James could not read English, so his mother translated the letters into Scots for him.) When the service ended he and Margaret received Magnus and Ratcliffe in one of the oratories, and the envoys produced his uncle's presents—a cloth-of-gold coat and a jewelled sword. He wore them all that afternoon.

Next day, Magnus broached the question of James's marriage with the Lady Mary. Finding Margaret 'well disposed' and 'highly pleased' on this point, he asked why she had announced that she would not send an embassy into England if Angus returned. She appeared embarrassed, and said hastily, 'I regret it, it is an oversight. I will follow the King's counsel, though it be to my pain.'

This conference was interrupted by a loud knocking. One of Margaret's gentlemen was admitted—and told her that the Earl of Angus had crossed the Border.

Margaret turned furiously upon Magnus. She had been betrayed— who was responsible? The Archdeacon explained that his master was still supporting her, and pointed out that Angus had arrived un-accompanied. 'Your Grace has his life in your hands,' he concluded. Margaret said, 'I cannot be familiar with him. But I wish he and my Lord of Arran could be reconciled,' she added, the thought of a Douglas-Hamilton feud and further danger to James uppermost in her mind. Magnus then asked her to set Beaton free, and she con-sented. 'Ask my brother', she said, 'to desire the Pope not to support the Duke of Albany.' Magnus replied that he would do what he could, and they parted on excellent terms.[12]

Next day, he found the Queen 'very gracious', and was congratulating himself on the success of his mission when, suddenly, he realized that she was going back on her promise about the divorce. She ended by saying, 'I trust my son will be able to protect me against Angus.' In despair, Magnus withdrew to report his failure to Henry VIII.

The Archdeacon thought that Margaret's change of front had been brought about by Harry Stuart, 'who keeps the seals and rules everything', and was prejudicing her against her husband. He told Henry that when he tried to give her Angus's letter she refused to receive it; he put it on a table, and spoke warmly of the Earl's height and good looks, and of the improvement in his manners. Margaret remained unmoved, and he was dismissed. She then opened the letter, in which Angus besought her to be 'a good and gracious lady unto me ... If I have offended Your Grace in any manner of way,' he concluded, 'I shall reform it at the sight and pleasure of Your said Grace.' Margaret re-sealed the letter, sent it back to Magnus, and wrote to Wolsey that she had been monstrously treated. 'I am resolved I will not be overset,' she added, and forbade Magnus to see James alone. The Archdeacon and Ratcliffe agreed in advising Henry to stop her allowance, only to find that the Scots Parliament supported her in refusing to admit Angus, and so, 'she persists in her wilfulness'.[13] Magnus reported that James followed her lead in everything—except in his attitude towards Harry Stuart, whom he seemed to resent. Margaret's disregard of this very natural jealousy was to have dire consequences for herself. She trusted too much to her power over a boy of strong character and advanced intelligence.

Although Margaret had disappointed Magnus she treated him as an honoured guest, and he could not resist her attentions. She gave a party for him and Ratcliffe at Leith, where James jousted, sang and danced. 'His princely doings and acts be so excellent for his age', Magnus reported ... 'that it is not possible they should be amended.'[14] He resembled his uncle rather than his mother, they both thought. When he said, 'I like England better than France,' they were delighted, and told Wolsey that the Queen should not 'be sharply dealt with', and the reconciliation with Angus held over for the moment. Deploring her subjugation by Harry Stuart, Magnus resolved to speak to her 'as a priest, for the weal of her soul', on this point. She listened courteously, 'but showed little appearance of amendment'.[15]

This mild treatment vexed Wolsey, who ordered Norfolk, as from the King of England, to warn Margaret that, 'unless she looked better to herself — and that betimes — she should have cause to repent ... and be sorry that ever she was born.' Norfolk refused to pass on this message; if he did, he told Wolsey, Margaret would resort to Francis I.

On November 14th, 1524, Parliament confirmed her regency, and she told Magnus that Angus would not be allowed to take his seat in the Tolbooth; she then suggested that as the envoy's mission was now at an end, he might as well leave Scotland. Magnus replied that he must stay until he was recalled. He felt himself useless: Arran refused to see him, he was mobbed by the Edinburgh women (they said he had the evil eye), and desired by Margaret to leave the city. After a short absence, he returned to Holyrood.[16]

At four o'clock on the morning of November 23rd, he was awakened by shouts, gunfire and the tramp of armed men. Angus, with four hundred followers, was marching towards the Castle. Failing to take it, he returned to the Market Cross, and there proclaimed his loyalty to James, whom he had come to rescue — the usual slogan — from his evil advisers.

Holyroodhouse, although well protected, had only three cannon. When Margaret ordered the guards to open fire, Magnus begged her not to start a war against her husband. She rounded on him. 'Go home!' she exclaimed, 'and do not meddle with Scottish affairs.'[17] The first salvo killed four people; this caused Angus to retreat to Tantallon. With James, Margaret then occupied the Castle; at her dictation, the King wrote to Angus, ordering him to leave Scotland, and to Henry VIII, asking him to recall the Earl. Margaret also wrote to Henry, begging him to further her son's marriage with the Lady Mary, and pointing out, it seems tactfully, that what she had predicted had come to pass. Angus was collecting his forces for a rebellion, and James was in great peril; of her own danger she said nothing.[18] At last, Henry was convinced. It might well be, he told Wolsey, that Angus was a French agent, and although he could not now be recalled, he must no longer be supported. Then, once more, the whole situation changed.

Angus was still urging Margaret to receive him (evidently he did not feel himself strong enough either to kidnap James or to occupy the capital). Suddenly, it occurred to her that this subservient approach might be used. She would be outwardly reconciled, she said, if he agreed to a divorce. While considering this proposal, Angus wrote sadly to Wolsey of his wife's enmity and of her threats. Meanwhile,

Magnus described her as 'blinded with folly' in her adherence to Harry Stuart and turning towards France for help. For Francis I had sent her 30,000 crowns in the hope of her accepting the hand of the recently widowed Duke of Albany. She told Magnus of this, adding, 'It will be long before I have as much from England.' A few days later, she said, 'I hope Angus will come to a better way than was thought.'[19]

What could she mean? Magnus confessed himself quite bewildered. In the first week of January 1525 he gathered that, while pressing on with the English marriage, Margaret was considering a French bride for James, and about to be reconciled to her husband. Events rushed past the Archdeacon so rapidly that the basic situation was obscured — namely, that there were now three parties in Scotland, all more or less equal numerically. Margaret and Arran headed one, the pro-French lords the second and Angus and his allies a third.

On January 24th Magnus reported that Margaret had rejected the French alliance, and that the people were in favour of James marrying the English Princess. The Queen had been ill, but was in good spirits, and had withdrawn, with her son, to Stirling. It seemed to Magnus that she changed her mind every week; he never knew when she was lying to him, or how he would be received. He was momentarily cheered by her cold reception of Gonzolles, the French ambassador, who, well snubbed, withdrew to pay court to her ladies. Their noisy laughter displeased Margaret, and she signed to Harry Stuart to intervene. He took Gonzolles by the arm and offered him the choice of leaving the castle or being thrown downstairs.[20] While disapproving of these ill-bred methods, Magnus could not help being amused by the Frenchman's discomfiture.

Like most favourites, Harry Stuart took unseemly liberties, and made himself very unpopular. Yet there was no real harm in him; he was the kind of handsome, lively, inadequate young man who attracts women older and more masterful than himself. Although impertinent and acquisitive, he was neither ill-natured nor cruel, and he had more courage and less cunning than his predecessor. His attitude towards Margaret was necessarily one of self-interest; yet at first he remained loyal to her when he could have profited by the bribes of her enemies. She came to despise him: but that was not his fault. His approach, once so pleasing, was bound to pall; and his judgment must always have been hopelessly inept.

When Magnus complained of Harry Stuart's power, he assumed

that any woman must be dominated by her lover. In this case, Stuart was rather a supporter than an adviser; he could be relied on to agree with Margaret's decisions—as when the Council asked her to arrange a truce between Arran and Angus, to break off her relationship with himself and permanently to establish James in Edinburgh. She replied, 'The King my son will remain in what place he pleases ... Your demand is unbecoming ... I will follow your counsel [in the other matters] when you are obedient to my son.'[21] She then told Magnus, who found her at the head of an army in Stirling, that she might make war on the lords, in which case the English marriage would probably fall through.

When Angus entered the town and asked to see her, she sent him an offer of 10,000 marks on condition that he agreed to the divorce. As he made no reply, she decided to leave for Edinburgh, and from there entered into correspondence with Albany and Francis I. 'I will take your part against all, except my son,' she wrote. 'If I were separated from Angus, I could do more against him.'[22] She then told Magnus that she might take Angus 'into favour', and he suggested arbitrating between them. Margaret consented—and so, after five years of hatred, she and Angus met again. It was agreed that he should attend the opening of Parliament on February 23rd.

Margaret's hand had been forced to her own detriment; for this reconciliation was too hollow to be of use—and too late. Now Angus had begun to rally his clan, and was nearing the point when he could make his own conditions. He concealed his intentions with the graceful courtesy which had become automatic. Another, perhaps more urgent reason for Margaret's capitulation was Angus's seizure of their daughter, the eight-year-old Lady Margaret Douglas. The Earl of Moray, one of the Queen's most valuable allies, had made an offer for her hand; and so her mother wanted to remove her from the Douglases, who might be planning a marriage with an enemy. Angus had no intention of releasing the child; as the niece of Henry VIII, she was a potential asset.

The procession headed by Margaret and James V was outwardly correct. Angus carried the crown, Arran the sceptre and Argyll the sword. During the course of the session a truce was agreed on between Angus and Arran; a regency council included these two noblemen, Margaret, several bishops and Lord Lennox. Twenty years later, Lennox's heir, Matthew, married Lady Margaret Douglas, became the father of Darnley and, eventually, the father-in-law of

Mary Queen of Scots, Margaret Tudor's only surviving grandchild.*

After the ceremony Margaret entertained her husband with every appearance of amiability; in private, they discussed the divorce; but Angus wanted more money and land than she was willing to provide. He agreed to say nothing of any arrangements they might make to Henry VIII, and Margaret sent Harry Stuart back to Stirling. Angus immediately reported the gist of their talks to Wolsey. A few weeks later Magnus's spies discovered Margaret's correspondence with Francis I. The Archdeacon then sent copies of her letters to her brother.

With Magnus's report Henry received the news of Francis I's defeat and capture by Charles V at Pavia. This did not lessen his enraged resentment of Margaret's double-dealing. He ordered Magnus to announce the collapse of her ally in public, and to present his personal indictment in private audience. Margaret managed to conceal her dismay during the first interview, which took place at St Johnston. Magnus then asked her to see him alone, and gave her Henry's letter. 'After Her Grace had looked over ... the first five or six lines of the same', the Archdeacon reported, 'her countenance altered in such manner that it was a full hour before she could sober herself from excessive weeping. And long it was, and with much pain, ere that Her Grace could read the letter to the end.' When she sobbed out, 'Such a letter hath never been written to any noblewoman!' Magnus replied, 'Note every part of it—and be as well content with it as the King was with Your Grace's letter [to Albany].' He then described her dealings with Francis I in detail. 'I deny favouring Albany,' was all she could say. 'Ask my son.' Aware that before he could do so, James would be primed by her, Magnus said nothing, and she then accused him of lying about her to Henry. Again, he was silent; she went on, 'I forbid you to bring any more such letters from my brother—if I do read any more, it will be my death!' adding that if she did reply, it would be 'too sharply', and dismissed him.[23]

A few days later Henry wrote to her again, less severely. Margaret replied insisting on the divorce, and told Magnus that Angus had been cited to Rome on that account. The Archdeacon consulted Angus, who complained of Henry's forbidding him to seize Margaret's properties. He added that, although he was doing his best to win over James by presents of hawks and hounds, Margaret continued to make mischief between them. After a talk with his mother,

* See genealogical table.

the boy would 'look down, and gloom and glower' upon the Douglas faction. (This saddened Angus—he was trying so hard to do his best.) James was inclined, Magnus wrote, to be rude and disobliging. He gambled and swore, was often unpleasant, and sometimes cruel. When he did approach his stepfather, it was only to ask for his agreement to the divorce. 'I will not agree without the consent of the King of England,' Angus replied, and withdrew to one of his private strongholds till April 1525, when he joined James and Margaret at Dumfermline, as if assuming that they were all on the best of terms.[24]

No news of the divorce came from Rome, and Angus was rapidly gaining allies among the lords; then he and Arran were reconciled. Margaret made the best of an increasingly dangerous situation by treating Angus so courteously in public that their reconciliation was expected; in fact, she was more than ever determined on the divorce, and sent James to him again. 'I will promise you boundless favour', said the King, 'if you will consent,' and received an agreeably non-committal answer. James then asked Magnus to order him an English buckler—'not as for a child', he added, 'and a man-size sword'.[25]

Then Margaret, made desperate by delay, had a new and ingenious notion. She had reason to believe, she said, that James IV was still alive when she married Angus; so that union was invalid, and she was free to marry again. When Magnus pointed out that that would prove her daughter's illegitimacy, she abandoned this scheme, and put forward another. If she and Angus were divorced, she told Magnus, she would support her ex-husband in every possible way. The horrified Archdeacon refused to consider such a proposal; it was not only improper, but ridiculous. Margaret then fell back on Angus's pre-contract to the Lady Jane Stuart of Traquair. This attack also failed.[26]

When Parliament met in July, Margaret did not attend; she was now afraid of being captured and imprisoned by Angus, who, having gained a majority in the lords, declared his intentions. 'Her Grace', he told them, 'shall be harmless of me ... *as long as we are divorced,*' and urged them to enforce her return to Edinburgh. When she refused, the Council passed sentence upon her. His access to the Queen, they told James, was now forbidden, and her regency cancelled. Very much shaken, he attempted to plead with them, saying, 'I trust my mother hath not so highly offended as to deserve such treatment.'[27] All he obtained was an abeyance of three weeks, during which time Margaret toured the north in order to raise an army, and so invade Edinburgh and rescue her son. In January 1526 Arran and

several other chieftains deserted Angus and joined her. That nobleman was unmoved, for he held the King, whose safety was now
essential to his policy. He chose to ignore James's hostility to himself,
maintaining a courteous serenity.

Magnus, trying to mediate between the factions, begged Margaret
not to influence James against the Council. When she and the King
were allowed to meet — 'Take this advice in good part,' he said. 'Give
His Grace your loving blessing,' apparently thinking that she and
James had been estranged. Margaret replied that Angus would have
her put away — he dared not injure her son — if she entered the capital.
'Your Grace might rule him as your servant, if you would be kind to
him,' Magnus persisted.[28] Margaret did not trouble to contradict
him. She was in touch with James, and a plan of rescue had been
formed by herself, Arran and the Earl of Moray. Alarmed by these
preparations, Angus then agreed to the divorce, promised not to
'trouble' his wife, and appealed — in vain — to Henry VIII for re-
inforcements. Henry no longer trusted him, and would have turned
to Margaret, if she had consented to give up Harry Stuart; he
realized that she would not do so.

On January 17th, 1526, Arran and Moray set forth to deliver James,
halting to collect their forces at Linlithgow. Margaret remained in
the castle. This must decide the issue. She was now sure of regaining
the regency.

NOTES

1 *L. & P.*, vol. IV, pt. 1, p. 199.
2 Ibid.
3 Op. cit., p. 206.
4 Op. cit., p. 199.
5 Op. cit., p. 206.
6 Op. cit., p. 239.
7 Ibid.
8 Green, vol. IV, pp. 385–6.
9 *L. & P.*, op. cit., p. 298.
10 Green, op. cit., p. 387.
11 *L. & P.*, ibid.
12 Ibid.
13 Ibid.
14 Op. cit., p. 239.
15 Ibid.
16 Ibid.
17 Ibid.
18 Op. cit., p. 387.
19 Op. cit., p. 408.
20 Op. cit., p. 429.
21 Op. cit., p. 454.
22 Op. cit., p. 488.
23 Op. cit., p. 534.
24 Ibid.
25 Op. cit., p. 605.
26 Op. cit., p. 646.
27 Op. cit., p. 696.
28 Op. cit., p. 889.

# XV
## *Defeat*

AT THIS time, battles between the clans appear to have been decided by the smaller army flying before the larger as soon as serious fighting began. So it was that when Angus's 7,000 men advanced upon Arran's and Moray's numerically inferior force, Angus's victory was instantaneous, with the result that Arran and Moray deserted Margaret and were admitted by Angus to the Council. Lennox and a few other chieftains remained with her; and Angus, surer now of his own strength, allowed her to visit James, while taking over her lands and revenues as he needed them. He seems never to have become agitated, or boastful of his triumphs.

Naturally, Margaret was in great distress; but her resolute optimism and the fact that Henry VIII was no longer supporting Angus—he told Magnus that he thought she had 'sufficient reason' for divorce[1]—led her to hope that she might eventually defeat her husband. Meanwhile, James suffered more than she did, not only from his stepfather's rule (he had always hated Angus, and now feared him) but through Margaret's reminders of his responsibility for her status. As he neared his majority—he would be fourteen in April 1526—the enmity between her and the lords so alarmed James that he wept openly, and dared not show his affection for his mother. His only friend was Patrick Sinclair, who reported him to Henry VIII as being better mannered and more inclined to intellectual pursuits. James had taken to writing poetry and plays; he resembled his uncle in looks (he was fair, with aquiline features) and shared Henry's tastes for music and learning. Angus gave him anything he asked for, while keeping him under restraint, making it clear that he was being used, and frightening him when necessary. So James, aware of his mother's helplessness, arranged, through Sinclair, to write to Henry, imploring him to rescue them both.[2]

Angus was then reported to be setting about James's corruption. Albany, whose interest in Scottish affairs revived during the autumn

of 1526, was informed by his agents that the young King, now ruler
*de jure*, was surrounded by 'profligate, greedy and wicked men', who
encouraged his violent tendencies. When Lennox and Margaret made
further attempts to rescue him and failed, his deterioration became
so pronounced that Patrick Sinclair took him to task. James appeared
'somewhat ashamed', and promised to do better.[3]

Angus then forced the boy to announce that he was perfectly
content, and that his mother need not be alarmed about his circumstances. A few weeks later, his secret letters to her described his
misery; he begged her and Lennox to attack again; they did so in
vain. During this skirmish Angus allowed James to ride in the rear-
guard, under George Douglas's charge. As the battle was joined, the
King, seeing a chance of escape, spurred on his horse. Douglas
snatched at his rein. 'Bide where you are, Sir,' he said. 'For if they
get a hold of you, be it by one of your arms, we will seize a leg and
pull you in two pieces rather than part from you.'[4]

On this occasion Lennox was killed (by accident, according to the
Douglases), and Angus captured Stirling Castle in order to imprison
the Queen; warned just in time, she escaped, no one knew where. She
was still corresponding with Albany; all he could do was to ask the
pro-French lords to give her the regency; they were defeated by
Angus's majority in Parliament.[5] Once more, his persuasive tactics
had triumphed.

Angus was now in a position to pose as an injured yet generous
husband. He had consented to the divorce (most unwillingly, he told
Magnus) but desired nothing so much as friendship with his wife,
whom he asked to attend the opening of Parliament in November
1526. Accompanied by James, he met her outside the city, and with
graceful deference conducted her to Holyroodhouse. A few days
later, she was given the choice of exile or consent to his conditions.
These were hard; she had to accept them, or be permanently
separated from her son.

Although Margaret and James were allowed to be together, neither
could move without Angus's permission, and Harry Stuart was told
to leave Stirling Castle, which Angus, courteous as ever, restored to
the Queen. Stuart departed in December 1526, with the result that
James reported favourably on his mother to Wolsey's envoy, and
never left her side, unless he was hunting.[6] Patrick Sinclair then
described Angus and Margaret as being outwardly on excellent
terms; but he believed that she was 'circumventing' her husband,

and that this would end in Angus's defeat and the return of Stuart.
Henry and his nephew were at one in their determination that this
ought not to be be allowed; as if to seal their agreement, Henry sent
James a present of hounds. A few weeks later, James announced that
he intended to banish Harry Stuart from Scotland; when Margaret
suggested that her lover and his mother should return to court,
James refused.[7]

Margaret was enraged. She told James that if he persisted in ban-
ning Stuart, she would leave for France. This, their first quarrel,
became public knowledge, and in April 1526 the French Ambassador
told Henry VIII that Margaret would marry again as soon as she was
free. Henry was horrified by what he described as his sister's 'foolish
and evil' behaviour. 'She hath made herself a shame and a disgrace
to all her family,' he went on. 'It is impossible for anyone to lead a
more shameful life,' adding that James was now old enough to be
independent of both his mother and his stepfather.[8]

A month later, Henry told Katherine of Aragon (she was now forty,
and no longer capable of bearing another child) that he was approaching the Vatican about a divorce, on the grounds of the invalidity of
their marriage. Bursting into tears, she declared that she would not
co-operate in so sinful a scheme.* Henry and Wolsey then began the
process which, after six years of conflict, ended in the King's final
breach with Rome and his long-planned union with Anne Boleyn.

By this time Margaret had left Edinburgh for Stirling, where she
remained during the spring and summer of 1527, while Harry Stuart
began proceedings for his divorce, and she continued to correspond
with Albany about hers; she seldom came to the Court now
dominated by Angus, who had become the virtual ruler of Scotland.
She and James then began to assemble a party against him. In the
autumn, news came of Clement VII's consent to and ratification of
her divorce—and in the last week of December the requisite papers
arrived. She at once presented Parliament with the proofs of her
freedom. Then she returned to Stirling, where Harry Stuart was
waiting for her. They were married in March 1528.

Henry VIII, who did not receive the official news of Margaret's
divorce until the following April, wrote her a shocked and indignant
letter. Although he must have known that she and Stuart were
married, he chose to assume that she was able to rescind the divorce,
and begged her, for her daughter's sake, to do so. 'Turn to God's

* See p. 203.

word,' he went on, ' ... and for the weal of your soul, avoid eternal damnation ... Relinquish the adulterous company of him that is not, nor may not be, of right, your husband.'[9]

In a tactful reply, Margaret made no reference to her brother's dealings with Clement VII, and asked him for aid against Angus, who was beginning to lose his hold on the government. Henry's matrimonial affairs were no concern of hers; all her energies were bent on driving out the Douglases and establishing James's rule. Her son's co-operation was temporarily halted by his disapproval of her third marriage; but as his hatred of Angus far outweighed his resentment at being forced to accept a second stepfather, he summoned Angus and his brothers in order to accuse them of encouraging the inroads of the 'thieves and broken men' on the Border, ill-treating the French ambassador and placing their kindred in official positions.

Deferentially, that smiling villain promised to raid the Border, and began to call up his forces. James came to the conclusion, as did Margaret, that Angus intended to kidnap him; as he and his mother were now supported by a number of powerful nobles who were assembled at Stirling, the King took advantage of Angus's departure to escape, disguised as a groom, from Edinburgh, and joined Margaret and their allies on May 30th, 1528. He then wrote to Henry describing Angus's treasonous plans. In July he issued a proclamation forbidding the Earl to come within seven miles of the capital, and with his mother, her husband and the royalist clans re-entered Edinburgh in triumph. He created Harry Stuart Earl of Methven and Master of the Ordnance, 'for the great love I bear my dearest mother'.[10]

A few days later, James and Margaret returned to Stirling Castle, where they remained strongly guarded. In September the Douglases were put to the horn and their estates confiscated. Neither Margaret nor James seized any of these; she merely retrieved what Angus had taken from her. Methven—his title, pronounced Meffen, came to be written and spoken as Muffin—was rewarded with a few properties. Meanwhile, Angus was appealing to Henry VIII, who ignored his letters. When Magnus pleaded for him with Margaret, she replied, 'I will do him no hurt if he and his friends be good to my son.'[11] Angus, with their daughter, then fled into England. In Christmas week peace between England and Scotland was signed at Berwick. This emboldened Margaret to write Henry a long, affectionate letter, and to urge on James's marriage with the Lady Mary.

So all her troubles seemed to have ended. She was happily married, on good terms with a son whose authority she had established, and allied, so she believed, with her brother. Then news came from England of Angus's reception and re-employment by Henry VIII; with the Earl of Northumberland, he was now Warden of the Eastern Marches, in place of Dacre, who had died in 1526. When James realized that this odious rebel was once more his uncle's agent, he told Magnus that he had been betrayed. If Henry did not dismiss Angus, then the Anglo-Scots alliance was meaningless, and he could no longer consider marrying his cousin. Horrified, Margaret assured Magnus of her own loyalty and devotion to his master, and tried to persuade him that James was still friendly towards England. But when Henry's seventeen-year-old bastard, Richmond, wrote to plead with her for Angus, her anger burst forth. 'How much I marvel', she wrote, 'that the King your father and yourself have such great regard for the Lord Angus, when we ... sustain such great dolour and wrong. We greatly marvel, considering his offences made to us,' she repeated, adding that Angus had further injured her by taking away their daughter. 'I bear no rancour to the said Earl,' she went on. 'But ... I advise him to keep ... out of the way of the King my son.'[12]

At this time, James and Margaret were on good terms – his dislike of Methven seems to have been overcome – and spent much time together. Yet their policies diverged. James, now approaching his seventeenth year and intensely conscious of his regality, would not accept his uncle's double-dealing; Margaret hoped to sustain the English alliance through the marriage James wanted to reject in favour of a French princess. Within a year, they were on the verge of another quarrel. Then, with the visit of Clement VII's nuncio in the summer of 1529, they began to enjoy the festivities and entertainments provided by the chieftains.

The most outstanding of these was that given by the Earl of Atholl, who spent £3,000 on a fête lasting many days. He prepared for his guests 'a fair palace in the midst of a green meadow', so constructed that 'no man knew whereon he stood, but as if he were in a garden'. This huge wooden building was hung with tapestries, 'lighted with fine glass windows', and divided into suites of flower-lined rooms for the royal party. 'All manner of meats, drinks and delicates' were served on gold plate, 'so that Queen Margaret wanted of her orders no more than when at home'. The final proof of Atholl's splendour came with his guests' departure. Turning for a last look, they saw the palace in flames. The nuncio, exclaiming in horror, was reassured by

James. 'It is the custom of our Highland men,' he explained, 'be they never so well lodged at night, they burn their lodging the next morn.'[13]

Shortly after James returned from the Highlands, he made Sir David Lindsay Lyon-King-at-Arms. There had been several disputes between Margaret and the retired Chamberlain; but she was too deeply involved in James's marriage plans to concern herself with trivialities. Henry's offer of the Lady Mary's hand had not materialized; and now an alliance with Catherine de Medici, the Pope's ward and the greatest heiress in Europe, was suggested; but Francis I prevented further negotiations by securing the young lady for his own son, afterwards Henry II. Meanwhile, James's inclination towards his cousin diminished as it became clear that if Henry VIII's divorce from Katherine of Aragon was granted, the Lady Mary would be declared illegitimate. To Margaret, no other marriage seemed so desirable; but as James's gifts of land to Methven increased—and with them that nobleman's appetite for more—her attitude became less insistent, although she still tried to keep the peace between England and Scotland. Angus's ravages of the Border infuriated James; then the Earl's bribing of the nobles in that district caused them to offer Henry VIII the crown of Scotland. James managed to crush this movement; but the breach between himself and his uncle was slowly widening.

At seventeen, James was acting independently of his mother. While assuming his agreement with her on political issues, she was hardly in a position to criticize his private life, and during the next two years she tolerated his mistresses and the birth of five illegitimate children, all by different mothers; but this development increased her eagerness for the English marriage.

James was now more than usually secretive, and so Margaret seems not to have known about his increasing hostility to Henry VIII, nor that he was preparing, just as his father had, to invade England with French support. While corresponding courteously with his uncle, he continued to protest about Henry's patronage of the Douglases. That monarch, exclusively occupied with his divorce, left Scottish affairs to the Earl of Northumberland, whose raids on the Border increased James's wrath. Meanwhile, Margaret insisted that all was well.

Superficially, this was the case. The arrival of an English embassy in the summer of 1531, headed by Lord William Howard, inaugurated a series of contests in wrestling and archery between hosts and guests. Margaret and James betted a hundred crowns and a tun

10

of wine each, she on the English, he on the Scots; when she lost, he gave her countrymen a banquet. During the rest of that year the English marriage was discussed, but no progress resulted, and Margaret retired into contented privacy with Methven. His acquisitiveness —with James's permission, she gave him the fortress of Newark and Ettrick Forest—did not, then, affect her love for him. This peaceful interlude was not destined to last.

In the autumn of 1532 James sent Henry an ultimatum. He must either dismiss Angus and stop Northumberland's depredations, or prepare for war. James then demanded the return of his father's body, which still lay unburied, so he had been told, at Richmond. He added that he had expelled the English residents from Scotland, called up all his male subjects between the ages of sixteen and sixty, and established a large force, supplemented by Irish and Danish troops, on the Border. Through the Venetian ambassador in London, he let it be known that he was in communication with Francis I, contemplating an alliance with the Archduchess Isabella of Austria, and supporting Charles V in his condemnation of Henry's divorce.[14] All plans for marriage with his cousin were now abandoned.

As so often, Henry's immediate response to threats of violence was disconcertingly bland. Adopting what might be called a boys-will-be-boys attitude, he informed the Venetian envoy that he had no quarrel with his nephew, but that he was not going to be browbeaten. 'Considering you as my son,' he wrote to James, 'I do not wish for war, but I am not afraid, nor do I doubt ... to be able to injure my enemies.'[15] But when James's herald came to warn Henry of his master's intentions, the Tudor King lost his temper, and threats were exchanged, just as in the camp at Thérouanne, eighteen years before. Henry then dismissed the Scotsman, who turned to say, in what an onlooker described as a haughty manner, 'If Your Grace possesses riches and treasures, my King hath braver and more valiant subjects. The English', he went on, 'will greatly deceive themselves if they rely on the Earl of Angus, who is a rebel to his King and detested by all in Scotland.'[16]

In January 1533 Henry sent 6,000 men to meet James's forces on the Border. They halted the Scots, who would not attack; then James himself came to lead them. This skirmish produced further imploring letters from Margaret to her brother, who replied that James had become his enemy and was set on war. 'I cannot', he concluded, 'sue for remedy, but must demand it by the sword.'[17]

Northumberland wrote in the same strain, hinting that Margaret had wasted her time in trying to mediate, and she withdrew from the dispute. In the course of the following year it became clear that neither Henry nor James was ready for open warfare, and Lord William Howard's second embassy arrived. James seems to have been under the impression that his uncle was cowed; in fact, Henry's intentions were subtler. He had now married Anne Boleyn and was the father of the future Queen Elizabeth, so needed Scots support of his Supremacy over the English Catholic Church. Peace was patched up, and Howard (he was Anne's uncle) presented James with horses and suits of clothes.[18]

Lord William then proposed that James should meet Henry and Francis I at what would now be called a summit conference in York. This piece of flattery was followed by a plea for the Douglases. As Margaret began to realize that peace between her son and her brother was unlikely to last, she wrote to Henry's Lord Privy Seal, Thomas Cromwell, asking if she and Methven might come to England. In December 1534 she received presents from Queen Anne, but no reply to this suggestion. She now faced the fact that she was no longer needed by Henry — or by James.[19]

In the same month a Black Friar criticized Henry's divorce and re-marriage in a sermon at Edinburgh. Enraged, Margaret told Cromwell that she would remember this insolence 'as cause requireth',[20] and so began to take in the beginnings of the religious controversies which were to end in the triumph of Lutheranism in Scotland.

Caring little for the spiritual issue, Margaret took the opportunity to show her loyalty to Henry by siding with the heretics, and thus further estranging James, whose adherence to Rome was part of his continental policy. Still she hoped that Henry would receive her; she had worked for England for thirty years — surely she deserved some reward. None came. Her daughter, having joined Angus (it is possible that he was genuinely attached to her), had been placed by Henry in the Lady Mary's household; and so, except for Methven and a few nobles, Margaret was alone. She assured Henry that 'I can do more [for you] than anyone in Scotland',[21] and was sent £400 and several bales of silk — but no summons to his Court. In November 1535 these presents were followed by an approach — to James — of a different kind. 'God hath revealed to me,' Henry wrote to his nephew, 'by study, and contemplation with famous clerks, the thralled captivity and usurped power of the Bishop of Rome and his ungodly laws ... I desire to allure you to the favourable embracement of God's word.'[22]

James evaded this magniloquent invitation by telling his ambassador, Sir Adam Otterbourne, tactfully to indicate to Henry that his 'new constitution of religion' was not acceptable. These orders were secret from everyone but Margaret, with the result that her opposition to James's religious attitude increased, as did his resentment of her interference. Even then, their disagreement might not have lasted very long; but in the spring of 1536 Margaret became aware that her son was about to ruin all her plans and hopes by making a love-match—and with a mistress! The ex-wife of the Earl of Angus could imagine no greater folly, no more disastrous self-abandonment to caprice. She prepared to fight this crazy scheme with every weapon she possessed.

---

## NOTES

1 *L. & P.*, vol. IV, pt. 1, p. 889.
2 Op. cit., p. 1081.
3 Op. cit., vol. IV, pt. 2, p. 1143.
4 Op. cit., vol. V, p. 519.
5 James V, *Letters*, p. 132.
6 *L. & P.*, vol. IV, pt. 2, p. 1186.
7 Op. cit., p. 1345.
8 Strickland, *Queens of Scotland*, p. 231.
9 Op. cit., p. 238.
10 Green, vol. IV, p. 475.
11 *L. & P.*, op. cit., p. 2154.
12 Strickland, op. cit., p. 239.
13 Op. cit., p. 241.
14 *Ven. S. P.*, vol. IV, p. 355.
15 Ibid.
16 Ibid.
17 *L. & P.*, vol. VI, p. 145.
18 Op. cit., vol. VII, pt. 2, p. 512.
19 Op. cit., p. 553.
20 Op. cit., p. 571.
21 Op. cit., vol. VIII, p. 266.
22 Op. cit., vol. IX, p. 248.

# XVI

## *The Player Queen*

THE former mistresses of James V had not succeeded in holding him. When he met Lady Douglas of Lochleven, he fell in love with her; their son was his favourite child, and he planned to legitimize him by marrying his mother. But first, she must be divorced from Sir Robert Douglas, and this was done before Margaret realized James's intentions; although she was somewhat taken aback when he called the boy Lord James Stuart. (As Earl of Moray, Regent of Scotland and the half-brother of Mary Queen of Scots, he was to acquire a rather sinister fame in the 1560s.) In her correspondence with Cromwell and Henry VIII, Margaret complained of her son's obstinacy—'he will not be dissuaded from marrying a divorced gentlewoman'—[1] while lamenting his lack of enthusiasm over meeting his uncle and Francis I. When James seemed to agree, but suggested Newcastle, as being more convenient for himself, and Lord William Howard replied that his King preferred York, Margaret insisted that James should give in, speaking 'very plain', and a violent quarrel ensued. There were other reasons for disagreement, both personal and political.

Although there is no record of James, now in his twenty-fifth year, reminding his mother of her behaviour over her second and third marriages, he must have done so when she objected to his marrying Lady Douglas. He then discovered that she had reported his secret instructions to Sir Adam Otterbourne to Henry VIII; she told her brother that James loved Henry 'better than any man living', and would obey him in all things. In a fury, James dismissed Margaret from Court, and threatened her with imprisonment. It was not much of a reward for all she had suffered in the past; but she did not complain, merely retiring to Doune, whence she wrote to Henry imploring him to let her take refuge with him. 'I am weary of Scotland,' she told Cromwell—and was informed that it would be a breach of etiquette for her to leave without her son's permission.[2]

In July 1536 Margaret returned to Court, under the impression that

149

Henry and James — Francis had withdrawn — would meet in August. She was, as ever, in debt, partly because the Border fighting had destroyed the source of her revenues. When she asked Henry to help her, he replied, 'You must not ask me to disburse notable sums merely because you are my sister,' reminded her of her ample (but long-spent) dowry, and pointed out, not unreasonably, that her son should support her.[3]

James, who had no intention of meeting his uncle, then abandoned his scheme of making Lady Douglas his wife, and departed for France in order to marry Francis I's eldest daughter, the Princess Madeleine, leaving Margaret as Regent. A few weeks later, she heard that Lady Margaret Douglas had betrothed herself, without Henry's permission, to Lord Thomas Howard, and that Henry had sent the young couple to the Tower. Margaret begged him to let her daughter return to Scotland. 'If this is done,' she wrote to Cromwell, 'I will answer that my daughter shall never trouble my brother more.' The twenty-one-year-old Margaret remained in England; when Lord Thomas died in the Tower, she was released. If his niece behaved herself, Henry told Margaret, he would treat her well; he expressed his approval of James's marriage, adding that he was distressed about his treatment of his mother. He concluded, 'There shall, on our behalf, want no loving and kind office which we think may tend to your relief.'[4]

Henry's sympathy stopped there. What Margaret most needed was money to buy new gowns for the reception of her future daughter-in-law. Her standard in dress was no longer catered for in Scotland; and now she had to face a worse disaster — the failure of her marriage; for her husband was copying his predecessor. As Muffin succeeded Anguish in disappointing and deceiving an ageing but strong-willed wife, Margaret's position became intolerable. Once more, she appealed to her brother.

Several years earlier, Margaret had given Methven the management of her estates. His appetite for property and wealth grew with her bounty; and in January 1537 she discovered, not only that he had stolen 8,000 marks in rents, but that he was the lover of Lord Atholl's daughter, Janet, who bore him a son. Margaret at once set about a divorce, asking Henry not to allow her 'to be wronged'.[5] As his agent, Sir John Campbell, could not confirm these charges, Henry replied that the reports from Scotland were so contradictory that he was sending another emissary, Ralph Sadler, to confer with her; Sadler was followed by a third envoy, Harry Ray. Both men interviewed Margaret, and supported her account of Methven's behaviour; Sadler added that James had treated her with great unkindness, and that she was in need of protection. Henry sent her £200, and desired Cromwell to write sternly to Methven. As soon as Sadler returned to England, Henry sent him to France to remonstrate with James. Meanwhile Methven, alarmed by Henry's threats, asked Cromwell to assure his formidable brother-in-law that he 'was ready to serve him before all princes in the world', saving James.[6]

In her first talks with Ray, Margaret gave him the impression that she was planning a fourth marriage. 'I met her', he wrote to Cromwell, 'alone in a gallery, no person knowing of the interview.' She complained that her brother had not answered her letters, adding, 'I trow my friends forget me—but there shall be nothing done in the realm but the King my brother and my lord of Norfolk shall have knowledge of it.' The gossip about her next husband centred on John Stuart of Arran; but there seems to have been no foundation for this, as Ray did not mention him in his report to Cromwell.[7]

Margaret's value as her brother's agent now increased, owing to the northern Catholic rising, known as the Pilgrimage of Grace: for the rebels had called upon the Scots to help them, and it was essential for Henry and Norfolk to find out if they were going to do so. Margaret was able to reassure her brother on this point. 'But,' she told Ray, 'I pray you, if ye intend war, say that I pray my lord of Norfolk that he make no war until I and Harry Stuart be divorced.'[8]

With the return of James and his frail young bride in May 1537 — Madeleine had been warned not to risk her health by leaving France, but was determined to be a queen—Margaret's complaints died down. James, absorbed in the marriage festivities, did not know that his mother's arrangements for divorcing Methven had come to a head during his absence, nor that Henry VIII was supporting this plan, for his relations with his uncle were superficially amiable, and his embassy to London had been well received. When Margaret informed him that twenty-four 'famous folk' (whom she did not name in her letters to Henry) had agreed to ratify her divorce, James at once quashed the proceedings, and a bitter dispute ensued.[9] This was temporarily halted when Queen Madeleine died of tuberculosis in July. While sharing her son's grief, Margaret was still determined to get rid of her husband and leave for England. Methven then offered James a large sum of money to prevent the divorce; Margaret outbid him with that of the rents from her Dunbar estates. James accepted his mother's bribe and promised her her freedom, but changed his mind. Margaret at once travelled south in the hope of crossing the Border, was followed and brought back to Stirling. A little later, she and her son achieved a makeshift armistice.

If James had not been a king, he might have become as viciously degraded as the worst of his nobles; but he had been brought up to feel himself responsible for his people. Cultured tastes and a highly developed intelligence rather enhanced than diminished his aggressive instincts; this was, of course, the result of a tormented childhood. Alternately flattered, terrorized, bewildered and courted — hailed as a potentate one day and reduced to cringing submission the next — his maturity produced a series of ineffective attempts at domination which were to end in the defeat of his armies at Solway Moss, his collapse and undiagnosed death. That he remained fond of the mother who did not perceive the nature of his development, that he became deeply attached to both his wives and to his first two children, is rather surprising. As the sinister aspect of his temperament (vividly reproduced in his portraits) had effect, so he achieved an unpopularity rare among Scottish monarchs; and thus his need of affection and loyalty drove him to seek satisfaction among his humbler subjects. His inclination towards low company and posing as the people's King brought him no happiness; he found some contentment in family life: but that did not last. His vain pursuit of what he no doubt thought of as glory, his uncle's ruthless manipulation of his follies, his private losses and public defeats — all contributed to a profound and ineradicable melancholy. A neurotic, living without hope, James was fortunate in his early death. A longer life might have driven him into insanity.

He now had to consider marrying again; and in April 1538 became the husband, by proxy, of a tall, heavily built widow, Marie de Longueville of Guise-Lorraine, who had just refused to marry Henry VIII. She landed at Fife in the following June, and their first child, another James, was born in May 1539. Meanwhile, Margaret had been badgering Henry and Methven for their co-operation over her divorce. A curious and unexpected aspect of her character was then revealed.

Like all the Tudors, Margaret admired men of action. She rated energy higher than virtue. And now, the unfortunate Methven, so aptly nicknamed, had not only exasperated but humiliated her by his steady absorption of her income. She might, perhaps, have forgiven even his unfaithfulness if he had shown either ability or ambition. But no; inert and feeble, he merely opened his mouth and swallowed whole anything that came his way: her rents, Lady Jane's favours, English patronage. This attitude was the opposite of his predecessor's; and so it came about that Margaret began to taunt him by contrasting his sluggish greed with Angus's executive villainy. What form her goading took is not clear; but Methven came to the conclusion that she intended to re-marry Angus as soon as she succeeded in disposing of himself—and he informed both Cromwell and James of his suspicions.[10]

As this volte-face became a further cause of dispute between Margaret and James, she accused Methven of lying about her. To Cromwell she wrote, 'I am now forty-nine years old, and should not travel like a poor gentlewoman, following my son from place to place. I shall never have another husband, and unless I get some remedy I shall pass to some religious place, and bide with them ... The King my son is more unkind to me daily, and I had liever be dead than treated as I am.'[11]

Although the idea of re-marriage with Angus may have been a momentary impulse, later reports indicate that Margaret continued to hanker after her first love, and to regret her own behaviour. Through some intricate and obscure process of reasoning, she ended by blaming herself for her hatred of the man who had endangered her son's life, murdered her allies, confiscated her properties and betrayed his own country. Also, practical as ever, she may have seen Angus as co-agent with herself for her brother—for she was as appalled now as she had been twenty-four years ago at the thought of war between England and Scotland. She knew, none better, that such folly must end in defeat. That James's attitude towards his uncle had become increasingly belligerent was her greatest anxiety; this did not affect her welcome of his second French bride, for whose arrival she made eager preparations, suggesting silver plate for Henry's wedding present while ordering more new gowns for herself.[12]

With Marie's entry into their lives, James and his mother ceased to quarrel. Margaret and her new daughter-in-law had much in common, for the younger woman was sophisticated, intelligent and warm-hearted. She treated Margaret with great courtesy, tactfully inquiring, 'What news hath Your Grace of King Henry?' 'But short since I heard from him,' Margaret would reply. In her reports of these conversations she described her pleasure in Marie's company, adding, 'She treats me honourably,' while begging Henry to write more often.[13]

A few weeks before the birth of her first grandson, Margaret was outwardly reconciled to Methven, although still secretly determined to divorce him. She liked being Queen-Dowager, and rejoiced in the health and strength of the baby Prince. In July 1539 Marie was once more pregnant, and on the same excellent terms with her mother-in-law; her only worry was the spread of Lutheranism in Scotland. 'The young Queen', Norfolk reported, 'is all papist, the old Queen not much less.'[14] The Duke underestimated Margaret's indifference. Her principal object was, as always, a firm and lasting alliance with England. When told by Ralph Sadler that if her three-year-old nephew, Prince Edward, Henry's son by Jane Seymour, died, James would have the reversion of the English throne, she was slightly sceptical. 'How is the Queen your mistress?' [Katherine Howard] she asked, and went on, 'I take it unkindly that I have had no letter from the King, for it is a small matter to spend ink and paper upon me. I should be better regarded here, if it was seen that my brother regarded me.' A few days later, she joyfully told the envoy that 'the King my son was never better inclined, and I am made much of by the new Queen.'[15]

With the birth of a second Prince in April 1540, Sadler took advantage of the general rejoicing to suggest that James might support the Reformed Catholic Church of England by abjuring his allegiance to the Pope. The King was too happy to refuse outright; he passed over the approach with a joking rejoinder, and Sadler did not raise the matter again.[16] Margaret and Methven then retired, in seeming amity, to Stirling, but were often at Court. James marked his approval of his mother's changed attitude by especially favouring her husband, as did his wife. So, at last, tranquillity and contentment enclosed their family life, and Margaret achieved her apotheosis. She was with a son and daughter-in-law who loved and respected her, and may even have been grateful for what she had done for them; and perhaps her grandsons partially replaced the children she had lost. She became resigned to a restful old age. Although James was more than ever determined to withstand Henry VIII's sovereignty, he did not involve his mother in the turmoil of Anglo-Scots relations.

Henry's motives were still devious and predatory. Noting the rise of what later became an extreme form of Protestantism in Scotland, he went on urging his nephew to destroy monastic and clerical power in the kingdom he still thought of as a vassal state. James ignored these demands, and continued to burn heretics and execute his uncle's spies. He then began to realize that he was not in a position to make war, but could only resist Henry's advances, whether of seeming friendship—such as a second invitation for a meeting at York— or of attacks on his own authority. The future of his sons was now his chief concern. In the last week of April 1541 both children died within a few hours of one another.

The stricken parents turned to Margaret for support; they would not let her leave them in their misery. Apologizing to Henry for her scrappy letters and 'evil hand', she explained that she had 'done great diligence to put ... my dearest son and the Queen his wife in comfort', and must remain 'ever in their company ... Whereof', she concluded, 'I pray Your Grace to hold me excused that I write not at length ... because I can get no leisure.'[17]

Thenceforward, James sank into a tortured gloom, as of one asking, in vain, what he had done to deserve this blow. His wife's youth and vigour—she became pregnant again seven months later—gave him no hope. He was haunted, specifically by the avenging shade of Angus's sister, Lady Glamis, whom he had burnt for high treason and heresy some four years earlier; for he was almost sure, now, that she had been falsely accused. Nothing could rouse him—and so he did not observe that his mother's health was beginning to fail; when she left Edinburgh for her castle of Methven he seems to have been unaware of any change.

There, in her fifty-third year, Margaret, alone but for her attendants—her husband remained at Stirling—had a stroke. She was not in pain; when warned by doctors and priests that she should prepare for death, she refused to do so. On October 18th, 1541, she realized that she was dying, and sent for James, who was at Falkland.

Margaret had no fear—no Tudor ever had—of moving on to the sphere occupied by the patron of her family. But one aspect of her state distressed her—her treatment of Angus. To the friars kneeling round her bed she said, 'I desire you to beseech the King of England to be gracious to the Earl of Angus.' A few minutes later, they heard her say, 'I ask God for His mercy that I have so offended the Earl.' She added that her daughter was to receive her goods—she had made no will, for there was almost nothing to leave—and that she hoped James would be kind to his half-sister. Then she sank into a coma.

She died without regaining consciousness some hours before he reached the castle.[18]

James ignored his mother's last requests, and told her attendants to lock up such valuables as remained. Her cash assets, which he seized, came to 2,500 marks. He then made arrangements for an elaborate funeral, and put all his courtiers into new and expensive mourning. Margaret's coffin was placed in the vault of the Carthusian Abbey in Perth, among those of the earlier Stuart Kings.[19]

No one was much concerned when, in 1559, a troup of Calvinists fell upon the royal tombs. They burnt Margaret's skeleton, and scattered her ashes in the ruined precincts of the abbey. A blue slab marks the spot where once she lay.

Angus continued alternately to betray and work for Henry VIII, who died in 1547. Methven married Lady Janet. Lady Margaret Douglas remained in England until, in her thirty-second year, she became the wife of Lord Lennox. On November 23rd, 1542, James fled from the holocaust of Solway Moss, dying at Linlithgow a fortnight later. His week-old daughter, Mary of Scotland, lived to fulfil a darker destiny in the Castle of Fotheringhay, formerly the birthplace of that Plantagenet King whose crown Margaret's father had taken from a thornbush on Bosworth Field.

---

## NOTES

1 *L. & P.*, vol. X, p. 355.
2 Ibid.
3 Op. cit., vol. XI, p. 50.
4 Strickland, *Queens of Scotland*, p. 254.
5 *L. & P.*, vol. XII, pt. 1, p. 197.
6 Ibid.
7 Strickland, op. cit., p. 257.
8 Ibid.
9 *L. & P.*, vol. XII, pt. 2, p. 226.
10 Op. cit., p. 327.

11 *Cal. S. P.* (Scottish Series), vol. I, p. 38.
12 Op. cit., p. 39.
13 *L. & P.*, vol. XIII, pt. 1, p. 558.
14 Op. cit., vol. XV, pt. 1, p. 243.
15 Op. cit., pp. 89–92.
16 Ibid.
17 *Cal. S. P.*, op. cit., p. 40.
18 *L. & P.*, vol. XVI, p. 601.
19 Ibid.

# MARY TUDOR

Accours, jeune Chromis, je t'aime et je suis belle;
Blanche comme Diane et légère comme elle,
Comme elle, grande et fière; et les bergers, le soir,
Quand, le regard baissé, je passe sans les voir,
Doutent si je ne suis qu'une simple mortelle;
Et, me suivant des yeux, disent: 'Comme elle est belle!'

*André Chénier*

# I

## *The First Betrothal*

JUST as princesses in fairy-tales have always been both good and beautiful, so the loveliness and virtue of kings' daughters in real life were, for many centuries, assumed—unless the young lady in question was actually deformed, in which case it did not matter whether she was virtuous or not. It therefore becomes increasingly difficult to find out, even through careful study of a portrait, whether a sitter of royal blood could have claimed the looks she was supposed to possess.

With the passage of time, changes in fashion proscribed certain types. After fifty years—or less—it was often impossible to find anything to admire in the likeness of one formerly described as the wonder of her day. So it happens that neither portraits nor drawings, nor the reports of eager and assiduous officials are acceptable guides to the beauty of persons long dead. The only proof of this asset is that created by the impact of the owner on a disinterested observer, who records it without concern for posterity.

Mary Tudor's exquisite appearance became, indeed, a legend, unsupported by the hard, flat productions of contemporary artists. Yet there is no question as to its existence, nor that it was set off by a natural vitality and a sweetness of character which no painter, then, attempted to convey. Such attributes are now lumped under the heading of charm; and of that again there can be little doubt. This princess allured and dazzled nearly all who beheld her; her grace and warmth of heart were immediately felt and permanently sustained. Like her fabled prototypes, she went through a time of trial, and then lived happily—or almost happily—ever after. In this respect her story breaks away from tradition; for she married twice: and both her husbands were, although differently, unpleasant—and rather degraded.

She was born at the Palace of Richmond in March 1496, making the fourth member of a group of five children: the others were Arthur Prince of Wales, Margaret, Henry Duke of York, and a baby,

Edmund. At the age of three she had her own household; this included a number of gentlewomen, a tutor, a physician, and a Lady Governess, 'my mother Guildford', on whom she chiefly relied. By the time she was three, her wardrobe was that of a grown person, and comprised, among other items, black, crimson and green velvet gowns, furred with ermine.[1] She was a delicate child; doctors were constantly in attendance for the first twelve years of her life. The only languages she learned were French and Latin. She was a fair performer on the lute and the regals; her dancing was faultless. She had little or no taste for outdoor sports, perhaps because her health prevented her joining in them.

Mary's first appearance in public took place in 1500, when she was four, at the Palace of Eltham, where she, Henry and Margaret received Erasmus and Sir Thomas More. While her elders conversed, she played on the floor, unreproved by her nurse, who was carrying Prince Edmund. Neither visitor spoke to her; but More, remembering her golden hair and brilliant colouring, described her, three years later, as 'bright of hue' in a poem lamenting her mother's death. This loss was one of a series in her childhood. In her fifth year Edmund died; and the wedding of Arthur with Katherine of Aragon was followed by his death in 1502. In 1503 Mary lost her mother and an infant sister. Then Margaret left to become Queen of Scotland.

Indirectly, Mary profited by Arthur's death, for the sixteen-year-old Katherine, now installed at Durham House in the Strand, became devoted to her, and, with Lady Guildford, created a family life for her little sister-in-law. Mary was much indulged by both ladies, and by her father, who was already planning her marriage. A Portuguese prince was considered, and then rejected for a greater alliance, that with the future Emperor Charles V, grandson of Ferdinand and Isabella of Spain, and nephew of Katherine of Aragon. He was six — four years younger than Mary — when the betrothal negotiations began, and continued until and after Henry VII's death. The resultant wrangling and delay, combined with failing health, overwork and the loss of his wife, caused the King's decline into invalidism, accompanied by outbursts of temper. Mary was his favourite child; but even she did not always escape his irritable censure.[2] This had little or no effect on her determination to get her own way. She seems to have shared her father's eagerness for her betrothal to Charles, which would have hung fire indefinitely, if his parents — Philip of Austria and Joan, Queen-Regent of Castile, Katherine's elder sister,

HENRY VIII *(Holbein)*

later known as Joan the Mad—had not been wrecked on the
Dorset coast in 1506. For several weeks they had to remain in
England.

Henry was delighted. Now he would be able to pin down this
rather elusive pair, both as to terms and the date of Mary's betrothal
to their son. On February 1st Philip left Melcombe Regis, while his
wife stayed to recover from sea-sickness at Wolverton Manor, where
her present of mahogany panelling is still to be seen. At first, Philip
was an unwilling guest. 'We shall stay here as short a time as possible,' he wrote to his father-in-law, soon after his meeting with the
fourteen-year-old Prince Henry, who received him at Winchester
and escorted him to Windsor.[3]

Here he was greeted by Henry VII a mile from the castle, entering
it to the sound of trumpets and sackbuts. Passing through galleries
lined with bowing nobles, they came into the great dining-chamber
arm-in-arm, where Katherine, Mary and their attendants awaited
them. Before taking his place beside Henry on the dais, Philip kissed
the two Princesses and their ladies. 'You have come', Henry told
him, 'to your father's house,' and commanded the musicians to play.[4]
With one of her gentlewomen, Katherine danced for her brother-in-
law; then it was Mary's turn; her performance was perfectly sustained. Katherine, now sitting beside Philip, asked him to take the
floor with her. He refused; she persisted. 'I am a mariner', he said,
presumably in joking reference to his recent experiences, 'and yet you
would make me dance.' He and Henry walked over to the fireplace
and continued to talk while Mary danced again. Required to play, she
did so, first on the lute and then on the regals. 'She played very well,'
according to one of Philip's gentlemen, 'and she was greatly praised ...
In everything, she behaved herself very well.' He found this rather
surprising, for Mary was only ten; he may have thought her even
younger, for she was then small for her age.[5]

During the next few weeks Henry persuaded Philip to agree to
three alliances—that of Mary with Charles, of Henry, now Prince of
Wales, with Charles's sister Eleanora, and of himself with Philip's
sister, the Archduchess Margaret. None of these marriages materialized. Then the two Kings set off for London, while the Eton boys
ran out to see them go.[6] A year later Philip died, and Joan's eccen-
tricities made it necessary for Charles's grandfathers, Ferdinand of
Aragon and the Emperor Maximilian, to proceed with the negotiations, which were concluded—or so it seemed—at Calais. It was

agreed that the proxy marriage between Mary and Charles should take place in the spring of 1508; their wedding was to be celebrated six years later, in Flanders. Henry decided to recoup his expenditure on Mary's dowry by marrying Philip's widow. When told of her mental condition, he replied that that would not prevent her bearing children; but nothing came of this proposal.[7]

Meanwhile, as Ferdinand seemed to be postponing the final arrangements for his grandson's marriage, Henry asked Fuensalida, the Spanish ambassador, what his master's intentions were. 'That marriage', Fuensalida replied, 'may come later.' 'I have been deceived [about Joan],' Henry said, 'and I will not be deceived about my daughter.' 'One should not impede the other,' protested Fuensalida. Henry exclaimed, 'But they do — you shall not have one without the other —' and left the room in a rage.[8] He then set a date for the betrothal ceremony without consulting Ferdinand, who forbade Katherine of Aragon to attend it, but gave in a month later, with the result that his deputies and the proxy bridegroom, de Bergues, arrived in December 1508 and received a magnificent welcome.

On December 17th the marriage was celebrated at Richmond Palace. De Bergues had brought with him the Emperor's wedding present for Mary, a diamond fleur-de-lys. A few weeks later, Henry received a bill for it of 50,000 crowns.[9]

The King had planned his daughter's reception of the Hispano-Flemish Commissioners with his usual care for display. At eight o'clock in the morning he led them into the late Queen's presence-chamber, which was hung with cloth of gold. He sat on the dais, and they took their places below him. After some minutes' suspense, the trumpets sounded, the doors were flung open and the twelve-year-old Mary, escorted by Katherine and followed by a group of peeresses, appeared, saluted her father and was conducted to a dais opposite his. There she stood, alone; her sister-in-law sat on a stool below her canopy of state.

The chronicler's ecstatic account of Mary's beauty and grace may be partially discounted; yet beneath the flattery there is a hint of surprised delight in her 'modesty and gravity'.[10] She remained standing while the speeches of welcome and gratitude rolled out, from the Archbishop of Canterbury, the President of Flanders and several other officials. The Sieur de Bergues then approached her dais and, in French, described his eight-year-old master's devotion to her, concluding with the marriage vows. Mary replied in the same lan-

guage. Taking de Bergues's hand in hers, she accepted 'the Lord
Charles' as her husband, promising to 'hold and repute him' as such,
'during my natural life'. Her share in the ceremony was short, and
she had of course learnt her speech by heart. Yet she was unsure of
herself, and there were long pauses between each sentence; no one
dared to prompt her, and nervousness spread through the audience,
to the point of bringing tears to the eyes of those fearing that she
might break down.[11] When she concluded, de Bergues stepped forward, kissed her on the lips and placed the wedding ring on her finger.
After the contract had been signed by the foreign principals, the
King, five bishops and twenty-one English peers, the women
separated from the men and High Mass was celebrated, while Mary
and Katherine dined in private, rejoining the guests for a tournament.
This lasted three days, to a musical accompaniment.

Before leaving to hunt with Henry and his nobles, Ferdinand's
ambassadors were received by the Princess of Castile, as she was now
called, for their presentation of jewels. Besides the diamond fleur-
de-lys and a cabochon ruby, Charles had sent her another diamond,
set in pearls and inscribed, in Latin, with the text, 'Mary hath
chosen the better part, which shall not be taken from her.' The
envoys then gave her a letter from him, beginning, 'Ma bonne
compagne', in which the boy Prince recommended himself 'as
cordially as I can', informed her of his health, which was excellent,
and hoped that hers was equally good. Begging God to bless them
both, he signed himself 'Votre bon mari'.[12]

Mary's replies were similarly correct, and no doubt dictated.
Meanwhile, her father, who had only four months to live, made a new
will, confirming her dowry of £60,000, and adding that if this marriage fell through she was to wed again, at once, 'out of the realm'.[13]
In April 1509 Henry VIII succeeded; he married Katherine three
weeks later.

Mourning for the old King was short—Henry VIII's coronation
took place six weeks after his father's death—and Mary's black garments were discarded for new and magnificent dresses provided by
her brother, together with a number of jewels. He removed her
diamond fleur-de-lys from the wardrobe and wore it in his hat, rather
to her annoyance;[14] but, as second lady in the kingdom, she was so
splendidly apparelled and so much in demand that her complaints
ceased as she prepared for a series of masques, jousts, banquets and
balls. Henry was proud of her beauty, and delighted to appear

between her and Katherine, whose delicate prettiness and gentle
dignity set off her sister-in-law's more exuberant charms.

The two girls now had to leave their indoor games and music
practice to rehearse the ballets and mimes planned by the seventeen-
year-old King's Master of the Revels. Even Hall, whose rapturous
descriptions of such displays occupy so many pages of his *Chronicle*,
eventually declares that 'it were too long to tell' all the items of these
performances; yet he could not resist recording those which adorned
the first years of Henry's reign. On one occasion, Mary and her ladies,
in russet gowns and gold caps, guarded a fortress successfully
besieged by gentlemen, who then led them out to dance; on another,
their faces veiled in black gauze, they were concealed in a mountain
covered with satin flowers and trees, emerging to be seized by 'wild'
men, clad in velvet moss. Many forms of fancy dress — Portuguese,
Italian, Spanish, Egyptian — were designed for Henry and his
courtiers, and a movable 'chamber of disguises' was built, so that the
King could change from one outfit to another during each show.
Before taking their places to watch a joust, Mary, Katherine and their
ladies might enter on horseback, carrying hoses which sprayed liquid
silver over their cavaliers. After the tilting, which lasted some three
or four hours, they would hurry away to dress as Virtues who, miming
belligerence, defeated a team of Vices, and so led their partners into
the banqueting-hall, where the feast concluded with more dancing,
and the sudden entry of Henry and his suite, masked; sometimes they
were dressed as shepherds, sometimes as gipsies or Turks. When they
unmasked, the delighted amazement of the audience was unfailing.

Amidst all these excitements Mary's betrothal, although assured by
the Spanish ambassador and supported by Katherine as her father's
agent, showed no signs of developing into the marriage, of which the
long-fixed date seemed to have become uncertain. The bridegroom
ceased to write, and his paternal grandfather, Maximilian, was now
oddly vague about the bride's identity, sometimes referring to her
(incorrectly) as Madame Marie of England, and sometimes as the
Lady Margaret, thus confusing her with her sister of Scotland.[15] Still
Katherine was sure that her father's promises would be kept; but a
coldness sprang up between her and Mary, for the younger girl was
told that the Emperor's negligence and King Ferdinand's elusiveness
had been encouraged by the Queen.[16] Then, with Henry's approaches
to the Archduchess Margaret of Savoy — Maximilian's daughter and
Regent of the Netherlands — the breach was healed. The Archduchess

wrote and spoke of Mary as Prince Charles's future wife, upon which Henry sent her a company of archers to help repel the invasion of French troops; this resulted in an Anglo-Spanish-Austrian alliance against France, and, in June 1513, Henry's capture of Thérouanne and Tournai. On his way home he visited Margaret of Savoy and Prince Charles at Lille. They declared their eagerness for the marriage, and in a letter to the Pope Henry described his future brother-in-law as a well brought-up and intelligent youth.[17] He returned to England with a number of hostages, of whom the most important was the Duc de Longueville.

Prince Charles and Mary then resumed their correspondence, and her trousseau was put in hand. Erasmus, no flatterer, visited her at this time, and was entranced. 'O! thrice and four times happy our illustrious Prince,' he wrote, 'who is to have such a bride! Nature never made anyone more beautiful; and she excels in goodness and wisdom.'[18] But the Prince had now reached the age agreed on for the marriage, and still nothing was said about the Princess leaving for Flanders, then Spanish territory. Henry's protests were met with further reassurances from Fuensalida, who, having watched Mary dance, wrote to Ferdinand, 'I think never man saw a more beautiful creature, nor one having so much sweetness, both in public and in private.' This letter reached Spain in March 1514. In April, for no ostensible reason, the marriage was again postponed, and again Henry protested, only to be informed by Prince Charles, that, although he had not yet seen his betrothed, he was deeply in love with her—an *amour courtois* statement that deceived no one. Then his portrait arrived: but nothing more was said of the marriage—and a rumour reached England that King Ferdinand had made a separate truce with Louis XII.[19]

Henry was enraged; once more, Fuensalida managed to soothe his injured pride. Visiting Mary in June of this year, the Spaniard took care that his report should be read by her brother. 'I have never seen so beautiful a lady,' he wrote to Ferdinand, 'or one so exquisite in dancing and walking.' She was lively, he added, but not learned. Distressed to find her portrait of Charles a poor likeness, he praised his looks to the Princess, who seemed to enjoy hearing about her future husband.[20] Then the Franco-Spanish truce was made public. Henry at once announced that his sister's betrothal must be dissolved, and the Duc de Longueville, who was a guest at the English Court, suggested that Louis, now a widower, should replace the Prince of

Castile. Louis's offer followed, with promises of a much larger settlement than that of Ferdinand and Maximilian, and an Anglo-French truce was proposed.

Yet there were complications. The English people objected to their beautiful Princess's marriage with an hereditary enemy, and petitioned against it. Henry's pro-Spanish ministers pointed out that an invalid of fifty-two — 'a feeble and pocky man', according to Fuensalida[21] — was a poor substitute for the youthful heir to the Austro-Spanish Empire. Henry then made it a condition that when Louis died, Mary should return to England with her dowry and all the jewels bestowed on her by the French. Finally, before any documents were signed, she must publicly renounce the Prince of Castile.

At eighteen, Mary's character was fully developed and set. Although not intellectual, she was quick-witted and independent — and as obstinate as any of her family. She differed from them in her truthfulness, and an incapacity to deviate or to deceive herself. She now met Henry with a strong and wholly unexpected objection to the French alliance. She detested the thought of marriage with a valetudinarian three times her age; she did not want to leave England. Henry ordered her to obey him. She wept and pleaded. At last she gave in — on one condition. When Louis died — and that would surely be soon — she must be allowed to take a second husband of her own choosing. She mentioned no names; and Henry, it seems hastily and perhaps absently, agreed. So Mary got her way. She did not tell her brother that she had fallen in love with his best friend, whom she intended to marry as soon as she was free.

---

## NOTES

1  *L. & P. Henry VII*, vol. I, p. 400.
2  Mattingly, p. 84.
3  T. Miller, *The Castle and the Crown*, p. 249.
4  Ibid.
5  Green, vol. V, p. 4.
6  Miller, p. 250.
7  *L. & P. Henry VII*, op. cit., p. 196.
8  Mattingly, p. 91.
9  *L. & P. Henry VII*, op. cit., p. 206.
10  Green, op. cit., pp. 11–13.
11  Ibid.
12  Ibid.
13  *L. & P. Henry VIII*, vol. I, pt. 2, p. 2.
14  Strickland, *English Princesses*, p. 3.
15  *L. & P.*, vol. I, pt. 1, p. 2.
16  Mattingly, p. 91.
17  Green, vol. V, p. 18.
18  *L. & P.*, vol. I, pt. 2, p. 512.
19  Op. cit., p. 186.
20  Op. cit., p. 1185.
21  Hall, p. 569.

# II

## *Queen of France*

CHARLES BRANDON, whom Henry VIII created Duke of Suffolk in 1514, was twenty-nine when Mary's betrothal to Louis XII came under discussion. His father, a country squire, who had joined Henry VII in 1485, became that monarch's standard-bearer, and achieved the rather gloomy distinction of being killed by Richard III's own hand at Bosworth Field. Henry VII then adopted Charles, and he was brought up with the royal children. The orphaned boy and the future Henry VIII became close friends, and with the latter's accession Brandon received a series of titles and places.

He and Henry looked much alike, and had some tastes in common. The Duke, a tall, broad, red-haired athlete, was practical, energetic and jolly — what would now be described as an extrovert leader of men; but he was almost illiterate, and had neither moral courage nor subtlety of mind. As he reached maturity his power over women was marked by a trail of broken marriages which left him a free man when Mary fell in love with him.

In the reign of Henry VII Brandon had begun by marrying Anne, the daughter of Sir Anthony Browne; this union was annulled on the grounds of consanguinity. He then married a rich widow, Margaret Mortimer, discarding her through a multiplicity of grounds in order to re-marry Anne Browne, by whom he had two daughters. When she died, in 1512, Brandon was contracted to an heiress, Elizabeth Grey; this marriage also, was annulled. So, although legally single, Brandon had two ex-wives in his background, when he and Mary Tudor came to a secret understanding.

In 1513 he accompanied Henry to France as Squire of the Body and Marshal of the army, returning, with the King, via Lille, to be entertained by the Archduchess Margaret. Described to that lady as 'a second king', by one of her gentlemen,[1] Suffolk, encouraged by his master, made flirtatious advances to her during the visit, and greatly distinguished himself in the jousts celebrating Henry's arrival at her

Court. The King then suggested that his much married favourite should become the Archduchess's husband, and urged her to accept him. In a private conversation between the three, Suffolk knelt and offered Margaret a diamond ring. She laughed, and accused him of stealing it—'Vous êtes un larron,' she said. Suffolk, whose French was poor, asked Henry to translate the joke, which was Margaret's way of politely turning down an impertinent approach. Henry persisted, presents were exchanged, and Margaret's courtiers began to say that she was going to marry the Englishman. Seriously displeased, she desired Henry to contradict these rumours, which he did after he and Suffolk reached England.[2] Yet his attempts to secure the Archduchess's hand for his friend may have encouraged the Duke in thinking that, when Mary was widowed, he might become her husband. As Henry proceeded to transfer his sister from Prince Charles to Louis XII, this question did not arise—except in Mary's mind. There it remained. Neither Henry nor any of his intimates—not even Wolsey, now a predominant figure—then had the least suspicion of the Princess's plans and hopes when, in the presence of Suffolk and a number of other nobles, she annulled her contract to the Prince of Castile. This ceremony took place in July 1514.

The Duke was cautious; he made no public advances to the Princess; but it seems that, somehow, he managed to convince her of a devotion which cannot have been entirely disinterested. Sure of Henry's favour and of his apparently unlimited tolerance, Suffolk had no notion of what his understanding with Mary would entail, nor of how perilous his circumstances were to become. No doubt he assumed that her marriage to Louis would last some years; and during that time anything could happen. She might die in childbirth; he might be killed in the next war, or in a tournament.

Meanwhile Henry, resolved that this alliance should not meet with the fate of that to Prince Charles, hurried on the arrangements, and on August 13th, 1514, the proxy marriage was celebrated at Greenwich. The Duc de Longueville, as bridegroom, and attended by his suite, was ushered into an upper room hung with cloth of gold, where Henry, Katherine and their courtiers, of whom Suffolk was the principal, were waiting to receive him.

Mary then made her entrance. She wore a petticoat of pale-grey satin, with a purple overskirt, and glittered with jewels, of which the most conspicuous was Louis's wedding gift of the 'Miroir de Naples', a diamond valued at 60,000 crowns. After High Mass and a Latin

sermon preached by the Archbishop of Canterbury, the marriage
vows were exchanged and the ring was placed on the Princess's
finger.[3] The ceremonies did not end there. To make assurance
doubly sure, Henry had arranged that symbolic intimacy should take
place. Surrounded by his court and the foreign ambassadors—all
except the Spanish, who had not been invited—he talked informally
with de Longueville, while Mary left to change her dress for a robe
giving the effect of a nightgown. When she reappeared, Katherine
and her ladies led her to a state bed, on which she lay down. De
Longueville then advanced, pausing at the foot of the dais to take off
one of his scarlet boots, thus revealing a bare leg. Lying beside the
Princess, he touched one of her legs with his naked foot. His gentlemen then replaced his boot, and he came down into the hall, while
Mary retired again to change into a ball-dress.[4]

The ladies dined apart from the men, rejoining them for a dance,
which lasted two hours and became so animated that Henry and his
courtiers had to throw off their velvet doublets.[5] Next day, de
Longueville left for France, so as to join Louis in welcoming the
bride, whose departure was set for September 15th. During the next
three weeks the Parisians prepared an elaborate and magnificent
reception for 'the bedding of the Queen's Grace with His Most
Christian Majesty of France'.[6] Mary was to be accompanied by eighty
gentlewomen headed by Lady Guildford, some four hundred male
attendants and a company of archers.

By this time, the Earls of Worcester and St John had been established as Henry's representatives at the Louvre. Here they found the
semi-invalid King in a state of high excitement. He had heard much
of Mary's beauty, and was determined, he told Worcester, to make
her fond of him. That nobleman kept his opinion of Louis's appearance to himself. The Venetian ambassador did not need to do so. His
reports to the Signory create a picture of an able, kindly but rather
pathetic bridegroom who, entering on a third marriage, is dimly
aware that he may fail to please.

The contrast between Suffolk's handsome virility and gallant
manners and poor Louis's tottering approach and mumbled address
(he had lost many teeth and dribbled when he spoke) makes sad
reading. Unlike Suffolk, Louis was intelligent, sophisticated and
witty; his people called him their good father. As a young man, he
had been successful in warfare and with the sex; in middle life he
achieved his aims through unscrupulous diplomacy. Now, worn out

after a reign of fifteen strenuous years, he was greatly enfeebled and
in constant pain from gout and what seems to have been a weak heart.
He had two daughters, the elder of whom, Madame Claude, was
married to his cousin and heir-presumptive, the Duc d'Angoulême,
later Francis I, a showily brilliant youth of twenty, whom Louis
detested, partly because Francis was insolently sure of the succession;
for it seemed unlikely that the King and Mary would produce an
heir. Yet Louis was determined to succeed in this last venture, and
had prepared the way, he told Worcester, by collecting a mass of
jewels for his Tudor bride. Taking the envoy into his cabinet, he
showed him a staggering display. 'My wife', he said, chuckling, 'shall
not have these [all] at once, for I will have many — and at divers times
— kisses and thanks for them.' 'I assure you', Worcester wrote to
Wolsey, 'the King thinketh every hour a day until he seeth her; he is
never well but when he hears her spoken of. I make no doubt she
will lead a good life with him, by the Grace of God.'[7]

Mary disregarded this account of her bridegroom's efforts, and
refused to correspond with him. Eventually, urged by de Longueville
—'the King is very much disappointed that you do not write'—she
scribbled a few notes, promising to love him 'as heartily as I can', and
acknowledging his letters 'with great joy'.[8] To become a queen was
her *métier*; but she still believed that the assignment would be short,
and trusted in her brother's promise about her next marriage. No
doubt she took pleasure in the splendour of her trousseau and
appointments, which far surpassed those provided by Henry VII for
her elder sister.

In fact, no other English princess had ever acquired such a quantity
of jewels. In addition to the 'Miroir de Naples', Louis gave her forty-
six diamond-and-ruby ornaments, seven pearl necklaces and a
number of girdles and bracelets. Henry presented her with sixteen
dresses of cloth of silver and gold in the French style, six in the
Italian, and a quantity of sapphires, rubies and diamonds in the form
of Tudor roses and fleurs-de-lys. Mary's slender height, fashionable
pallor and streams of golden hair could well support these glories;
gazing at the result, her brother's courtiers had no need, almost
forgot, to flatter. Meanwhile, the people mourned her departure, and
the Spanish were deeply chagrined. The Archduchess Margaret's
disappointment burst forth in a sobbing fit; and the fourteen-year-
old Prince Charles rated his ministers for their negligence.[9]

Apparently resigned, Mary resumed her French lessons with her former tutor, John Palsgrave, author of *Éclaircissements de la Langue Française*, and practised conversation with a Flemish maid of honour, Jane Popincourt, who had become the mistress of the Duc de Longueville during his captivity in England, and was to accompany her to the Louvre. Horrified at this appointment, which had been engineered by de Longueville, Worcester informed Louis XII of the young lady's 'evil life'. 'As you love me,' the King exclaimed, 'speak of her no more, I would she were burnt!' and her name was struck off the list of Mary's attendants, much to the Princess's disappointment; she seems to have been consoled by Lady Guildford, on whom she entirely depended.[10]

So the day came for her to set forth. With the King and Queen, she and her suite were established at Dover Castle. In the bay nine galleons were anchored ready to receive them, and a group of French merchants had crossed the Channel to kiss her hand. She spoke to them in fluent French, and they described her to the Venetian ambassador as 'a nymph from Heaven', and the most beautiful creature they had ever beheld.[11]

Then a gale sprang up and a storm raged for fifteen days and nights. Mary became increasingly depressed; when at last the wind changed and she went down to the shore, she sobbed and cried, clinging to her brother and sister-in-law. Katherine, equally distressed, failed to comfort her. As Henry took her in his arms, she reminded him of his promise that, once widowed, she should return to marry whom she chose. Hurriedly assenting—he disliked scenes, and too much time had already been wasted—he kissed her and said, 'I betoken you to God, and to the fortune of the sea, and the governance of the King your husband.'[12]

On this rather ominous farewell Mary embarked. No sooner had the fleet stood out to sea than the wind changed again and another storm arose. On October 4th, after four days of misery and danger, they sighted Boulogne. By this time Mary's ship had been separated from the rest and was grounded on a sand-bank. She and some of her attendants were then lowered into a rowing-boat, but it was impossible for her to land, until the tallest and strongest of her gentlemen, Sir Christopher Gervase, took her in his arms and fought his way through the surf to the beach.[13]

Soaked through and incapacitated by sea-sickness, Mary entered her kingdom in a state of collapse. Some hours passed before the remainder of her suite, headed by the Norfolks, were able to join her.

On October 6th the procession formed and set off for Abbeville.
There Louis came to meet her, informally, and dressed, according to
custom, for hawking — a sport he had long abjured for reasons of
health.[14]

Some miles from the city Mary was received by Francis d'Angoulême and a party of nobles. Riding a white palfrey, and dressed in
white and silver with a jewelled coif and a red velvet hat, she was
followed by her suite and half-a-dozen chariots carrying her plate,
chapel furniture and tapestries. Presently Louis, accompanied by
Madame Claude, two hundred ladies and all his courtiers, was seen
approaching, and Mary prepared to descend. It then began to rain,
and the canopy under which she had been riding was drenched before
she and the King met; fortunately, her brocade gown was so stiff as
to keep its shape when she attempted to kneel, and was quickly raised
by the King, who kissed her cheek; flinging his arm round her neck,
he pushed her hat to one side, where it remained. As this ended their
private meeting, he then had to remount and ride before her into
Abbeville for their public appearance. When he turned for another
look, Mary kissed her hand to him, a gesture some of the onlookers
found rather too informal.[15]

Louis's appearance must have been a sad confirmation of her fears.
As shown in the illuminated manuscript of an eye-witness, Pierre
Gringoire (now in the British Museum), he is red-faced, bloated and
porcine; his hunched posture gives the impression of an asthmatic
invalid. In six studies of him and Mary, the artist seems to have been
struck by her downcast expression; although it is clear that throughout a series of processions she behaved correctly, she could not
achieve the radiance expected of a bride.[16]

At Abbeville, Mary was escorted by Francis and Madame Claude
to a house adjoining the King's. Next morning at seven o'clock, she
met him in the garden separating their lodgings, and two hours later
they proceeded through the city to the Cathedral. 'Her beauty', the
Venetian ambassador informed the Signory, 'exceeds description,'
adding that its only flaw was an extreme pallor. 'But,' he continued,
'she is a Paradise — tall, slender, grey-eyed, courteous and well-
mannered.' He was much impressed by the splendour of her suite,
and by the ruby-and-diamond necklace which Louis gave her when
they talked in the garden.[17]

For the wedding, Mary wore cloth of gold, trimmed with ermine
and blazing with diamond clasps; her hair fell to her waist beneath a

coronet of rubies and sapphires. 'She looked more like an angel than a human creature,' says an English observer, 'and the French so gazed at their new Queen's beauty as they could not cast their eyes from her.'[18]

At some point during the wedding banquet Louis gave Mary 'a marvellous great pointed diamond' and two cabochon rubies three inches long. A ball followed, lasting till midnight, for which the King, who had not danced for years, took the floor. In some pain, he then retired to his bedchamber to wait for his bride, whom Madame Claude and her ladies escorted to an adjoining room, where she was undressed and re-robed for the consummation of the marriage.

There was then no question of privacy in an event of European importance. Next morning, Louis, 'very joyous and gay', described his prowess to the Venetian ambassador in terms for which that functionary had to provide a euphemism. His Majesty *'crossed the river three times'*, he wrote, 'and could have done more —' rather maliciously adding that the King found himself unable to precede his wife into Paris, as had been arranged. They remained in Abbeville for three weeks.[19]

Three days after the wedding, Louis dismissed all Mary's attendants, with the exception of four maids, some half-dozen gentlemen, a physician, a secretary and a chaplain. He had taken a particular dislike to Lady Guildford, who left Abbeville almost before Mary realized what was happening. Her tears and prayers being of no avail, she dashed off a letter to her brother.

There was now no one left, she began, to advise her, or in whom she could confide. Without Lady Guildford, she was desperate. 'And if it be by any means possible, I humbly require you to cause my said Mother Guildford to repair hither once again.' Mary blamed Norfolk —just as her sister Margaret had, eleven years before—for yielding to Louis's decisions and failing in his duty towards herself. 'Would God', she concluded, 'my Lord of York [Wolsey] had come with me, in the room of Norfolk.' Knowing that Henry seldom answered letters, Mary wrote to Wolsey in the same strain. Her only hope lay in the fact that Lady Guildford was waiting at Boulogne; she believed that Wolsey might persuade Louis to let her return to Abbeville.[20]

In a long and tactfully phrased letter, Wolsey asked Louis to reconsider this dismissal, concluding, 'I have no doubt, Sire, that when you know her well, you will find her a wise, honourable and discreet lady.' He then wrote to Worcester, asking him to plead with the King.

As the Norfolks had now left for England, Worcester was able to speak frankly to Louis, who made it clear that his dismissal of Lady Guildford had not been entirely unreasonable.[21]

Louis explained that from the moment of his wife's arrival Lady Guildford had taken it upon herself to rule her mistress. She refused to leave him and Mary alone, with the result that his efforts to establish a relationship with the Queen were continually frustrated. 'My wife and I', he told the ambassador, 'be in as good and perfect love as ever any two creatures can be—and we are both of an age to rule ourselves.' He added that he alone must rule his bride, who would, he thought, have become attached to him at once, if Lady Guildford had not stood between them. Thus, it had been impossible for him to 'be merry'—i.e. to court Mary—although 'never man doth better love his wife than I do.' While admitting that his health prevented a sustained courtship, he pointed out that Lady Guildford had curtailed their intimacy; it was therefore obvious that, if she had stayed, the marriage would have failed; now, he could hope for an heir.[22]

Several days passed before Worcester was able to raise the subject with Mary—and then, much to his surprise, he found that her attitude had changed. All her life, Lady Guildford had ordered her comings and goings; now, as Queen of France, she was not only in sole command of the attendants given her by Louis, but free to behave as she wished. Louis did not trouble her unduly; she was beginning almost to like him. 'I love Lady Guildford well,' she told Worcester, 'but I am content that she come not, for I may well be without her—for I may do what I will.' She was, however, much concerned for her English attendants' salaries; then, with Worcester's help, she arranged for them to be recompensed in London, and through Wolsey obtained a benefice for her chaplain.[23]

The complaints of the dismissed suite were loud and bitter. As soon as they reached England, they so publicized their chagrin as to cause angry talk of French meanness and brutality. It was rumoured that grief and disappointment had caused the more sensitive to collapse—and that this had, in some cases, resulted in madness. Others, Hall solemnly declares, remaining destitute, had 'died by the way'.[24]

Within a day or two of their departure, Mary found herself becoming agreeably intimate with several French ladies, of whom the most engaging was Marguérite de Valois, Francis's brilliant poet-sister, known at Court as the Tenth Muse. Then Louis retired to bed with a severe attack of gout—and Mary's heart was touched by his sufferings and his kindness to herself. She sat by him most of the day, and did her best to distract and comfort him, while he, Worcester told Henry VIII, 'makes as much of her as it is possible for any man to make of a lady'. Mary then wrote cheerfully to Wolsey about the attentions paid her by Francis, his wife and their courtiers.[25]

On October 26th Louis was well enough to begin the journey to Paris. He and Mary made their first stop at Beauvais, where they remained for several days so that he could rest. On the 27th they were joined by a party of English nobles, come to congratulate them on Henry's behalf. They were headed by Suffolk. He at once asked for, and obtained, a private audience with the King and Queen.

---

## NOTES

1  Green, vol. V, p. 18.
2  L. & P., vol. I, pt. 2, p. 1186.
3  Ven. S. P., vol. II, p. 199.
4  Green, op. cit., p. 30.
5  Ven. S. P., ibid.
6  Op. cit., p. 193.
7  H. Ellis, Historical Letters, vol. I, p. 237, 2nd Series.
8  Green, op. cit., p. 34.
9  Ven. S. P., op. cit., p. 199.
10  Ellis, vol. II, p. 40, 2nd Series.
11  Ven. S. P., op. cit., p. 95.
12  Hall, p. 570.
13  Ibid.
14  Ven. S. P., op. cit., p. 202.
15  Op. cit., pp. 202–4.
16  Vespasian MS. B. 11.
17  Ven. S. P., ibid.
18  J. Speed, Chronicle, p. 75.
19  Ven. S. P., ibid.
20  L. & P., op. cit., p. 1413.
21  Green, op. cit., p. 48.
22  Ellis, vol. I, pp. 244–7, 2nd Series.
23  Ibid.
24  Hall, p. 570.
25  Ellis, ibid.

# III

## *Suffolk's Diplomacy*

IN THE weeks that passed between Mary's proxy marriage to Louis and her departure for France, her intention of eventually marrying Suffolk had become known to Henry VIII. Although he had promised to allow it, he would have had no scruple about going back on his word if the political situation made it necessary. As Queen-Dowager of France, Mary would be a trump card, and her second marriage a European issue; for Henry knew that, once widowed, she would again head the Austro-Spanish list of brides for Prince Charles. Yet this consideration was not paramount, as compared with two others: the first being Henry's resolve that when she did return — and the reports of Louis's health gave the impression that this might be sooner than had been expected — she should bring back her settlement and all the jewels given her by her husband. Finally, Henry had to consider her marriage with his friend; here, his plans were known to Wolsey alone. He had no objection to the union, as such; but it must be viewed, both by his sister and the Duke, as a possibility, or rather, a goal, which they could only achieve under conditions profitable to Henry's power and detrimental to England's ancient enemy.

So it was that Suffolk — whose rival, Norfolk, was busily intriguing against him — came to Beauvais as Henry's representative, on the understanding that he was to help cement the rather precarious alliance between England and France. No one could tell how much longer Louis might live, or if Mary was likely to become pregnant; and if Francis succeeded, war could break out again. The situation being fluid, Suffolk must behave as a courtier — a mere envoy — with whom Mary should have no personal dealings.

Suffolk himself was more than willing, indeed eager, so to present himself. His hopes of marriage with Mary were, at this time, subordinated to his desire to please Henry, to impress Wolsey with his abilities as a diplomat and to defeat Norfolk's faction. His account of his reception by Louis shows that he took the greatest possible care

LOUIS XII *(artist unknown)*

to maintain a correct, and therefore distant attitude towards the
princess whose heart he had won before she became a queen.

Summoned by Louis's herald, Suffolk was conducted to his bedside
to find Mary sitting by him. After he had made his reverences and
knelt down, Louis signed to him to rise, kissed him on both cheeks
and held him in his arms 'a good while'. 'You are heartily welcome,'
he began. 'How doth mine especial good brother, whom I am so much
bound to love above all the world?'[1]

Suffolk replied suitably, adding that he had been commanded to
convey his master's thanks for Louis's 'honour and love' of the Queen.
'I will spare nothing to do His Grace's pleasure,' Louis replied. 'I
reckon that I have of him the greatest jewel that ever one prince had
of another —' and after some further compliments, Suffolk was dismissed. In his report to Henry, he stressed the perfect propriety of
Mary's — and therefore of his own — behaviour, 'the which,' he added,
'I assure Your Grace, rejoiceth me not a little. *Your Grace knows
why* —' thus making it clear that any rumours of himself and Mary
maintaining a secret agreement were false; for he knew that Norfolk
would hasten to use such reports against him. He then described
Mary and Louis as a devoted and happy couple, concluding, 'And
so says all the noblemen in France that have seen her demeanour.'
Mary kept her thoughts to herself; and Henry sent Louis an affectionate letter, ending, 'Our will, pleasure and intention is that ... she
should persevere from good to better, if she wish and desire to have
our love and fraternal benevolence.' Meanwhile, Suffolk wrote to
Wolsey, begging him not to heed the Norfolks' suggestion that he
should return. 'I know', he added, 'their drifts.'[2]

With remarkable self-control, Mary did persevere. Preceded by
Louis, Suffolk, the Marquess of Dorset and a number of French and
English nobles, she left Beauvais for her coronation at St Denis; this
would inaugurate her entry into the capital. Watched by her husband
from a concealed alcove, she was conducted by Francis to the high
altar to be anointed and enthroned. The crown-matrimonial having
been placed on her head, she remained seated during the celebration
of High Mass. The huge diadem was unbearably heavy; seeing her
discomfort, Francis, who stood behind her chair, held it over her till
the end of the ceremony.[3]

Next day, she and Louis entered Paris in state — a process lasting
some six hours — pausing to receive addresses and hear recitals of
indifferent verse, accompanied by a wealth of symbolic pageantry.

12

Angels, pagan deities, saints, heroes and kings, with their attendant
Virtues and Graces, descended from cardboard heavens and castles,
pouring out songs of praise. The Parisians were in raptures; Louis,
too exhausted to attend the banquet, which lasted almost as long as
the procession, retired to the Palais de Tournelles in the Place
Royale.[4]

In the great hall of what later became the Palais de Justice, Mary
sat down to the sound of trumpets with Madame Claude, Marguérite
de Valois and their ladies to a display of culinary 'subtleties' so contrived as to move before being served. These included a phoenix
which, beating its wings, lit the fire that consumed it; the fight of a
cock and a hare; and St George on horseback leading a damsel.[5] Next
day, she attended Mass and a reception given by the City fathers
before joining Louis, who was still prostrate. Then followed the
climax, the ultimate splendour of welcome, a tournament, in which
the English nobles were to meet the chivalry of France. It at once
became obvious that knightly courtesy was to have no share in a
series of furious contests.

Knowing that Suffolk was one of the most celebrated jousters in
Europe — his combats with Henry VIII, who equalled him in strength
and skill, had been compared to those of Hector and Achilles —
Francis determined that he and Dorset, another champion, must be
defeated. (Then, as today, there was no question of what is now called
sportsmanship or seemly behaviour in international competitions.)
Francis, a lightweight athlete, appears to have believed that his team
was the more accomplished, and himself sure to excel. He therefore
opened the proceedings by giving Suffolk a personal challenge as soon
as Mary and Louis had taken their places.

Their entry caused some delay, partly because the greater number
of the spectators now had a close view of their new Queen for the
first time. Again and again she had to stand up, to be greeted by prolonged cheering, while Louis lay on a couch at her side. Advised by
Wolsey, she had had her hair dressed in the French fashion, and
looked so beautiful that 'all wondered', according to the chronicler,
and would not let her sit down. When she did, Francis and his
knights, preceded by the heralds and followed by Suffolk and Dorset
with theirs, made the tour of the arena; as they passed the royal
stand they bowed so low that their plumed helmets touched their
stirrups.[6]

Suffolk then ran fifteen courses, and was the victor in all but two.

Next day, and the day after that, he and Dorset were equally successful. Francis, wounded in the hand, had to retire, together with two of
his best men, whose hurts were more severe, and may have been
fatal. By the end of the fourth day, it looked as if the French were
thoroughly beaten.[7]

But Francis, ever resourceful, had in reserve a gigantic German
mercenary disguised as a French knight, whom he now sent into the
lists in the certainty that not even Suffolk would be able to withstand
him. 'The same great German', says Hall, 'came to the bars fiercely …
and bare his spear to the Duke of Suffolk with all his strength.' Suffolk
then so belaboured him that he was unhorsed, and the combat continued on foot. Forcing the huge creature against the barriers,
Suffolk battered and pummelled him, until, seeing the blood stream
from his visor, the judges intervened. A rather awkward situation was
created by the fact that the German dared not raise his helmet and
thus reveal his employer's underhand methods; so he was smuggled
out of the lists. Mary then gave the prizes to the English team.[8]

Louis was privately delighted by his cousin's humiliation. 'Ce grand
gaillard gâtera tout,' he said to Mary, when Francis's ferocity defied
the laws of chivalry. Later, in Francis's presence, he rallied Suffolk
and Dorset about bringing their French allies to shame, and Mary
joined in his teasing.[9] By this time, Francis's courtly approaches to
her had become rather warmer than custom required – or his stout,
plain little wife could approve. He masked his amorousness by
addressing Mary as his mother, and was always at her side, until his
real mother, Louise of Savoy, the only person of whom he stood in
awe, intervened. His anger against Suffolk died down; and he chose
to ignore Mary's shrinking reception of his gallantries.

The jealousy of Madame Claude, Louis's increasing ill-health and
Mary's ignorance of French etiquette began to worry her. She therefore asked Suffolk and Dorset to consult with her husband's ministers
about advising her, so that she might 'best order herself to content
the King'. The Duc de Longueville and the Bishop of St Pol were
chosen to 'counsel her on every behalf', and she reported this arrangement to her brother in a grateful and contented letter.[10] The English
nobles then left – all but Suffolk, who, as Ambassador Extraordinary,
remained to discuss Henry's 'secret business' with Louis. He was
thus constantly entertained by Mary – sometimes in her husband's
absence – 'which charge', says a French contemporary, 'he undertook
willingly, for … he did not wish ill to the sister of his master.'[11]

These interviews took place at St Germain-en-Laye, where Louis
had planned a series of hunting expeditions. He was now sufficiently
rested — so he believed — not only to dance and hunt, but also to adapt
his early hours to those kept by his wife. 'He was not man for such a
thing,' according to an observer, 'but he deceived himself,' and so
defied the orders of his physicians. Eventually, he had to let Mary
receive a series of congratulatory visits in Paris, while he stayed in the
country. In the evenings she returned, to sing and play to him, and
they seemed to be on good terms. But, the Spanish ambassador told
Wolsey, 'Charon will soon carry him in his boat,' unkindly adding that
His Majesty's habit of licking his lips and swallowing the spittle had
much increased. The Venetian envoy described him as an old, sick
man, whose senile infatuation for his lovely young wife would soon
end his days.[12]

On December 14th, 1514, Suffolk returned to England, and Louis
and Mary left for Paris, where, Louis wrote to Henry, 'She so con-
ducts herself towards me that I know not sufficiently how to praise
her — I ever more love, honour and hold her dear.' He concluded with
high praise of Suffolk — 'his virtues, manners and goodwill' — and
wrote enthusiastically about his next visit.[13] Then he commissioned
Mary's portrait. She sat twice to the anonymous artist, wearing a
quantity of pearls, an overskirt of purple velvet furred with ermine and
a gold-fringed amber satin petticoat. Her unbound hair indicates that
she was still a virgin, but this rather startling arrangement may have
been caused by Louis's pride in her beauty. Her gentle kindness to
him did not fail. They were always together, and every day he gave
her some jewel. Then the Venetian ambassador asked for an
audience, in order to present the Signory's gift of diamonds and
pearls. Mary, hearing of it, was looking forward to this new acquisi-
tion; but the prudent Doges, anticipating Louis's imminent death,
told the envoy to keep their present in reserve for the next French
queen.[14]

The Christmas celebrations were curtailed as Louis became weaker.
On January 1st, 1515, a great storm broke over Paris, 'the most
horrible', according to a French chronicler, 'that ever was seen.' In the
afternoon of that day, Louis died in his Palace of Tournelles. He and
Mary had been married eighty-two days.

Robed, crowned and sceptred, he lay there in state till January 10th.
Then his corpse was conveyed, through streets hung with black, to
Notre Dame, and laid beside that of his second wife, Anne of Brittany.

A magnificent monument was set above them, which survived until the Revolution of 1789.

Meanwhile, Mary had retired, according to custom, to the Palais de Cluny. Here, dressed in the white mourning then decreed for Queen-Dowagers of France, she had to receive Francis I every day. On January 13th he asked her if she was pregnant, and she gave him an incoherent answer. On the 27th he asked her again, adding that Queen Claude was expecting a child. Bursting into tears, Mary replied that she was not, 'I know of no other King [of France] but you!' she sobbed out.[15] She had already written to Henry and Wolsey in desperation—what was she to do? When might she come home? Francis then said that he was arranging a marriage for her with his cousin, the Duke of Savoy.

On January 29th Suffolk's arrival was announced. Officially on an embassy of condolence, he had been instructed by Henry to prevent the Savoy alliance, and to arrange for Mary's return, while negotiations were set in hand for her next marriage, either to Charles of Castile, or to his grandfather, the recently widowed Emperor Maximilian.

## NOTES

1 *L. & P.*, vol. II, pt. 2, p. 1422.
2 Op. cit., p. 1413.
3 Hall, p. 574.
4 Vespasian MS. B. 11.
5 Green, vol. V, p. 59.
6 Hall, p. 575; Green, op. cit., p. 62,
7 Lord Herbert of Cherbury, *Henry VIII*, p. 53.
8 Hall, p. 578.
9 *L. & P.*, vol. I, pt. 2, p. 1451.
10 Ibid.
11 Green, op. cit., p. 65.
12 *L. & P.*, op. cit., p. 1445.
13 Green, op. cit., p. 71.
14 *Ven. S. P.*, vol. II, p. 216.
15 Green, op. cit., p. 78.

# IV

## Suffolk in Danger

BEFORE Suffolk left for France he was interviewed by Henry and Wolsey at Eltham, and desired to take an oath that he would not propose marriage to Mary. The Duke obeyed without hesitation; his attachment to her was still subordinated to his ambition and to his awe of her brother. (It did not occur to him how soon and in what manner his loyalty would be put to the test.) This precaution was the result of some indiscreet talk, presumably on Suffolk's part. By the time his embassy left England, most of Henry's courtiers knew that he had intended to ask for the Queen-Dowager's hand.

A few days after King Louis's death Henry told Mary to refuse all offers of marriage until she knew his wishes, thus indicating that any alliance put forward by Francis was not be be considered. She replied, 'Whereas you require that I should make no promise ... I trust ... you will not reckon me in such childhood.'*

Rejection of Francis's candidates was the least of Mary's difficulties. His personal advances were so persistent that she dreaded his visits, and was constantly in tears. As he had replaced her English attendants with his own people, she was helpless, for his status forbade their intervention; also, her three weeks' retirement as *la Reine Blanche* made it impossible for her to appeal to his mother. At last, she decided to tell him that she intended to marry Suffolk, and thus eliminate Savoy, the Duke of Lorraine (another of his relations) and a liaison with himself. Before she could bring herself to do so, Francis continued his attack with a threat and another advance. If she did not give in, Henry would marry her to Charles of Castile; and once more he proposed to become her lover. Mary then said, 'Sir — I beseech you that you will let me alone, and speak no more to me of these matters. And if you will promise me by your faith and troth, and as you are a

* The contemporary sources for this Chapter and Chapter V are from *Letters and Papers of Henry VII and Henry VIII*, vol. II, pt. 1, pp. 5, 25, 27, 33–4, 46, 48, 52, 67, 73–4, 103, 111, 133, 223.

true prince, that you will keep counsel and help me, I will tell you all my mind.'

Francis agreed. She then told him that she and Suffolk were promised to one another. She also revealed the 'ware words', or secret code they had used before she left England. This convinced him that she was not to be won, either as the bride of a relation, or as his mistress. Concealing his chagrin, he replied, 'I will help you to the best of my power.' Mary said, 'I cannot think but that the King my brother will be displeased with me,' and asked for Francis's help in obtaining Henry's support. He promised to plead with the English King, adding that his mother and his wife would write to him to the same effect.

Francis's sudden change of front was the result of some quick thinking. If Mary married Suffolk, all danger of an Austro-Spanish match would be removed. So he decided to support her, to the point of forcing Suffolk's hand, if need arose.

A few days later Friar Langley, one of Norfolk's employees, came to the Palais de Cluny and suggested that Mary should confess to him. Guessing from whom he came, she refused; he then asked for a private audience, and began, 'It is said in England that you should be married to the Duke of Suffolk. Beware of him, of all men, for he and Wolsey meddle with the Devil, and by the puissance of the said Devil, keep their master subject.' When Mary rejected this attack, Langley went on to say that Wolsey and Suffolk had poisoned Sir William Compton, one of Henry's closest friends. As this courtier had in fact died of the sweating sickness before she left England, Mary angrily dismissed the friar. She remained in great distress.

She then heard that Suffolk, with the invaluable Dean West and Sir Robert Wingfield, had landed in France. They were not in time to attend Francis's coronation at Rheims, but met him at Senlis on February 4th. Suspecting that his treatment of Mary was not as it should be—for his reputation was that of an insatiable lecher—the Dean said, 'Be to her as a loving son to his mother.' 'I may do no less, with my honour,' Francis blandly replied, adding that the Queen-Dowager would vouch for his kindness to her. He then summoned Suffolk to a private audience. Unaware that Mary had cut the ground from beneath his feet, the Duke made his reverence and waited for Francis to speak.

'My lord of Suffolk,' the King began, 'there is a bruit in this realm that you are come to marry with the Queen, your master's sister.'

Very much taken aback, Suffolk replied, 'I hope Your Grace will not reckon so great a folly in me — to come into a strange realm, and marry the Queen of the realm, without knowledge of Your Grace, or of the King my master. I have none such thing,' he continued, in his halting French, 'nor it was never intended, on the King my master's behalf, nor on mine.' 'It is not so,' Francis coolly replied — and as Suffolk began to protest, he went on, 'Since you will not be plain with me, I will be plain with you. The Queen herself hath broken her mind to me, and I have promised her my faith and troth, by the truth of a king, that I will help her, and do what is in me to obtain her desire.' As Suffolk continued in his denials, Francis added, 'And because that you shall not think I bear this in hand [am deceiving you], I will show you some words that you had to Her Grace.' He then repeated part of Suffolk's and Mary's secret code.

Appalled, Suffolk was silenced. Francis went on, 'I have promised that I should never fail you, but help and advance this matter with as good a will as I would for mine own.' Still the Duke remained, as he later told Wolsey, 'abashed', and speechless. Francis continued, 'And because you shall think no less, here I give you in hand' — extending his own — 'my faith and troth, by the word of a king.' Suffolk kissed it, and stammered out, 'I shall displease the King my master.' 'Let me alone for that,' Francis replied. 'I and the Queen [Claude] will so instance your master that I trust he will be content. And because I would gladly put your heart at rest, I will, when I come to Paris, speak with the Queen, and she and I will both write letters to the King your master, with our own hands, in the best manner that can be devised.' Suffolk was then dismissed.

On February 10th West, Wingfield and the Duke were received by Mary at the Palais de Cluny. In the presence of her English attendants, whom Francis had now restored, they told her that Henry had forbidden her to marry again, or to remain in France. She replied, 'I were an unkind sister, if I did not follow His Grace's mind and pleasure. I count every day an hour till I can see His Grace.' Supper was then announced, and West and Wingfield left the room. Mary desired Suffolk to remain.

Her white robes and black velvet hood were very becoming. (The Venetian ambassador, seeing her thus attired, reported her as 'the most beautiful and attractive woman ever beheld', but noted her restlessness; it seemed that she could not keep still.)[1] When Suffolk asked how Francis had treated her, she described that monarch's 'importunate and dishonourable' advances, adding that he had now promised to help her; but, she went on, she might be forced to marry Charles of Castile. Suffolk said nothing. She burst out, 'I would rather be torn in pieces!' and began to cry. ('I never saw woman so weep,' Suffolk told Wolsey.) 'There is no such thing—' he began, but the sobs went on; she would not heed his attempts to soothe her. Then, pulling herself together, she announced, 'I will be short with you, and open to you my pleasure and mind. If you will be ordered by me, I will never have none but you. If you will not marry me—at once—I will never have you, nor never come into England.'

Suffolk was a man of great physical courage; he had proved himself many times—in the lists, and before Tournai and Thérouanne. Yet, though he did love this imperious and passionate creature, he feared her determination almost as much as he feared the wrath of her terrible brother; furthermore, he shrank from breaking his oath. So the man who had beaten down the German giant and faced the French cannon stood aghast. He was trapped. He guessed how cunning old Norfolk would manipulate the coil which now entangled him; he saw the block and the axe being made ready. At last he managed to say, 'If Your Grace would be content—to write to His Grace and obtain his good will—I will be content. Else—I durst not—for I have made His Grace a promise.'

'You are come to 'tice me home,' Mary cried, 'to the intent that I may be married [to Charles] in Flanders. Which I will never—even to die for it! And so I possessed the French King ere you came.'

Between the upper and the nether millstone, poor Suffolk found nothing to say. Mary then remarked—and surely there was in her tone something of her brother's cold menace—'If you will not follow my end, look never after this day to have the same proffer again.' She added, 'I put you in choice, whether you will accomplish the marriage in four days—or else you shall never enjoy me.' Once more, Suffolk reminded her of his oath. She replied, 'If the King my brother is content—and the French King—I will have my desire.' She then repeated her fear of being ' 'ticed' into the Spanish marriage, adding her now-or-never conditions.

In a somewhat inadequate reply, Suffolk consented to an immediate wedding. His first letter to Wolsey describing Mary's proposal ends simply, 'And so she and I was married,'—it seems a few days later, in the little chapel of the Palais de Cluny. There were ten witnesses— all French, for the marriage was not favoured by Wingfield and West

—of whom Francis was one. 'The Queen', Suffolk rather ungallantly informed Wolsey, 'would never let me rest till I had granted her to be married; and so, to be plain with you, I have lain with her heartily, in so much as I fear me that she be with child—' presumably hoping to make their union appear irrevocable. Still in great fear, he had nevertheless committed himself, utterly and completely. He and Mary then set about composing their letters to Henry—a task which threw her, as it did him, into a state of cringing supplication.

Henry had of course anticipated this development. His plan was to put Suffolk in the wrong through his broken oath, and then to give his consent to the marriage, on condition that Mary's French jewels and the revenues settled on her by Louis XII fell into his hands. This bargaining was to be Suffolk's test; his reward would be his master's favour and the enjoyment of Mary's patrimony. If the Duke did not succeed in wresting these properties from Francis, he and Mary would be separated, their marriage annulled and Suffolk arraigned for high treason. It was not necessary for Henry to outline this aspect of the matter; Wolsey could do that. He himself intended to adopt a benign and gracious attitude, while observing the progress of Suffolk's negotiations.

---

NOTES

1 *Ven. S. P.*, vol. II, p. 237.

# V

## *Cloth of Frieze*

THE letters of Mary and Suffolk to Wolsey show that they continued to ask for Henry's permission to marry after they had become husband and wife. (In fact, that private ceremony in the Palais de Cluny would hardly have amounted, in his eyes, to a legal union.) Knowing his sister's strength of purpose, Henry must have guessed that Suffolk would play into his master's hands. This characteristically devious planning was combined with that for the retention of Tournai, which Suffolk had already discussed with Louis XII. Francis I's prestige required the return of that fortress. Henry intended to make him pay for it, not only in cash, but by handing over Louis's wedding gift of jewels, of which the 'Miroir de Naples' was the principal item.

This complicated bargaining would have defeated Suffolk, if he had not been supported by Dean West. Francis also was cunning, but less experienced and over eager to show himself the equal in diplomacy of his predecessor. And he was still afraid of Henry combining against him with Ferdinand and Maximilian by annulling Mary's marriage to Suffolk and giving her to Charles of Castile. So his endeavours to retain her French revenue and jewels were more easily combated than Suffolk had anticipated. The Duke did not grasp all the aspects of his own situation. He only knew that, having broken his word, he was hopelessly in the wrong; but he believed that Wolsey would help him. He did not realize that that minister was merely playing the part of mediator between himself and the King, under Henry's direction, any more than Mary did, when they continued to ask him to obtain her brother's favour.

Mary's principal aim was to shield Suffolk from Henry's wrath by pointing out that it was she who had proposed marriage. 'I know well', she wrote to him, 'that I constrained [the Duke] to break such promises as he made to Your Grace.' Meanwhile, Suffolk implored Henry to forgive him for consenting, and promised the return of Mary's dowry with her plate and jewels, adding, 'If I have not done

my best, it were pity that I lived ... for it is Your Grace that hath
made me and holden me up hitherto ... I trust I shall be found a true
gentleman,' he went on, begged for 'some word of comfort' from his
master, and ended by saying that both he and Mary were ill from
anxiety and suspense.

As this state of mind was just what Henry desired to create, he
maintained it by an ominous silence. Then Wolsey wrote to Suffolk,
at length and reassuringly. He thought that Henry was, on the whole,
in favour of the marriage. But—and this portion of his letter was
underlined—Suffolk had many enemies at Court, who were working
against him. Wolsey was his 'fast friend'; nevertheless, he and Mary
must have patience until the matter of Tournai and all her possessions
had been settled.

Suffolk replied with a frenzied account of his sufferings. His spelling, generally phonetic, now became maniacal, and must have cost
Wolsey some hours of study, as he interpreted 'wosbound' for
husband, 'dyllewar' for deliver and 'dysskrasseun' for discretion.
Meanwhile, Mary reminded Henry that she had married Louis 'for
your pleasure', adding that if she were not allowed to become Suffolk's
wife, she would retire to a nunnery (thus eliminating his disposal of
her hand), 'the which I think Your Grace would be sorry of, and your
realm also'. She followed up this threat by imploring Henry to send
for her—'for my singular desire and comfort is to see Your Grace,
above all things in the world'.

Suffolk then wrote to Wolsey describing Paris as 'a stinking prison
... I and the Queen', he went on, 'would rather be out of the world
than abide his Grace's anger ... For the passion of God ... I would
His Grace would receive us.' He enclosed a note to Henry which
ended, 'My heart is with you—you wot why.'

Suffolk could not begin discussions with Francis I until that
monarch had made his state entry into the capital. With other foreign
envoys, he watched the procession from a stand opposite the Louvre,
while Mary observed it from a private house near by. At the banquet,
Suffolk sat next to the papal nuncio, and was then formally received
by Francis. Some days later, Mary again asked Henry to allow the
marriage, and the Duke told him that 'Her Grace and I shall never
be merry', till they were called home. At last, Suffolk began talks with
Francis, which met with so little success that Wolsey wrote warning him
that Henry would become 'cold and remiss' if the Duke were not more
persistent. Any failure, Wolsey added, 'will rejoice your enemies'.

Some of the jewels were then handed over to Mary; as proof of Suffolk's endeavours, she sent Henry the 'Miroir de Naples', and promised to give him everything Francis let her take away. Hearing of this, Queen Claude made a fearful scene. The 'Miroir de Naples' was the hereditary property of the Queens of France, and must be sent back at once; but Francis, who was offering Henry other lands in return for Tournai, let it go.

As Suffolk's negotiations appeared to be succeeding, Henry decided to step up his demands. The result was a complete volte-face, outlined in a terrifying letter from Wolsey to the Duke. The King now knew about the marriage, and had taken the news 'grievously and displeasantly'. Recalling Suffolk's oath, Henry had exclaimed, 'I would not have believed he had broken his promise, had he been torn with wild horses!' This made Wolsey very anxious; but there was a faint chance, he thought, of Suffolk's regaining favour, if he made Henry a yearly payment of £4,000 during Mary's lifetime. 'I am so perplexed', Wolsey added, 'that I can devise no other remedy … Cursed be the blind affection and counsel that hath brought ye [to the marriage] … Such sudden and inadvised dealing shall have sudden repentance.' He ended by saying that if Francis let Mary keep both dowry and settlements, Tournai might be returned—at a price. But until that was agreed, the guilty couple must remain in France. Meanwhile, Suffolk's danger was 'the greatest ever man was in'.

After talks which lasted till the beginning of April, Francis agreed that Mary should return with her dowry, but not with all the revenues of her French properties; nor was she to keep her plate, nor the remainder of the jewels given her by Louis XII. Later he promised to release a few of these, and to pay back the dowry by instalments. She and Suffolk were to leave Paris on April 16th. In fact, they had caused Francis, his mother and Queen Claude so much trouble that he was anxious for them to go.

Wolsey then informed Suffolk that Henry expected to receive all Mary's dowry, and that he must extract from Francis 200,000 crowns on account, adding, 'This is the way to make your peace … Trust not too much to your own wit.' Meanwhile, the Council, headed by Norfolk's faction, were using Suffolk's marriage to destroy him; they told Henry that the Duke was working against him with Francis, and should be extradited and beheaded. Wolsey's announcement of this attack produced a pathetic letter from Suffolk to his 'most dread and sovereign lord … Alas, Sire … that it should ever be thought or said that I should be [a traitor].' He admitted his fault in marrying Mary, and went on, 'Alas, that ever I did this! For afore this done, I might have said that there was never man that had such a loving and kind master.' In his next letter he declared himself ready 'with most humble heart ... to do with my poor body Your Grace's pleasure', while continuing to haggle with Francis, who promised to disgorge plate and jewels to the value of 100,000 crowns and to pay the expenses of Mary's return journey.

Francis was very angry about the loss of the 'Miroir de Naples', and tried to get it back — 'there is much stickling thereat', Mary told her brother — which caused further discussion and delay. Finally, he allowed her to keep twenty-six large pearls, twenty diamonds, and a number of rings described as 'of no great value' by Sir Robert Wingfield. He accompanied Mary and Suffolk as far as St Denis, and sent a party of nobles with them to Montreuil. When they reached the English colony of Calais, no word had come from Henry, and so they waited for his leave to cross the Channel. Mary then wrote to him with respectful firmness about her determination to stick to Suffolk, adding, 'and the same, I assure you, hath proceeded only of mine own mind, without any request or labour of my said Lord of Suffolk.' Once more, she reminded Henry of his promise that her second husband should be of her own choice, and that her first marriage had been to 'an aged and sickly man ... for the peace of Christendom'.

At last permission came for her and Suffolk to cross, and they reached Dover on May 2nd, 1515. Still they did not know how they would be received, but were reassured by the appearance of Wolsey and a number of courtiers. They then proceeded to Barking, where they were to stay the night at one of the royal manors. And there, surrounded by his Court, was Henry, seemingly in the best of humours, and 'rejoicing greatly', according to an eye-witness, 'at [their] honourable return'.[1]

It was then arranged that Mary and Suffolk should be publicly married at Greenwich on May 13th, and Francis's approval was formally bestowed on their union. But, says Hall, 'against this marriage many men grudged, and said it was a great loss to the realm that she was not married to the Prince of Castile.'[2] Indeed, the English garrison in Calais so resented what they thought of as Suffolk's insolent seizure of the King's sister, that he had had to barricade his house against them, and dared not venture out of doors.

Henry VIII was delighted to welcome his friend — no one else equalled him in the lists, or was a better companion—and celebrated the wedding with a tournament, in which Suffolk excelled himself. Gradually, the general disapproval of the marriage died down, for 'the Duke so behaved himself, that he had the favour of the King and the people [by] his wit and demeanour.'[3] Suffolk then commissioned a portrait of himself and Mary, and, for the first and only time in his life, burst into poetry. His verse was inscribed beneath the painting.

> Cloth of gold, do not despise,
> Though thou be matched with cloth of frieze.
> Cloth of frieze, be not too bold,
> Though thou be matched with cloth of gold.

Grasping and ruthless, Henry yet rejoiced in his friend's triumph and his sister's happiness. They had had to do what he required of them—for he was England. And England must be enriched and glorified by despoiling her ancient enemy. A more brutal ruler would have dissolved the private marriage—a comparatively easy matter—and given Mary to the Austro-Spanish powers. Henry felt himself able to withstand those powers, while threatening Francis with the triple alliance of his kingdom and theirs. Having retrieved the greater part of his expenses over Mary's marriage to Louis, he kept her and her splendid husband to adorn his court and share his pleasures. When Francis continued to demand the return of the 'Miroir de Naples', Sir Robert Wingfield was desired to inform him that it was 'but a small thing', and in any case, Mary's 'own by right'. No doubt Henry seized it for himself; Mary cared little for that, or for the plate and jewels left in France, or about her diminished income. Suffolk was equally carefree, partly because he regarded his promise of yearly payments to his master as one that need not be scrupulously kept.

So Mary Tudor, twice married by proxy and twice in reality, was a Queen-Duchess, and more radiantly beautiful than ever. In July 1515 she became pregnant. She and Suffolk then retired to their estates in East Anglia.

---

## NOTES

1 Green, vol. V, p. 102.    3 Ibid.
2 Hall, p. 582.

# VI

## *Court and Country*

S H E had ordered him to marry her; and he had obeyed at considerable
risk to himself. Thenceforth, she required his compliance with such
of her demands as did not infringe on her brother's; this also she
obtained. Finally, she expected him to be faithful and loving; and
that aspect of their union was shown by the permanently sustained
companionship of a popular and lively couple.

Mary Tudor had all her family's common sense; as long as Suffolk
behaved as became her rank and his—courteously, attentively and
with respect—she could hardly have expected him to love her as
passionately as she loved him. After the dangers he had escaped, he
knew better than to jeopardize his position by neglecting or dis-
pleasing his master's favourite sister; and his adherence to her wishes
was helped by their having many tastes in common. Suffolk had less
heart and was more self-seeking than his wife; his interests lay in
warfare, sports and political power, hers in the country pursuits
hitherto unknown to her, in domesticity and in dressing up for
masques and balls. Both were granted all these things: for a time, at
least.

Meanwhile, their enormous and rapidly increasing debt to Henry
VIII was coolly disregarded. Open-handed, sociable and gay, neither
of the Suffolks had the faintest notion of economy; and both had been
brought up to believe that their expenditure was the responsibility of
the state. Having achieved marriage, they trusted to Henry's favour
to support their standard of living—how, then, could they be expected
to pay him £4,000 a year? Suffolk's numerous properties in the county
from which his title derived were liabilities rather than assets; his
manors in Warwickshire, Hampshire and elsewhere, his London
houses and his suites of rooms at Greenwich, Eltham and Windsor
required an upkeep commensurate with his status as the King's
brother-in-law, minister and marshal of the army. When not at court,
the Duke preferred to hunt and shoot from his Suffolk residences—

MARY TUDOR AND THE DUKE OF SUFFOLK *(artist unknown)*

Westhorpe Hall, Donnington Castle, Wingfield Castle and Lethering-
ham Hall. He owned Castle Rising in Norfolk, and in London the
newly built Suffolk House (which contained two parks and a maze)
and the medieval Palace of Stepney. He and Mary spent more than
half their time in East Anglia, where they lived in rather ramshackle
splendour, enhanced by the adoring loyalty of their tenants and the
eager hospitality of the great abbeys, whose rulers hurried to welcome
them, whenever they and their suite dropped in for a meal or a few
nights.

The Suffolks were presently joined by one of the Duke's daughters,
the Lady Anne Brandon, whom he had placed at the Court of
Margaret of Savoy. This was Mary's doing; she insisted on making a
home for her, while looking round for a suitable husband. Suffolk
had taken little or no interest in his children by Anne Browne; all his
hope was for an heir by the Queen-Dowager of France—whom he
usually referred to in this manner. He had intended, he told the Archduchess, to leave the Lady Anne with her—'but the Queen has so
urged and prayed me to have her, that I cannot contradict her'[1]—so
he was sending two of his gentlemen to bring her home; and at
Westhorpe Hall, Mary's favourite manor, their family life began.
Presently they were joined by Suffolk's second daughter, the Lady
Mary Brandon; a few years later Anne was married to Lord Powis
and Mary to Lord Monteagle.

In the early sixteenth century, Suffolk was a wild, sparsely inhabited county, then, as now, austerely beautiful. When Mary came
to live there, the arts of the Renaissance had not touched its archi-
tecture. All was Gothic: speckled flint churches and abbeys, grey
stone manors, whitewashed, oak-beamed cottages and farms. Like
galleons riding the seas of meadow and marsh, the great monasteries,
battered by gales from the North Sea, dominated the scene. Sprawling
forests alternated with sweeps of barren land, draped, every now and
then, in icy mists from estuaries and rivers. When the traveller left a
town—when the last, low-built house, the last squat tavern had been
passed—he might face an undulating waste, marked here and there
with a half-ruined Norman castle, a church spire, a turreted priory,
or such a manor-house as Westhorpe Hall. And everywhere the
shapes of monks, friars and nuns made a recurrent pattern; for in
East Anglia the list of ecclesiastical buildings ran into three figures.
That superabundance may account for the almost unquestioning
acceptance of the reformed faith in later years; it seems that the

destruction of monastic wealth and power was neither deplored nor withstood; it may even have been regarded as a release.

Enclosure was then limited. Ocean-trading, fishing and sheep-farming constituted Suffolk's most profitable industries, whose owners spoke in a dialect comprehensible only to themselves. So it was that their magnificent Duke, King Henry's comrade, the most envied ornament of his Court, the ruler, and—when it suited him—the champion of some thousands of peasants and small-holders, used two languages: that of the south and that of his own district. His highly individual spelling shows that he sometimes thought and spoke like the humblest of his tenants; this partly accounts for his popularity and fame. Mary became beloved for her charities; but Charles Brandon's legend, that of a warrior, a great hunter and a casually generous landlord, was more enduring. Local sculptors recorded memories of them both. Two heads remain, looking down from the roof of St Edmund's Chapel, in Southwold. Already the Duke has begun to put on weight; a huge, striding figure is hinted at in a carving which must have been a likeness. The portrayal of his wife is conventional, medieval—her head-dress is that of the fourteenth century—and without beauty. It is as if the craftsman, never having seen her, placed her beside him as a matter of form.

Mary's first stay in the country was cut short by her brother's sending for her and Suffolk to join in the Maying from Westminster: an elaborately rustic affair. Early in the morning, she and her husband rode out with Henry, Katherine and their courtiers to Paddington Fields and so to the woods of Shooters Hill. There, Robin Hood, Maid Marian and their troupe (players trained by the Master of the Revels) were waiting for them. When the royal party had dismounted, the chieftain advanced, bowed and began, 'Will Your Grace come into the greenwood, to see how the outlaws live?' Henry turned to the ladies. 'Dare you adventure into the wood, with so many outlaws?' he asked. Katherine replied for them with, 'If it please Your Grace, I am content,' and they were ushered into an arbour by Robin Hood, who announced, 'Sir—outlaws' breakfast is venison, and therefore you must be content with such fare as we use.' Henry was more than content—and they all sat down on the grass for a picnic feast. As they finished eating, a procession of chariots carrying pretty girls emerged from the trees. Then followed dancing and singing.[2]

While Henry went on progress in the West, the Suffolks left London for a reception given by the Mayor and burgesses of Yar-

mouth. They remained in the country till October, and then returned
to Greenwich for the launching of the King's new galleons, headed
by the *Virgin Mary*, a ship carrying 207 guns and accommodation for
a thousand soldiers.

Here the French ambassador, Bapaume, was waiting, in some
anxiety, to speak to Suffolk. Henry had received him with marked
coldness, he said; and his King had been disturbed by the news of
these warlike preparations — what did it portend? The Duke exerted
his charm. 'I am more indebted to the French King than to all but
King Henry,' he said, 'and I will serve him all my life.' The English
people, he then explained, wanted war with France; but His Grace
had no intention of obliging them. He desired peace; and the new
fleet consisted merely of 'pleasure-ships' for the two Queens, who
had dined on board the *Virgin Mary* a few days ago. Another naval
party was then organized, attended by Bapaume and his gentlemen,
who watched Henry act as pilot, in a sailor's dress of cloth of gold,
wearing a gold chain inscribed *Dieu et Mon Droit* with a large whistle,
'which he blew as loud as a trumpet'. Noting the quantities of
artillery, bullets and gunpowder, Bapaume again fell into mistrust,
and asked Wolsey for an explanation. Laying his hand upon his breast,
the minister repeated Suffolk's assurance; then they all went up to the
poop deck for the celebration of High Mass.

When they returned to the palace, Wolsey and Suffolk drew
Bapaume aside and asked him about the remainder of Mary's jewels —
why had they not been dispatched? Before Bapaume could reply,
Wolsey went on to Albany's 'shameful treatment' of Queen Margaret,
adding that if that nobleman left Scotland, then his King would not
consider war. 'His Grace's words', Bapaume replied, 'are gracious
enough — if not misinterpreted — but he has written to my King with
great discourtesy.' Suffolk then suggested that his wife should write
to the Duke of Albany on her sister's behalf; Albany replied to her
entreaties with a gallantry which recalled their brief acquaintance in
Paris.[3]

The Suffolks were then visited by the Venetian ambassador, who
opened the conversation with a congratulatory message — in Latin —
from the Doges. The Duke replied firmly in English. 'I love the
Signory,' he said, and went on to warn the envoy about Francis I.
As the Venetian seemed to have difficulty in understanding him, he
repeated, 'very earnestly' — 'The King of France longs for glory — he
is a rash young man.'[4]

Both the French and the Venetian ambassadors were impressed by
Suffolk's supremacy, and by Henry's dependence on him. Wolsey,
they observed, was paying him and the Queen-Duchess every attention. When that minister's cardinalate was confirmed by the Vatican,
Suffolk took first place (with Norfolk, much to the senior Duke's
disgust) in the procession escorting Wolsey to Westminster Abbey;
with Henry and Katherine, he and Mary were the principal guests
at the Cardinal's banquet that same evening. A few days later, having
asked for a private audience, the Venetian found Henry practising
the new dances with the two Queens and their ladies.[5]

Katherine and Mary, both pregnant, had eagerly renewed their
intimacy; yet the contrast between them was, from the older woman's
point of view, a sad one. Katherine still held her husband's affection,
but she had borne him five dead children and cannot have been hopeful
about the survival of the next one; also, she had lost her looks. On
February 15th, 1516, her only surviving child, the Lady Mary, was
born. The Queen-Duchess's state gave her husband no anxiety; on
March 11th the longed-for heir was born in Suffolk House.

Two days later the baby was christened Henry. Twelve gentlemen
carrying torches lined the corridor ('well gravelled and meetly
rushed') which led to the chapel. The King, Wolsey and an ancient
Plantagenet aunt, Lady Devon, were godparents; some forty esquires,
knights and nobles followed 'the young lord' to the font. Mary's
reappearance at Court coincided with the arrival of the Queen of
Scotland; then she and Suffolk left for the country. Her first visit was
to Butley Abbey, where the prior received her 'with as much honour
as he religiously could'. She rejoined her husband at Westhorpe Hall
to find that Wolsey had sent him a bill for £5,000.

The Suffolks decided to remain where they were, giving Mary's
health (she had had an attack of malaria) as an excuse. They wrote to
Henry, suggesting that he should visit them at Donnington, but
nothing came of this plan. In October 1516 Mary became pregnant
again, and no more was said of Suffolk's debts. Then Queen Katherine
asked them to accompany her on a pilgrimage to Walsingham. They
were setting off to join her at Bury-St-Edmunds, when Lady
Jerningham, one of Mary's attendants, announced that she had
betrothed her daughter to Lord Berkeley, Suffolk's ward, without
asking the Duke's leave, 'which is no little displeasure to me', he
informed Wolsey—and the match was broken off.[6]

On their return from Walsingham Henry sent for Suffolk; but

Mary forbade him to leave without her. A few weeks later the Duke suggested that they should both come to Court, combining their stay with a visit to his lawyers, in order to raise money for part payment of his debt. Permission given, they reached London to find themselves faced with the apprentices' 'Evil May Day' revolution. In July 1517 they returned to Westhorpe for the birth of their second child: a daughter, Frances. The eighteen-month-old Lady Mary was god-mother; she was represented by one of the Queen's gentlewomen, Anne Boleyn, whose elder sister, Lady Carey, had been the mistress of Henry VIII. The Boleyns were related to the Norfolks and the Ormondes; but Sir Thomas's city connections gave them the reputa-tion of climbers, and they never achieved popularity. Mary, who was devoted to Katherine, had resented her brother's relations with Anne's sister; and the rumour (unfounded) that Lady Boleyn, also, had been his mistress, seems to have prejudiced her against the whole family. Suffolk did not share this feeling.

---

## NOTES

1 L. & P., vol. II, pt. 1, p. 298.      4 Op. cit., p. 258.
2 Hall, p. 582.                          5 Op. cit., p. 304.
3 L. & P., op. cit., p. 294.             6 Op. cit., p. 117.

# VII

## Cloth of Gold

As the Boleyns gradually emerged from prosperous obscurity, dis-agreement between Henry and Mary about that family's progress did not immediately arise. Suffolk's affiliation with them was then super-ficial, and tolerated by his wife; for Henry's relationship with the elder sister had come to an end, and his passion for the younger not yet begun. Sir Thomas's power at court was based on the fact that he was Norfolk's brother-in-law; meanwhile, the senior Duke's hatred of Wolsey strengthened his opposition to the Suffolks, who still believed that the Cardinal had saved their marriage.

Shortly after the birth of their second daughter, Eleanor, the Suffolks, with the King and Queen, were Wolsey's guests of honour at the banquet he gave to celebrate the betrothal of the two-year-old Lady Mary to the infant Dauphin in the summer of 1518. A feast, 'the like of which', according to the Venetian ambassador, 'was never given by Cleopatra or Caligula',[1] preceded the appearance of twenty-four masked ladies and gentlemen, dressed in green and gold and led by a couple who were greeted with loyal amazement when Henry and his sister revealed themselves. Everyone then sat down at tables loaded with gold and silver vessels, dishes of comfits and bowls of ducats and dice; after a formidable succession of courses, they danced, resuming their seats for a mime, which opened with the appearance of a man on a winged horse from a castle he described as the rock of peace; he was followed by nine armed couples, set to defeat a band of Turks whom the guests pelted with sugar-plums; then supper was served, and dancing continued till the small hours. The Suffolks returned Wolsey's hospitality with a more modest display a few days later.[2]

In the following week one of Plautus's comedies was performed at Greenwich, after which the Suffolks and Henry retired to change into Egyptian costumes of black and gold. The resultant expense neces-sitated the Duke and Duchess retiring into the country for several months, where again Mary fell ill with a pain in her side. 'She has taken such a fantasy', Suffolk wrote to Wolsey, 'that she should not do well without she should come up to London for remedy, insomuch that she weeps every day, and takes on so, that I am afraid it should do her harm.' Rather than open up Suffolk House, he begged leave to establish her at Westminster—'an it be but one chamber'—enclosing a letter from Mary to the King to the same effect. They both remained at Court while plans for the Field of Cloth of Gold were set in hand. Then Mary's former fiancé, Charles V, arrived at Dover; for this meeting, she and her ladies were given new dresses by Henry, and a series of balls and banquets took place at Canterbury.[3]

Mary appeared in great beauty; and the effect on Charles, who was still a bachelor—he was betrothed ten times before he eventually married a Portuguese princess—caused much comment. Sinking into embittered gloom at the spectacle of what he had missed, he refused to dance, and sat staring at the Queen-Duchess in silent chagrin.[4] He left England in May 1520, a few days before the two Queens, Henry and Wolsey crossed the Channel with a suite of 5,000 persons, 6,000 workmen having preceded them to prepare for the meeting with Francis I. The Suffolks were accompanied by five chaplains, twenty-four ladies and gentlemen, fifty-five servants, and thirty horses with their attendant grooms.[5]

The English Court was established at Guines, and that of Francis at Ardres, a few miles away. Heading their respective armies, the two Kings then met and embraced in the Val d'Or, while their wives remained in the pavilions especially built for them. Mary occupied a suite of three rooms between those of Wolsey and Queen Katherine. Later, dressed in cloth of silver, she walked behind her brother and sister-in-law to meet Queen Claude. As the days went by in a series of masques, jousts, masses and displays of fireworks, she was acclaimed as *la Reine Blanche* by the French, and appeared in a litter bearing King Louis's arms. Thenceforth, she led the dances with Henry, while the other two Queens looked on. The Field of Cloth of Gold was her peculiar triumph, whether she watched the jousts, or visited Queen Claude or talked with Francis. The Venetian ambassador observed that Henry preferred the company of 'the beautiful Lady Mary' to that of his plain and ageing wife.[6]

Meanwhile, Suffolk subordinated himself to Wolsey, holding the basin and towel for the ceremonial washing of the Cardinal's hands.

The Duke of Buckingham, required to share this duty, showed his resentment by spilling water over Wolsey's slippers. Suffolk, who would have cheerfully washed the minister's feet, as long as his protector remained powerful, was one of the peers called to pronounce sentence on Buckingham, when that nobleman's claim to the throne brought him to the block a year later.[7]

Returning via Calais, Henry and Mary spent four days with Charles V and the Archduchess Margaret. Then the Suffolks' finances reached a crisis; and as the Anglo-French peace became shakier, Mary and her husband began to worry about her French revenues. When war broke out in 1522, and the Duke left England to take up his command, she received Charles V at Suffolk House, afterwards retiring to the country; but economy was beyond her. Beset by place-hunters, she distributed presents of land; then she set about re-modelling the gardens at Westhorpe Hall, and entertained the local clergy and nobility, regardless of expense. Suffolk's successes in battle were rewarded by grants of manors from Buckingham's estates; later, the enforced retirement of his armies displeased the King, who refused to see him, until persuaded by Wolsey and Mary to take him back into favour. A tournament celebrated Suffolk's reappearance, during which he came near hideous disaster.

He entered the lists against Henry wearing a new visor which prevented a full view of his opponent. This would not have mattered, if the King had not forgotten to lower his helmet. The appalled spectators, Mary among them, then saw the Duke, deaf to shouts of 'Hold—hold!' charge his master. As the King's helmet fell, smashed to bits, Suffolk reined back, staring in horror. Then he dismounted, flung himself at Henry's feet in tears, crying, 'I will never more run against Your Grace!' and began to disarm. Henry said, 'None is to blame but myself,' ordered Suffolk to remount, and ran six more courses. This escape was followed by an attack, which Norfolk may have engineered; it amounted to an assault on the succession.[8]

Henry's hopes of a son were beginning to fade. After fifteen years of marriage, his only surviving child was the eight-year-old Lady Mary, whom he betrothed to Charles V in 1524. The next heir was James V of Scotland, whose accession would never have been ac-cepted by the English people. The remaining male candidate was Suffolk's nine-year-old boy, whom Henry had created Earl of Lincoln. And now the Duke's marriage to Anne Browne was said not to have been properly annulled, in which case his children by Mary were illegitimate. After a series of hearings, Suffolk proved the authenticity of his original dispensation; but this issue was to recur, on other grounds, five years later.[9] His third wife, Elizabeth Grey, had died before this setback.

More troubles followed. War expenses caused the tax of a sixth on all goods, ironically described as the Amicable Grant. The townsfolk seem to have grumbled and paid; the peasants of East Anglia were so exacerbated by this inroad on their meagre holdings that they rose in strength, and the Dukes of Norfolk and Suffolk had to combine in dealing with them. Norfolk, one of the most corrupt and merciless potentates of his day, endeared himself to his tenants by listening to their protests ('It is our Captain, Necessity, that hath brought us to this,' he was told) and promising to plead for them with the King. Suffolk simply obeyed orders and punished those refusing to pay, until Henry, realizing that this revolt might end in rebellion, rescinded the Amicable Grant, announcing that it had been engineered by Wolsey; he himself, he added, had known nothing of it, and was much distressed for his faithful people. Wolsey thereby acquired the reputation of an ogre, and Norfolk became known as the Good Duke by his tenantry. Rather belatedly, Suffolk championed his dependents, and regained their loyalty as soon as the Grant was cancelled; his wife's careful and unfailing charities helped to restore his popularity.

In 1525 the defeat and capture of Francis I by Charles V at Pavia made it necessary for Henry to write to Queen Louise, who was acting as Regent, about his sister's French revenues and the arrears of her dowry. Eventually, Louise sent Henry 5,000 crowns on account, and promised to pay him this sum twice yearly; she then arranged an annual pension of 875 crowns for the Suffolks themselves. Even so, by the end of 1526 Mary's debt to Henry came to £19,333 6s. 8d. and Suffolk's to £6,519 3s. 11d.[10] Meanwhile, Mary's correspondence with her French friends included Jane Popincourt, who was now installed, presumably as de Longueville's mistress, at the Louvre. That young lady kept Mary informed about Paris fashions, sending her the newest head-dresses, with presents for her daughters.[11]

The third Anglo-French peace was celebrated by an outdoor banquet at Greenwich of great splendour, attended by Mary's ten-year-old namesake and niece. It was observed that the Queen-Duchess took precedence over the heiress to the throne;[12] yet it occured to no one that Henry might be considering the divorce which would result in his daughter's being made illegitimate. He then went on progress through Kent, and stopped for some days at Hever Castle, now occupied by Sir Thomas Boleyn and his family.

Financial worries apart, 1526 had been a happy year for the Suffolks. That to come was to cause a breach between them.

---

## NOTES

1 *Ven. S. P.*, vol. II, p. 462.
2 Ibid.
3 Green, vol. V, p. 122.
4 Herbert, p. 98.
5 Green, op. cit., p. 123.
6 *Ven. S. P.*, vol. III, pp. 14–17.

7 Green, op. cit., p. 125.
8 Hall, p. 674.
9 *L. & P.*, vol. IV, pt. 1, p. 327.
10 *L. & P.*, vol. IV, pt. 2, p. 1225.
11 Strickland, *English Princesses*, p. 53.
12 Green, op. cit., p. 132.

# VIII

## *Taking Sides*

ANNE BOLEYN was in her twenty-first year when Mary realized that Henry's desire for her had become an infatuation, and thus a national issue; for Anne's refusal to be his mistress sprang from her grasp of the dynastic situation. Daring, cool-headed and supremely self-confident, she was playing for the crown-matrimonial of England. As it then seemed, a divorce might be a prolonged and complicated business, but also one based on the precedent of others in royal houses. Neither Henry nor Anne, nor their families, could have foreseen the repercussions of 'the King's Great Matter', nor its effects on the Church of which he eventually became the Supreme — and bigamous — Head.

Queen Katherine had tolerated his affair with Elizabeth Blount, and that with Mary Boleyn. But when, in June 1527, he told her that her marriage with his brother had led them, according to the Scriptures, into a sin for which God had punished them by denying him a male heir, she refused to co-operate. The Levitical dictum, 'If a man shall take his brother's wife, it is an impurity ... they shall be childless', was invalidated, she maintained, by the dispensation obtained from Julius II in 1504, and by the fact that her union with Arthur had never been consummated. She was his wife — of eighteen years' standing — and England's Queen; she would not leave his side. Dressing more elaborately than was her custom, she held her state, and appeared in public as usual. So the struggle which was to last six years began — and Mary Tudor's attitude towards it was uncompromising and sustained.

She was not, like Henry, of a religious temperament; nor had she any interest in or knowledge of the theological problems in which he delighted to exercise his subtlety of mind. She had always submitted to his deviousness and his caprices; but when the position of Queen Katherine, her equal in rank and her most intimate friend, was threatened by a young woman whose father had been a city merchant,

and whom Mary could not, in any case, bring herself to like—then
she took sides against the brother she had once herself defied. She did
not publicize her disapproval; nor does she seem to have considered
the dynastic difficulties, or the chaos which must have resulted if
Henry had died at this time. She saw only the cruelty, the injustice
of his treatment of the Queen. All she could do was to withdraw, not
too conspicuously, from a Court dominated by Norfolk and the
Boleyns. When Henry commanded her to appear, she obeyed, remaining with him for as short a time as possible. It presently became
clear that she was in disgrace.

Suffolk's situation was quite different. As he said himself, Henry
had made him out of nothing, and 'holden him up' in the face of his
enemies and rivals. He could not begin to contemplate withstanding
his master's desires and needs. And so he was drawn into an alliance
with the most formidable of all his adversaries—Norfolk, Anne
Boleyn's uncle, and as it were her manager in the imbroglio of her
relationship with Henry; a management shared, at first, with Wolsey,
who, working for the divorce, planned a French marriage for the
King. The Cardinal obliged Henry by putting an end to Anne's secret
engagement—it never became a betrothal—to Harry Percy. For the
next two years, he visualized her as the King's *maîtresse en titre*. By
the time he realized that both she and Henry were bent on marriage,
he had failed to obtain the divorce, once promised and then withheld
by the unfortunate Clement VII, whom Charles V, Katherine's
nephew, was holding in thrall.

Again, Mary Tudor was not concerned with these developments.
Her love for and loyalty to her sister-in-law continued to prevail;
meanwhile, she accepted, because she could not prevent, Suffolk's
disingenuousness; she may even have sympathized with an attitude
she refused to share. While he, with Anne's father, now Earl of Wilt-
shire, and the Duke of Norfolk, hunted, gamed and supped with
Henry, Mary remained in the country.

In July Wolsey made his first approach to Clement, and was super-
seded by Henry's dispatch of an independent emissary to the Vatican.
In August Suffolk returned to Westhorpe Hall, which he and Mary
left for Butley Abbey, where they stayed for two months. Then the
Duke set off to meet Henry in Essex, first sending his master a
present of a goshawk, with the request that Mary might be received.
Henry refused; and Mary stayed on, perhaps thankfully, at Butley,
where she made a practice of dining out of doors in the hot weather.

Her favourite picnic place was a garden, the especial care of Brother Nicholas. Long afterwards, he remembered her and her ladies being driven indoors by a storm, halfway through the meal, that when she left she gave each monk a sum of money, and presented the abbey with a canopy for the pyx and a vestment chest covered with cloth of gold.[1] She did not attempt to win over her brother; no doubt she believed that his displeasure would pass when he tired of Anne Boleyn, who, sitting at cards with the Queen, was told by her mistress, 'You have good hap to stop at a king, my Lady Anne, but you are not like others, you will have all or none.'[2]

A fearful outbreak of the sweating sickness during the summer of 1528 nearly solved both Anne's and Katherine's problems; a number of courtiers died, and it was rumoured that the 'goggle-eyed whore', as the London fishwives called Mistress Boleyn, had perished in the holocaust, which Henry avoided by moving from one country residence to another, while the Suffolks renewed their visits to the monasteries of Ely, Butley and Eye. In June they were hunting and picnicking at Slaverton and Sholgrove, when news of Cardinal Campeggio leaving Rome to interview Henry and Katherine about the divorce reached them, and Suffolk was summoned to Court, while Wolsey and Campeggio tried, in vain, to persuade the Queen to enter a nunnery. It was then recalled that Suffolk, with other noblemen, had attended Prince Arthur on the morning after his wedding, twenty-seven years ago, and that the boy had said to him, 'This night I have been in Spain.' Katherine stated that during their five months' marriage Arthur had slept in the same bed with her on seven occasions, but that she had been his wife in name only.[3]

The split between Mary and her brother was patched up during the Christmas festivities—stubbornly presided over by Katherine—and the usual series of banquets, Masses and jousts took place. Mary then returned to the country, where she remained until August of the following year.

Suddenly, another attack was made on the legitimacy of her children—this time on the grounds of the Duke's marriage to Margaret Mortimer—and she and Suffolk hurried up to London to consult their lawyers. Margaret Mortimer was still alive, and still—owing to the supposed invalidity of the dispensation allowing Suffolk to remarry Anne Browne—his wife: or so it seemed. Mary at once appealed to the Vatican, and, having obtained proof of the validity of her own marriage to the Duke, set about establishing the legitimacy of her step-daughters. She had both documents attested by the Bishop of Norwich, and copies made for the Suffolk archives. So it was that, in the event of the Princess Mary being declared illegitimate, the little Earl of Lincoln's claim to the throne would be assured.[4]

She and Suffolk then returned to their country pursuits in high spirits; their enjoyment was halted by Suffolk being summoned to appear before the Court of Blackfriars as witness in the hearing of Henry's petition for a divorce. Mary accompanied her husband, presumably hoping to influence him to support the Queen. Apart from Katherine and her ladies, no women were present; and so Mary was spared hearing Suffolk repeat his memories of Arthur's youthful boasting about his prowess as a husband.

In this portion of the evidence, Suffolk was associated with Sir Arthur Willoughby and Thomas Grey, Marquess of Dorset. 'Willoughby, bring me a cup of ale,' the bridegroom had announced, 'it is good pastime to have a wife.' 'Sir, you look well upon the matter,' he was told, and replied, 'Well enough, for one who has been in Spain.'[5] So Suffolk was committed, as became one entirely dependent on the King's favour.

In the final hearing, when Campeggio, supported by Wolsey and under instructions from Rome, refused to give a decision and postponed the next session till October, Suffolk demonstrated his loyalty in a highly dramatic manner. Prompted by Henry, he started up, banged his fist on the table and shouted, 'By the Mass! It was never merry in England while we had Cardinals amongst us!'

With unruffled dignity, Wolsey replied, 'Sir—of all men within this realm, ye have least cause to dispraise Cardinals—for if I, poor Cardinal, had not been, you should have, at this present, no head upon your shoulders, and no tongue wherewith you might make any such brag. You know best what friendship I have showed you,' he continued, as Suffolk remained silent, 'which I have never revealed to any person before now.' 'And therewith', says Cavendish, Wolsey's gentleman usher, 'the Duke gave the matter over, without any word to reply.'[6]

So did not Mary. She abjured controversy; but her attitude was unchanged. She could do nothing for Wolsey, whose downfall, partially engineered by Anne (she had not forgiven him for breaking off her engagement to Harry Percy), was now imminent. When Henry sent Suffolk to the Cardinal for the surrender of the Great Seal, Mary was officially neutral; she and the brilliant minister, who died in 1530, never met again. Meanwhile, her husband's temporary alliance with the Marquess of Dorset was confirmed by the betrothal of the twelve-year-old Lady Frances to Dorset's heir, Henry Grey.

The King then seized York House from Wolsey's estate, renaming it Whitehall, and took over Suffolk House for Anne Boleyn. Neither the Duke nor his wife dared protest, and Mary's hatred of the 'night-crow' remained unexpressed—but not for long.

As Henry's struggle with the Vatican entered its second and most discouraging stage, Mary became the principal figure at the fair of Bury-St-Edmunds, which was organized by the Abbot of that foundation. She entered the town in state, accompanied by her suite and her musicians, and took up her position in an elaborately decorated tent, where she received the local gentry. Her patronage enhanced the sale of two industries—hempen cloth and 'flet', or one-meal, cheese.[7] In the evenings she presided over the dancing, with her children, and her husband's wards—Henry Grey, who had succeeded his father as Marquess of Dorset, and an orphaned, half-Spanish girl, who was related to Katherine of Aragon, Lady Katherine Willoughby. The Dowager-Marchioness of Dorset had not wanted to part with her son; but when Suffolk urged the King to make him the boy's guardian, she had had no choice; and so the five children—two Henrys, Frances, Eleanor and Katherine—were brought up together.

In spite of Suffolk's absences, 1530 was another happy year for Mary; that summer he accompanied Anne's brother, Lord Rochford, on a mission to Clement VII. He dared not leave the Court for long, lest Norfolk should influence the King against him. Neither Duke realized that Henry's divagations were self-generated, and that only one person—Anne—could sometimes sway them. When he created her Marquess—not Marchioness—of Pembroke, and set her up in a household of her own, she was still clinging to and advertising her virtue; still Henry, despite her complaints, would occasionally spend the evenings with his wife; and still the wretched Clement, ground between the millstones of the Emperor's threats and Henry's hints that England might be 'lost' to the Vatican, prevaricated and fumbled over the King's Great Matter.

There is no evidence that Mary tried to influence her husband against his own interests; but in June 1531 Chapuys, the Spanish ambassador, heard Suffolk say to Henry that Katherine would obey him 'in all but two things, God and her conscience'. Chapuys informed Charles V that the Suffolks would combat Henry's second marriage, 'if they dared'.[8]

This was optimistic thinking. Whatever Mary's feelings — and they appear not to have changed during the last three years of her life — her attitude became one of withdrawal from a conflict in which Suffolk was wholly committed to the King.

As Henry began to achieve his Supremacy, and Anne's position to resemble that of a Queen-Consort, Katherine was forced to retire to the country, and Henry defied the papal nuncio. 'Let the Pope do what he will,' he shouted. ' ... I shall not mind it, for I care not a fig for his excommunications.'[9] A few months later, he accused the clergy of being 'but half our subjects, yea, and scarce our subjects' — yet still he could not break up the deadlock between himself, his bishops and the papacy. Meanwhile, Mary remained aloof, out of favour and slightly ailing. In April 1532 she appeared at Court, and in a conversation with the Venetian ambassador, 'reviled' Anne Boleyn.[10] Her remarks were repeated to the King, with the result that she had to return to the country, where she remained for the rest of that year.

In September Henry's anti-Spanish alliance with Francis I necessitated a renewal of the Field of Cloth of Gold, and preparations were made for a meeting which was supposed to include Anne as the French King's guest of honour; but Queen Claude and Marguérite de Valois refused to receive her. Desired to accompany her husband, Mary would not go; she did not even make her health the excuse, and Suffolk went to Calais without her.[11] Yet Henry's displeasure with his sister had no effect on the Duke's position; it merely separated him once more from the woman for whom he had risked so much. They were detached rather than estranged; the wedding of the Lady Frances and Henry Dorset in March 1533 saw them in good accord. Then Suffolk returned to London.

For the King's affairs were reaching a climax. At last, Anne yielded, and became pregnant. (Henry knew that their child would be a boy; he had been assured of it by a Higher Power.) Cranmer, Archbishop of Canterbury, pronounced the divorce, Henry and Anne were privately married, and Katherine was made Princess-Dowager by Act of Parliament. Mary, who had received a New Year's present of gilt bowls from her brother, remained at Westhorpe Hall, seeing little or nothing of Suffolk. Henry then sent him to tell Katherine about her new title, which she at once rejected, and a long and painful argument ensued. Much embarrassed, he concluded the interview by informing her that the King was now the husband of Anne Boleyn.

---

## NOTES

1 Green, op. cit., p. 136.
2 Mattingly, p. 190.
3 Op. cit., p. 197.
4 *L. & P.*, vol. IV, pt. 3, p. 2619.
5 J. Bowle, *Henry VIII*, p. 146.
6 G. Cavendish, *Life and Death of Cardinal Wolsey*, p. 91.

7 Strickland, *English Princesses*, p. 54.
8 *L. & P.*, vol. V, p. 138.
9 J. Scarisbrick, *Henry VIII*, p. 290.
10 *Ven. S. P.*, vol. IV, p. 332.
11 Op. cit., p. 351.

# IX

## *Reconciliation*

ATTENDED by Suffolk as Lord High Steward, Anne Boleyn was crowned on June 1st, 1533. It would have been impossible for Mary to absent herself from a ceremony involving the whole Court — and an audience of silently hostile citizens — if she had not been seriously ill. By the time Suffolk rejoined her at Westhorpe Hall, she had lost faith in the medicaments of 'Master Peter', the local apothecary; so she wrote to Henry, describing her state, and asking her 'most dearest and best beloved brother' whether she might accompany her husband to London for treatment from the King's physicians. 'I am rather worse than better,' she went on, giving no details, and adding that she 'had been a great while out of your sight ... The sight of Your Grace is the greatest comfort to me.'[1]

So Henry forgave his favourite sister for her abuse of his second Queen, no doubt because he knew that she was dying. They never met again. Mary returned to Westhorpe Hall, where she was joined by her husband and the Dorsets. On June 26th, between seven and eight in the evening, she died. The nature of her last illness is unknown.

She was embalmed, and lay in state for three weeks. Etiquette forbade the Duke's attendance as chief mourner. Authorized by Henry, he made arrangements for a magnificent funeral, and for Requiem Masses at Westminster and St Paul's. Such evidence as exists points to his having returned to London before Mary was buried. He had been fond of her: now his chief concern was the loss of her French revenues.[2]

After the embalming, Mary's body was enclosed in leaden wrappings, laid in a coffin covered with a blue velvet pall and placed in the chapel of Westhorpe Hall. The tapers surrounding it were renewed and guarded by a series of attendants. Her daughters and her seventeen-year-old son came to pray beside her, and attended Mass every day. On July 20th the mourners began to arrive, from London,

Paris and the neighbouring abbeys and manors. After a short service, the procession, headed by the Lady Frances, walking between her husband and her brother, and followed by the Lady Eleanor and the Lady Katherine Willoughby, was formed. The gentlemen of the household carried the coffin to the funeral car, which was drawn by six chargers draped in black velvet embroidered with the roses of England and the lilies of France. A footman knelt at each end of the car, which was hung with banners displaying the dun cow, the hawthorn bush and the portcullis of the Tudor dynasty. A golden pall then replaced the blue velvet covering; this framed a black-and-white representation of the Queen-Duchess, crowned, sceptred, and dressed in robes of state.[3]

The chief mourners, having entered their chariots, were met at the gates of the Hall by a hundred pensioners in black gowns and hoods carrying tapers, an ecclesiastical dignitary holding a cross, and a concourse of knights, barons, clergy and gentlemen of the King's household; these were followed by Clarencieux and Norroy Kings-at-Arms and the Suffolks' chamberlain, all on horses draped in black. They preceded the torch-lit car; Lincoln, Lady Eleanor and the Dorsets followed it. Behind them, in single file, rode ten of Mary's ladies, each attended by a groom; then came a party of maidservants on foot, a number of lesser employees – and, finally, 'all that would' joined the procession from the surrounding parishes.[4]

As the journey from the Hall to the Abbey of St Edmundsbury took all day, the funeral service began at two o'clock the following afternoon. The coffin was received by the Bishop of Lincoln and the Abbot and monks of Bury, and placed on an elaborately decorated hearse, of which the principal feature was the Queen-Duchess's 'device', with her motto, *La Volonté de Dieu me suffit*. The church, hung with heraldic banners and French and English escutcheons, was so filled with mourners that the Suffolk tenantry had to stand outside. After a preliminary service, the French poursuivant stepped into the aisle and cried, 'Pray for the soul of the right high and excellent Princess, and right Christian Queen Mary, late French Queen – and for all Christian souls!'

The whole company then left the church and entered the refectory for supper, 'in goodly order ... with all manner of delicacies', while monks and nuns watched over the bier. Next morning, two Low Masses were said, followed by a Requiem Mass in the afternoon, and another procession, headed by Lincoln and his sisters, who laid golden palls before the bier, returning to their stalls to listen to an address from the Abbot of St Bennett's, a neighbouring monastery. They were about to follow the coffin to the vaults when a disturbance was caused by the sudden irruption of Mary's step-daughters, the Ladies Powis and Monteagle, with their husbands, who had not been expected, and who now pushed their way to the head of the cortège.[5]

Without an unseemly struggle, it was not possible for Mary's children to oust the invaders. They withdrew to the great chamber adjoining the vault, while the coffin was lowered into what seemed to be its last resting-place. The officers of the household broke their white staves and, 'with great weeping and lamentation', threw them into the grave. After that, a funeral feast was provided for all the mourners, and 'for the poor people, a great dole, in four places of the town of Bury, having meats and drinks, come who would, and every poor body fourpence'.[6]

All her life, except when she was forced to marry against her will, Mary Tudor had been indulged. She was her father's favourite child. Louis XII petted and spoiled her because she entranced him. Suffolk submitted to her desires, because their happy relations had become the basis of his career. Henry VIII gave in to her, even when she displeased him. And so the splendour and elaboration of her funeral well became the last public tribute accorded to one whose appearance had always delighted the beholder. Like those fabled princesses — beautiful, beloved and kind — she was remembered as a figure of romance. Her gaiety and grace, her wilfulness, her many bounties, combined to create a legend; and because that legend stood for contentment and success, it soon faded. Mary had been neither disagreeable, nor awe-inspiring, nor tragic, nor doomed — and not even particularly clever. She was a symbol of impermanency: the admired of a single generation: the heroine of a love-story.

Meanwhile, Suffolk had had to recoup his losses, and he did so by a fifth marriage. In 1535 he became the husband of Katherine Willoughby. He then arranged for Eleanor to marry Lord Cumberland, but did not find a bride for the Earl of Lincoln, who died in 1544. A year later, the Duke died, leaving two sons by his last wife; they died in 1551, with the result that Frances and Henry Dorset became Duke and Duchess of Suffolk. They had three daughters — Jane, Katherine and Mary Grey. Lady Jane, the nine days' Queen, was executed in 1554 at the age of sixteen and a half; Katherine married into the Seymour family, and died of tuberculosis in her thirty-second year; Mary, married but childless, survived till the age of fifty-one. Katherine Grey's descendants, the Earls of Hertford, continue their line, as do those of Eleanor Cumberland, whose daughter Margaret became Countess of Derby and Queen in Man. So it was that in 1547, when Edward VI succeeded Henry VIII, eight girls—the Princesses Mary and Elizabeth, Frances, Eleanor, Frances's three daughters and Margaret Tudor's grand-daughter, Mary Queen of Scots—were in line for the throne. When Edward died in 1553, there was no male Tudor left alive.

In 1538 the dissolution of the monasteries made it necessary for the monks of Bury to move the Queen-Duchess's coffin (they had carved on it five crosses, representing the five wounds of Christ) to the neighbouring church of St Mary's. It was placed before the high altar under a stone slab so inscribed as to give the impression that it was merely a memorial. In 1781 this portion of the church was enlarged, revealing the coffin, which had rotted away. The corpse then had to be stripped of its leaden wrapping, on which was engraved, 'Marye, Quene of Ffranc, 1533.'[7]

Once again, legend became reality; for the embalmers (did Henry VIII send them down from London?) had done their work well; and after two and a half centuries his sister's body had a spectral loveliness which was partially veiled by the almost frightening growth of her hair. Still golden, it now reached her knees.[8]

There was, naturally, no question of respect for such a phenomenon. The antiquaries got out their scissors—and very soon locks of Mary Tudor's hair were sold at auctions, sent to collectors (one became the property of Horace Walpole) and displayed in shop-windows. In the nineteenth century they were still being advertised in catalogues, and knocked down to dealers as part of odd lots. Meanwhile the tomb, now removed to the left-hand side of the altar of St Mary's, had become defaced. In 1881 Queen Victoria ordered a commemorative window to be placed above it, and a marble slab, with Mary's name and the date, was set in the wall sheltering her dust.

A single, minute fragment of the Princess described by her contemporaries as a nymph from Heaven and a Paradise remains—in the museum of Bury-St-Edmunds. Inside a glass case, pinned to a card, is a slender ring of hair. In the course of four and a half centuries it has darkened. But it has not faded—and it looks as if it might spring away from the fastening that holds it down.

## NOTES

1 *L. & P.*, vol. VI, p. 21.
2 *Ven. S. P.*, vol. IV, p. 28. *L. & P.*, op. cit., p. 311.
3 Green, vol. V, p. 139.
4 Ibid.
5 Op. cit., p. 141. Strickland, *English Princesses*, p. 57.

6 Green, op. cit., p. 141; Strickland ibid.
7 Strickland, ibid.
8 Ibid.; Green, op. cit., p. 142.

# Epilogue

THE saga which begins with a handsome Welsh steward stumbling into the lap of a Valois Queen-Dowager, and ends with the greatest of all the Tudors lying dead, her head upon her arm, in the Palace of Greenwich, covers a hundred and eighty years of English history. That saga seems, in retrospect, so crowded, so overpowering, that Margaret of Scotland and Mary of Suffolk, significant personalities in their own day, are now seen as background figures. Because their respective granddaughters were beheaded in highly sensational circumstances — one in extreme youth, the other in middle age — the spotlight of historical narrative has moved away from these two sisters to their descendants.

Margaret's story was one of frustration, conflict and ultimate failure; Mary's that of triumph over a momentary set-back. Margaret's few successes were effected by strength of character against heavy odds. Wealth and ease, admiration and privilege were showered on Mary all her life. Margaret withstood danger and hardship by lying when she had to, and pleading as best she could, till both methods became second nature. Mary's comparatively rare deceits were unconscious; that the will of God sufficed her was the most absurdly false of mottoes. Eventually, all her demands were granted, while Margaret's were ignored, and her career was based on a combination of disingenuousness and revolt. Yet both were alike in their devotion to the brother who alternately used, indulged and neglected them, and in their refusal to become puppets in his or anyone else's hands. Bursting away from the conventions of their time, they appeared, briefly, in the foreground of the Tudor tapestry. Then they retreated, as became the daughters, consorts and sisters of kings. Their position in the family group is therefore one of deliberate withdrawal.

# Bibliography

Anglesey (Co. of), *Inventory of Ancient Monuments* (1927)
*Antiquities of Scotland*, vol. VII (Edinburgh, 1800)
*Archaeologia Cambrensis* (London, 1846)
Bacon, F., *Life of Henry VII* (London, 1627)
Bailly, S., *François I* (Paris, 1954)
Bowle, J., *Henry VIII* (London, 1959)
Brewer, J., *Reign of Henry VIII* (London, 1890)
Cavendish, G., *Life and Death of Cardinal Wolsey* (London, 1959)
Commines, M. de, *Mémoires* (Paris, 1903)
Cooper, C., *The Lady Margaret* (Cambridge, 1874)
Donaldson, G., *Scottish Kings* (London, 1967)
Drummond, W., *History of Scotland* (London, 1745)
Dunbar, W., *Works* (Edinburgh, 1884)
Ellis, H. (ed.), *Letters*, vols. I and II (London, 1834)
Evans, H., *Wales and the Wars of the Roses* (Cambridge, 1915)
Gairdner, J. (ed.), *Letters and Papers of Richard III and Henry VII*
    (London, 1843)
Godwin, F., *Annals of England* (n.d.)
Green, M. A. Everett, *Princesses of England* (London, 1854)
Grose, F., *Antiquities of Scotland* (Edinburgh, 1800)
Hall, E., *Chronicle* (London, 1809)
Herbert of Cherbury, Lord, *Henry VIII* (London, 1649)
James V, *Letters* (London, 1954)
Leland, J., *Collectanea* (London, 1752)
Lesley, Bishop, *History of Scotland* (Edinburgh, 1829)
*Letters and Papers of Henry VII and Henry VIII* (London, 1881)
Lewis, C., *English Literature in the Sixteenth Century* (O.U.P., 1954)
Lindsay, R., *History and Chronicles of Scotland* (Edinburgh, 1814)
Mackie, J., *James IV* (London, 1950)
Mattingly, G., *Catherine of Aragon* (London, 1942)
Miller, T., *The Castle and the Crown* (London, 1965)
Nichols, J., *Epistles of Erasmus* (London, 1840)
Pinkerton, J., *History of Scotland* (London, 1807)

Pollard, A. F., *Henry VIII* (London, 1905)
Rowse, A. L., *Bosworth Field* (London, 1967)
Scarisbrick, J., *Henry VIII* (London, 1968)
*Scottish State Papers, Exchequer Rolls and Acts of the Council* (various dates)
Sneyd, C. A. (ed.), *Relazione d'Inghilterra*
Society of Antiquaries of Scotland
Speed, J., *Chronicle* (London, 1846)
Stow, J., *Annals* (London, 1640)
Strickland, A., *Queens of Scotland*
              *English Princesses* (London, 1848–54)
Stuart, M., *The Scot Who Was a Frenchman* (London, 1940)
Tytler, P., *History of Scotland* (Edinburgh, 1824)
*Venetian State Papers* (London, 1891)
Vergil, P., *Anglica Historia* (Edinburgh, 1849)
Vespasian MS. (B. 11)
Wood, M., *Flodden Papers* (Edinburgh, 1933)

# Index

ABBEVILLE, 172–3

Albany, John Stuart, Duke of, 81–2, 84, 88–94, 96–106, 108–11, 113–16, 117–26, 127, 129, 140–41, 195

Alexander, Duke, brother of James III, 82

Alexander, Duke of Ross, son of Margaret Tudor, 83, 103–4, 117

Alexander VI, Pope, 28

André, Bernard, 26

Angoulême, Francis d', 172

Angus, Archibald, Earl of, 83, 84, 86, 95, 96–9, 101–2, 105–6, 107–8, 112, 114–16, 117–19, 127–39, 140–48, 153, 155, 156

Anne of Brittany, 65, 66, 71, 180

Argyll, Lord, 91

Arran, John Stuart of, 151

Arran, Lord, 48, 52, 65, 71, 81–2, 91, 101, 110–14, 117, 128, 130–32, 135, 136, 138–9, 140

Arthur, son of Henry VII, 18, 20, 21, 24, 25, 27, 29–30, 59, 159, 160

Arthur, son of Margaret Tudor, 54–5

Atholl, Earl of, 144, 150

Atholl, Lady Janet, 150, 156

Aubigny, Lord d', 53

Avondale, Lord, 126

BAPAUME, French ambassador, 195

Barham Down, battle of, 73, 75

Barton, Sir Andrew, 55–6

Beaton, Archbishop, 79, 89, 130

Beaufort, Joan, 28

Beaufort, Margaret, see Margaret of Richmond

Beauvais, 175, 176–7

Berkeley, Lady, 20

Berwick, 77–8, 143

Blacader, Bishop of Glasgow, 28

Blacater, 98–9

Blount, Elizabeth, 113, 203

Boleyn, Anne, 142, 147, 197, 203–5, 207–9, 210–11

Boleyn, Sir Thomas, 197, 198, 202, 204

Borthwick, Earl of, 125

Bosworth Field, battle of, 18

Bothwell, Patrick, Earl, 28–9

Boyd, Mary, 47, 66

Brandon, Lady Anne, 193

Brandon, Lady Mary, 193

Browne, Anne, 167, 193, 200, 205

Browne, Sir Anthony, 167

CAMPBELL, SIR JOHN, 150

Campeggio, Cardinal, 205–6

Carey, Lady, 197

Cassilis, Lord, 124

Caxton, William, 23

Chadworth, Father, 113

Chapuys, Spanish ambassador, 207

Charles V, Emperor, 137, 146, 160–66, 168, 170, 181, 182, 184, 187, 199–201, 204, 208–9

Charles VI of France, 14

Charles VIII of France, 17

Claude, Madame, 170, 172–3, 178–80, 181, 188, 199, 208

Clement VII, Pope, 142–4, 204, 207

Coldstream, Prioress of, 121

Collyweston, 21, 32

Compton, Sir William, 183

Comyn, Sir William, 68–9, 88–9, 93

Cranmer, Archbishop, 208

Cromwell, Thomas, 147, 149, 151, 153

Cumberland, Lord, 212

DACRE, LADY, 76

Dacre, Lord, 58, 74, 80, 88, 91, 92, 93, 98, 99, 101–6, 111, 114, 115–16, 117–21, 125, 127–30, 144

Dalkeith, 31, 33, 38

Damian, Abbot, 51–2

Davy, Alice, 24

De Bergues, Sieur, 162–3

De la Bastie, Sieur, 81, 89

De la Mothe, 65

De la Pole, John, 15

219

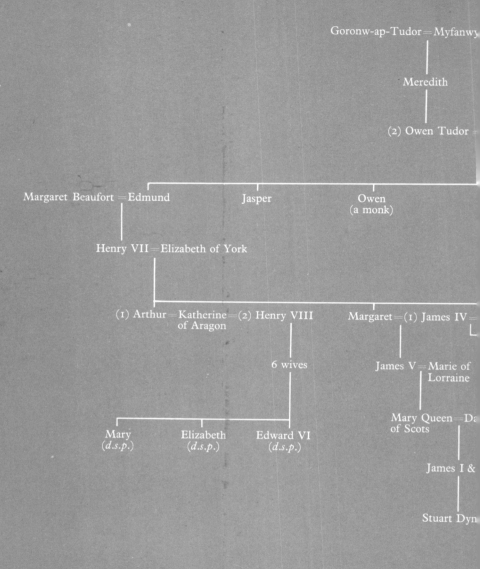

Goronw-ap-Tudor = Myfanwy

Meredith

(2) Owen Tudor =

Margaret Beaufort = Edmund      Jasper      Owen
(a monk)

Henry VII = Elizabeth of York

(1) Arthur = Katherine = (2) Henry VIII      Margaret = (1) James IV =
of Aragon

6 wives

James V = Marie of
Lorraine

Mary Queen = Da
of Scots

Mary      Elizabeth      Edward VI
(*d.s.p.*)      (*d.s.p.*)      (*d.s.p.*)

James I &

Stuart Dyn